TIES OF BLOOD
AND
FRIENDSHIP

The Complicated Life of Francis Lynn

by

Patrick Darby

For DWC.

CONTENTS

ACKNOWLEDGMENTS

My thanks for their help to the staff at the National Archives in Kew, Calista Lucy (Dulwich College Archivist), Carolyn Hammond (Brentford & Chiswick Local History Society), Rose Graham (Bacton & Cotton Local History Group) and Olive Geddes and Lynsey Halliday (of the National Library of Scotland, who provided me – almost by return – with a facsimile of Francis Lynn's 'diary'). Transcribed extracts from the 'diary' are printed by kind permission of the Countess of Sutherland.

The plan of Hall Place on p.31 is an adapted extract from a map of the Dulwich Estate in the Dulwich College archives, and the painting of Hall Place on p.253 is in the South London Gallery. Otherwise all the images in this book have been derived from Internet downloads, and I have acknowledged in footnotes at appropriate points those sources of which I am aware. My apologies to any not properly acknowledged – omissions notified to me will be corrected in any future edition.

On which subject, if any reader has additional information about any of the characters in this book, or any queries or comments on it, please contact me at tobaf@hitherwood.co.uk.

THE MAIN CHARACTERS
FEATURED IN THIS BOOK ARE…

Francis Lynn (1671-1731), son of John and Susanna Lynn, educated at Westminster School and Trinity College, Cambridge. Secretary to several Navy Boards and related bodies, 1695 to 1714. Chief Secretary of the Royal African Company, 1720 until his death. In 1697 he married …

Mary Thompson (c.1678-1756), daughter of …

Elizabeth Thompson *née* Newby (1649-1727), later Mrs Moreland, who in 1675 had married the deputy Governor of the garrison at Sheerness …

Lt. Robert Thompson (c.1649-1678), former Assistant Groom of the Privy Chamber, and son of …

Robert Thompson (c.1619-1697), Groom of the Privy Chamber to King Charles II and his successors 1660 to 1694, who in 1671/72 married, as her second husband (and his second wife) …

Elizabeth Thurman, *née* Vickers (c.1625-1699), whose first husband was …

Nicholas Thurman, merchant (c.1620-1671), by whom she had a daughter …

Mary Thurman (1659-1712), who in 1676 married …

Samuel Hunter (1651-1725), Clerk of the Cheque at Sheerness dockyard in 1678, subsequently a Commissioner of the Navy, and (in succession to the

Thurmans and the Thompsons) lessee of Hall Place, in Dulwich, which he left in his Will to Francis Lynn, whose "*best Friend*" was …

Captain William Morgan (c.1678-1744), Regimental Agent until 1714, thereafter Jacobite adventurer, and in business with …

Lt.-Gen. Robert Echlin (c.1657-1723), and with Francis Lynn, and with Lynn's younger brother …

Samuel Lynn (1675-1737), Muster-Master of the Marines to 1714 (and unofficially thereafter, to 1719). Owner of the manor and lands of Tidmarsh, in Berkshire, from 1715.

PREFACE

When I began writing this book, it was intended to be a history of a house in Dulwich called Hall Place, from its origins in the 13th century to its demolition in the 19th. I may yet produce such a book, but as the research for it progressed I realised that there was a particularly well-documented period in the history of the house in the late 17th and early 18th centuries, when it was successively occupied and/or owned (as lessees from Dulwich College) by four families – the Thurmans, the Thompsons, the Hunters, and the Lynns. Quite how well-documented I did not realise for some months. In the process I discovered some surprising, and indeed remarkable, connections between those families, which seemed to revolve around one man – Francis Lynn.

This was fitting, as what initially piqued my interest in Hall Place as a subject for further research, over half a century ago, was an intriguing sentence in William Young's two-volume '*The History of Dulwich College*' (1889), of which my father, William Darby, a noted Dulwich historian in his time, had borrowed a copy from the College (where he taught Classics). Young wrote:[1] "*One of the inhabitants of Hall Place, Captain Lynn (circa 1750), quarrelling with a neighbour, challenged him, and in the ensuing duel was killed by his antagonist, apparently somewhere close by the Old House.*" In his '*Dulwich History and Romance*' (1922), E. T. Hall repeated this story. My father alluded to the same passage on page 33 of his '*Dulwich – A Place in History*' (1967). I, from a combination of natural filial duty and laziness, used the same story in an article written in 1980 for the *Dulwich Society Newsletter* entitled '*Where was Dulwich's Manor House?*', without questioning its truth.

We were all wrong. Since I began research for this book, the only Captain Lynn I have been able to trace as being active in England in the late 1740s and throughout the '50s, whose first name also happened to be Francis, had nothing to do with Dulwich and was not killed in a duel. Captain Francis Lynn, R. M., no relation (except perhaps distantly) to our Francis Lynn, died in his bed at Greenwich Hospital in 1810, aged 84. Young cited no authority for his intriguing statement – it may have been a story told to him by local 'character' Tom Morris, whose grandparents had lived in Dulwich village – and successive students of Dulwich history uncritically accepted it.

That said, there *was* a deadly duel involving two individuals closely connected with Hall Place, and this book details the events leading up to it, and its surprising aftermath. Young, Hall, my father and I could all have claimed that, apart from getting the rank, name, date and place wrong, we were essentially

---

[1] '*The History of Dulwich College down to the passing of the act of Parliament dissolving the original corporation, 28ᵗʰ August 1857*', pp. 451-2.

right, but no-one should be convinced by that argument. An object lesson in why historians should always, as far as possible, check their sources.

"… as far as possible"… I have more recently been guilty of the same offence. In January 2016 I submitted an article, entitled *'Ties of Blood and Marriage'* to the *'Dulwich Society Journal'*, taking as its 'hook' the journey down to Exeter which Samuel Hunter and Francis Lynn undertook in November 1713. I rashly stated: *"There is no evidence that, prior to travelling together by stage-coach (as one supposes they did) … Samuel Hunter and Francis Lynn had more than a nodding acquaintance, if that."* Even before the *Journal* was published, I knew that I was mistaken. I did not know the extent to which I was mistaken until I made the chance discovery, a few weeks later, that Francis Lynn had kept a record of his life and that, almost miraculously, it had survived, in the National Library of Scotland. The very helpful staff there provided me with a copy of it, and it became one of the main sources for this book.

We are extremely lucky to have in this country a wealth of original documents of interest to national, local, and family historians, and once one has tracked down a source – a task made much easier since the advent of Internet search engines – one can of course go into almost infinite detail. In writing this book the chief problem I have encountered has not been finding the sources, but eliminating those which relate too indirectly to my main characters. Francis Lynn, as you shall learn, had a wide circle of relations, friends, acquaintances and antagonists. Some of those individuals knew each other, and in turn had their own circles, which may or may not have overlapped, and when they were borrowing money from each other the situation could get extremely complex, to the point where one can hardly tell who is the debtor and who the creditor. Indeed, long after Francis Lynn's death his heirs were to become embroiled in a legal dispute with the heir of one of his friends, which turned on precisely that problem.

That, however, comes much later. I will begin with Francis Lynn and his 'diary'.

CHAPTER 1

Westminster and Cambridge

"I was born the 2d. day of Nov: 1671, about 1 of the Clock in the Morning in Westminster, and bred up by my Father and two Elder brothers John and Charles, who were at Westm'. School, till between 9 and 10 Years old, and then, without having been at any other School, I was putt there[2] under the care of Dr. Busby, or rather of Mr. Knipe the second master, being admitted the very lowest boy in the school, which I passed quite through, and in the course was Captain of every form: I lodged and dieted at home, so the charge of my Schooling during the 8 Years from admission till I got into the College, being at 10th: a quarter was for 8 Years … … 16: 0: 0

To Dr. Busby[3] every X^{tmas} as a Gift }

---

[2] At this time Westminster School, under the formidable Rev. Dr. Richard Busby, headmaster from 1638 until his death in 1695, would have had about 240 fee-paying pupils.

[3] The payments, described as 'gifts', to Dr Busby, Mr Knipe and the Usher, are explained by W. Teignmouth Shore in '*Public School Life – Westminster*' (1910) thus: "*Such was the old system in every public school; the masters were entirely dependent for any income beyond their statutable salaries on the liberality of the parents of those boys who were*

one guinea ... ... }	*8:12: 0*[4]
To Mr. Knipe d°. half a guinea	*4: 6: 0*
To the Usher d°. 5ˢᵇ.	*2: 0: 0*
In all, besides Books	*£30:18: 0*"

Thus begins the remarkable 'Diary of Francis Lynn' (1671-1731), known to his intimates as Frank. Although various early histories of Westminster School suggest that Francis Lynn, most unusually, kept a diary while at school, the entries were not in fact made contemporaneously with the events they record, and the book is really more of an autobiography, compiled much later. This most fortuitous survival came, by what route I do not know, into the possession of a 19th-century Duke of Sutherland, and may currently be found in the Archives and Manuscripts Collections department of the National Library of Scotland,[5] deposited on long-term loan by the Countess of Sutherland in 1980. It first resurfaced in 1834, when a copy of it was sent, supposedly by Francis Lynn's executors (although by then he had been dead for over a century), to the editor of *'The Evening Mail'*, who published extracts from the early part of it which eventually came to the attention of successive historians of Westminster School, none of whom appear to have examined the original.

In fact, those are not the diary's actual opening words. On the flyleaf are three hand-written

---

admitted 'commoners' or 'oppidans', or under any other designation; and by degrees these gratuities became a matter of recognised custom and claim".

[4] At this date (and until 1717) a guinea was worth £1 1s 6d.

[5] Dep. 314/19.

quotations from Latin authors, which I give below (with their translations noted):

- Stemmata quid faciunt, quod prodest sanguine longo Censeri ? ---------- [6]

- Genus et Proavos, et quae non fecimus ipsi, vix ea nostra voco ---------- [7]

- Olim haec meminisse juvabit.[8]

And immediately before Lynn begins his life-story there is the following (which may have been written post-1720):

Having the Example of the best of Fathers to follow, I thought it proper to leave behind me the following Account of my self.[9]

Fra: Lynn

Below that, as if to make the statement more official, Lynn has appended his seal.

Despite the authors of those histories[10] of Westminster School almost all giving the impression

---

[6] 'Of what value are pedigrees, or to derive one's blood from a long line of lofty ancestors?' (Juvenal, '*Saturae*', 3.8)

[7] 'Birth and ancestry, and what we have ourselves not done, I would hardly call our own.' (Ovid)

[8] 'Sometime in the future it will be pleasing to remember these things.' (Virgil, '*Aeneid*', I, 203)

[9] This implies that Francis Lynn's father had also written a similar 'diary'. If he did, it does not seem to have survived.

[10] Including '*The Public Schools*', by W. Lucas Collins (1867); '*Westminster School, Past and Present*', by Frederic H. Forshall (1884); '*Memoir of Richard Busby DD (1606-1695)...*' by G. F. Russell Barker (1895); and '*Public School Life – Westminster*', by W. Teignmouth Shore (1910).

that the 'diary' was merely a record of Lynn's schooldays, it is very much more than that, and I am pleased to have the opportunity, after three centuries, of bringing it to a wider readership.

The final entry is dated May 1728, but entries after 1719, although undoubtedly in Lynn's handwriting, are in a slightly bluer ink and generally not so carefully written. The earlier entries were probably compiled when Lynn was enduring a spell of unemployment between 1719 and 1720, and (despite his claim to be copying the example of his father) mirror the form of a slender volume, intended for publication, on which his younger brother Samuel was working at the same time. This was essentially a treatise complaining of Samuel's perceived poor treatment at the hands of his employers, the Lords of the Admiralty and of the Treasury, and published in 1720.[11] The two works complement and corroborate each other, and in Francis Lynn's case are supported by numerous letters he wrote to a friend, William Morgan, between 1716 and 1721. These, and Morgan's replies – as well as some correspondence between Morgan and his wife up to 1740, and numerous receipts and statements of account and suchlike – were produced as evidence in a court case in the 1750s, and somehow found their way into the possession of a senior Chancery judge of the 1830s. He kept them, and they can be found today, catalogued as part of 'Master Brougham's Exhibits',[12] in the National Archives at Kew, where I had the opportunity to study and transcribe them.

---

[11] '*A Short Narrative of the Case of Samuel Lynn Esq;*'.

[12] TNA, ref. C 111/207.

But there is even more. Francis Lynn became friends with one Samuel Hunter, so much so that after Hunter retired in 1714 to his home in Dulwich, called Hall Place, Lynn took his family to live with or close to Hunter, and after moving to another Dulwich house temporarily when a neighbour of Hunter's made life too uncomfortable for him, Lynn moved back into Hall Place after Hunter's death, having been left the lease of it in Hunter's Will. 'Uncle Hunter', as Lynn refers to him in the 'diary', was not in fact directly related to Lynn or to Lynn's wife. However, Samuel Hunter's wife, Mary, was the only child of the occupants of Hall Place in the 1660s, Nicholas and Elizabeth Thurman, and when Elizabeth Thurman remarried following Nicholas's death in 1671, Mary became the step-daughter of Elizabeth's new husband Robert Thompson. Thompson's eldest son, also Robert, from a former marriage, became a lieutenant in the Royal Navy. Fate brought Lt. Robert Thompson and Samuel Hunter together at Sheerness in 1673, and Hunter met and married Lt. Thompson's step-sister. Before dying in tragic circumstances, Lt. Thompson married and fathered a daughter, Mary, who was eventually to marry Francis Lynn. Nicholas Thurman, Elizabeth and Robert Thompson, Samuel Hunter, Francis Lynn and Lynn's widow (the only child of Lt. Thompson), were successive lessees of Hall Place between 1662 and 1753. This may seem like the plot for an historical novel, or series of them, but it is all true, and documented in often startling detail.

For example, there are no fewer than 125 extant letters written (or at least subscribed) by Samuel Hunter to his Navy Office employers during his time in the Naval Dockyard at Sheerness. Furthermore,

Thurman, Thompson senior, Hunter, Francis Lynn, his wife, children and brother, and William Morgan, were all involved in court cases for which the original 'Bills of Complaint' and/or 'Answers', if not reports of the judgments, have survived, throwing fascinating additional light on crucial events in their lives. So all in all, what with parish, manorial, and probate records to fill many gaps, we have an astonishing treasure trove of documents, all hitherto largely untapped by historians. This book aims to rectify that omission.

That said, I have been unable to trace any record in any Westminster parish register of the baptisms of Francis Lynn or of his brothers John, Charles and Samuel and sister Elizabeth, or of the marriage of their parents. The church with which the family was most closely associated was St. Margaret's Westminster, which lies between Westminster Abbey and the Houses of Parliament, although both Francis and his brother Samuel were later to have some of their children christened at both St Margaret's and at St Martin-in-the-Fields.

By the age of 17 Frank Lynn, whose school career so far had been exemplary, was ready to progress further:

In May 1689 I was Elected into the Foundation as a Kings schollar, having been putt by two Elections[13] before for want of friends, but now standing Captain or Senior, I was elected in accordingly.

Here follows a particular Account of Expences whilst in

---

[13] An 'election', in Westminster School slang, meant a division of Scholars by year.

Westmʳ. College taken from my Fathers pocket book [14]

Although much of what follows is mundane stuff, the entries give clues as to what the well-dressed 'Westminster' was wearing, what he was reading, and how he was furnishing his accommodation.

May 16[89]		*£ s d*
3. [To e]ntertain my Schoolfellows upon }		
m[y bei]ng Elected, a usual custom …}		*0: 7: 0*
6. For my Theam[15] making … … … …		*0: 5: 0*
For an old Gown for common use …		*0:10: 0*
9. For a Trunk … … … … ... … … …	*0:14: 0 }*	
Nine Ells of Holland[16] for Surplice …	*1:14: 9 }*	
16 Ells of sheeting … … … … … …	*0:16: 0 }*	*3:13: 3*
a Yard & ½ of Kenting[17] … … … …	*0: 1: 6 }*	
a remnant more … … … … …	*0: 1: 0 }*	
A Kings schollars Cap[18] … … …	*0: 6 : 0 }*	
13. For admonishing money, i.e. }		

---

[14] It was of course Francis Lynn's father who provided his income and arranged most of his expenditure.

[15] I can only suggest that 'team' is intended.

[16] Holland cloth was a fine, plain-woven linen imported from Europe, particularly from the Netherlands, and was chiefly used for furniture coverings.

[17]'Kenting', or Kente cloth, was a brightly-patterned, hand-woven fabric produced by the Ashanti tribes of the Gold Coast. Francis Lynn was to become Secretary of the company chiefly responsible for importing this material into England, and his only surviving son Philip was to spend his last days in the heartland of the Ashanti.

[18] Strictly speaking, this should have been 'A King's and Queen's Scholar's Cap', as William and Mary were now joint monarchs.

forfeiture for speaking English[19]   *0: 0: 6* }

16. A bible, practise of piety, & a comb   0: 4: 7 } *2: 6: 1*

24. For a new Gowne ... ...   2: 1: 0 }

June 1689

10. This day I was admitted into ye College

 by the Dean, & putt on my Gowne.

11. For double Commons and Serv[ts] }

Fees as customary on this occasion }   *1: 0: 0* }

Pocket money & Candles ... ...   0:10: 0 }

New featherbed & bolster ... ...   1:13: 0 } *4:12: 5*

Bedstead, Cord, & Matt ... ...   0: 6: 0 }

A Rug ... ...   0:12: 0 }

2 New Blankits ... ...   0:11: 0 }

A new Table ... ...   0: 7: 0 }

A Canopy to the Bed ... ...   0: 7: 0 } *0:14:0*

--- Payd to the 8 Seniors for my Freedom }

  as customary for y[e] *Cap*[t]*. of y*[e] *Election ... ... ,* } *8:12:0*

And so on, and so on. The entries for December 1689 to the end of Francis Lynn's time at Westminster School end with the following statement:

May 12 [1691]. I was Elected away Captain of the School, to Trinity College in Cambridge, together wth the

---

[19] Westminster schoolboys were expected to converse in Latin. Nowadays this might be regarded as child abuse.

Honble. Dixy Windsor Esqr,[20] Wm Shippen,[21] Hugh James, & John Lambe. The same time to Oxford[22] were Elected, Wm Adams, Henry Brydges,[23] Adam Langley,[24] & Nicholas Burton.[25]

Lynn's account initially mentions his elder brothers John and Charles, and his younger brother Samuel (according to Samuel's memorial tablet in Tidmarsh parish church) also attended Westminster School. None of them, however, shone as brightly academically as did he, and none was elected as a King's Scholar, was School Captain, or went to university. Westminster's famous alumni living in 1691 included the Poet Laureate John Dryden, the philosopher John Locke, architect and founder member of the Royal Society Sir Christopher Wren, scientist Robert Hooke, Judge Jeffreys (of 'Bloody Assize' fame), and composer Henry Purcell. The government of 1714 would include five Old Westminsters – about a third of the Ministry – and although none of them would have known Francis Lynn personally at school, nevertheless this was a

---

[20] Dixey Windsor (1672-1743), M.P. for the University of Cambridge from 1705 to 1722.

[21] William Shippen (1673-1743) became an M.P. in 1707, and from 1715 until his death was Member for Newton, Lancashire. He later espoused the Jacobite cause.

[22] Westminster School held three Closed Scholarships to Trinity College, Cambridge, and another three to Christ Church, Oxford. Lynn was awarded one of the Trinity Scholarships.

[23] Later the Rev. Dr. Henry Brydges (1675-1728), the younger brother of James Brydges, 1st Duke of Chandos.

[24] The Rev. Adam Langley, M.A., became Vicar of Black Bourton in Oxfordshire in 1700.

[25] The Rev. Nicholas Burton became headmaster of Durham Grammar School in 1699, resigned in 1709, and died in 1713.

well-connected young man, with definite prospects.

Francis Lynn's time at school was over, and he now prepared to embark for university, and Trinity College, Cambridge. His 'diary' records that on 27th *June 1691 he "went down to Cambridge, and was admitted in Trinity College under Mr Thomas Powers*[26] *as my Tutor"*. He lists the *"Expenses attending it"* as 10*s* for *"Coachire"* (i.e. coach hire), 8*s* 6*d* *"on the road"*, 12*s* paid to College servants, 2*s* 6*d* paid *"To my Tutors Sizer"*, and another 2*s* 6*d* *"To ye Library keeper"*, in all £1 15*s* 6*d*.

Next comes a record of Lynn's expenses during his first three months at university, which he initially refers to as his *"1st Quarter"* but then renames *"Quarta 4ta"*, as the academic year did not start until October.[27] These comprised £1 for tuition, 7*s* 6*d* for books, 12*s* 6*d* for Chamber rent, 4*s* for his Bedmaker, 8*s* for shoes, 5*s* for laundry, 4*s* 10*d* for candles and stationery, £5 0*s* 6*d* to a draper for his gown and cap, gratuities of 1*s* each to the College Butler and Porter *"upon admission"*, 3*s* to a blacksmith, 3*s* 4*d* to a joiner, £1 3*s* for furniture and £7 12*s* 7*d* for upholstery. *"Sizings"* were £4 5*s* 6¼*d*, making the total expenditure for the three months to the end of September 1691, including those initial £1 15*s* 6*d*

---

[26] The Rev. Thomas Power (not 'Powers') had undertaken the somewhat thankless task of translating Milton's *'Paradise Lost'* into Latin, and published the first part of it in 1691. As Lynn later records, Power *"went abroad"* at Easter 1692. He became successively Rector of St Mary's, Antigua, and Vicar of St John's, Nevis. He died in the West Indies in 1698, and there is a well-preserved memorial inscription to him at St John's, Antigua.

[27] It seems that in those days there were four university terms, of approximately equal length, not three terms with a long vacation as nowadays.

expenses in going "*down*" to Cambridge[28], £25 2*s* 10¼*d*, paid of course by his father.

As at Westminster, Lynn paid for the services of a 'bedmaker'. (The 'bedmakers' at Cambridge were all female.) A 'sizar' (which Lynn spells 'sizer') was an impoverished student, "*performing menial tasks – bedmaking, chamber-sweeping, water-carrying, serving at table – in return for free 'sizes' or rations from the college buttery*",[29] and apparently Lynn was initially wealthy enough to employ one of those as well. He was certainly expected to pay, or at least to contribute to the cost of, his Tutor's sizar, as well as other College servants.

There is, however, some ambiguity about Lynn's accountancy, as he seems to lump together income and expenditure – there are items for "*Money*" or "*Moneys*" and "*Income*" scattered among what are obviously items of expenditure – so one cannot be entirely sure that after his second term Francis Lynn was employing a 'sizar' or being employed as one.

Sad events at home may have led to such a change in young Frank's financial circumstances:

… In Nov[r].[1691] my Father fell sick and after languishing about 6 weeks dyed the 18th of December, in the 60th Year of his Age, and was buryed at the New Chappell in Westminster, upon w[ch] occasion I came home, and it was under debate with my Mother and Relations, whether or no I should return to the College again; But it having been my Fathers

---

[28] A more recent convention among Oxford and Cambridge students was to refer to going "up" to and "down" from university.

[29] From '*The Reckoning – the Murder of Christopher Marlowe*', by Charles Nicholls (2002).

desire, that I should be a Clergyman, I had framed my studys accordingly, and by advice of D: *Jekyll*[30] *a Friend of my Fathers, it was agreed that I should go down again, and proceed in my studys, and as an encouragement to me, He soon after obtained of some Publick Company (I think it was the Fishmongers) an Exhibition of £10 a Year for me, which with another Exhibition of £6 a Year, I obtained from the College, by performing some exercise for it, was a good help towards my Maintenance there;*

"*My Father*" is nowhere named in his son's 'diary', but in the Westminster City Archives is a copy of the parish register for St Margaret's, Westminster, which records that four days later, on 22nd December 1691, a John Lynn was buried there. From this, and a later reference in the 'diary', we can deduce that Francis Lynn's parents were John and Susanna Lynn. Of John Lynn I have been able to discover very little, apart from the fact that between 1678 and 1683 "*John Lynn, Gent.*" earned £60 a year as Clerk to the Tax Office. In September 1678 he was awarded a special payment of £60 "*as reward for his service, he being formerly appointed clerk under the Agents for the better managing and bringing in the Hearth money, with the salary of 60l. p.a., which duty he performed with all diligence, and hath since taken great pains in writing certificates, engrossing large books of arrears of the Royal Aid, Additional Supply and divers other taxes, and hath performed several other considerable services relating to the*

---

[30] Searching for 'Dr Jekyll' on the Internet poses, thanks to Robert Louis Stevenson, almost insuperable difficulties, but the Rev. Dr. Thomas Jekyll, D.D., M.A., (1646-98), Minister of Tothill Fields Chapel, Westminster, seems the most likely candidate.

said taxes, for which he has had no fee or reward."[31]

John Lynn must have had private means to have been able to send four of his sons to Public School, but from what those means were derived I have not discovered.

Francis Lynn's diary details his income and expenditure for his remaining time at Cambridge. Since this makes for even more tedious reading than his accounts for his Westminster schooldays, I will refrain from reproducing them, and will merely comment that after October 1692 until he left Trinity College Lynn was in receipt of irregular payments "*for livery and wages*" and other unspecified income totalling £5 1*s* 4*d*, and from October 1693 was awarded an Exhibition (a form of minor Scholarship) of £6 a year, paid half-yearly. He also received from the kindly Dr Jekyll payments totalling £14 between October 1693 and February 1694[95] when he went down (or "up" as he would have thought of it) from Cambridge to London for the last time.

Lynn summarised his income and expenditure for his combined times at Westminster and Trinity as follows:

Abstract of the foregoing Accounts.

£ s d

*Charge at Westm*ʳ. *School from my* }

first going thither till I gott to be a }   30:18:0

Kings schollar ... ... }

[31] Entry Book: September 1678, in *Calendar of Treasury Books, Volume 5, 1676-1679*, ed. William A Shaw (London, 1911), pp. 1106-1120, *Money Book (General)* p. 309.

Charge whilst I was King'ˢ Schollar }
till I was Elected to yᵉ University .. }   *39:17:0*

Charge at the University till I }
took my Batchelors Degree, and}   *142:10:0*
came for London … … … … … … … }

    Totall for 14 Years Education -   *213: 5: 0*
NB.
Of this whole charge at the University, vizͭ͟ … *142:10:0*
My Tutor received for me by }
Exhibitions & Livery money }   *32: 2: 4*
And Wages … … … … … … … }

So that the real expence I }
putt my Friends to was but}   *110: 7: 8*
To wᶜʰ add the 2 former Summs …   *70:15:0*

    Totall is …   *181: 2: 8*

Lynn concludes the record of this early part of his life with the following:

> *… I continued till I took my Batchelor of Arts Degree, wᶜʰ: was in Febͬ: 1694/5, which being over, and I not under obligation of keeping any more Terms, the 25ᵗʰ: of that Month,*

I left the College and came away to London.

March 15:1694/5

My Bro: Samuel, who was a Clerk in the Warr Office, was appointed to go abroad to Spain with Brigad^r Steuart as Secretary to the Expedition & Deputy Judge Advocate of ye Forces sent to Palamos; And that he might have an opportunity of returning to his Desk again when he came back, I undertook to Supply his place whilst absent.[32] *This brought me by Mr John Thurstons assistance to the knowledge of George Clarke Esqr: Judge Advocate Gen^{ll} of the Forces and Secretary at Warr here at home, during K: Williams absence abroad, who was attended by M^r: Blathwayt.*

Aprill 10:1695

Just about this time was erected A Board of General Officers of the Army, who were to meet at the Horse Guards to redress abuses & greivances in the Army, and were attended by M^r. Clarke as Judge Advocate; And it being proposed to me by M^r: Clarke, to embark in that Service, as one of his Clerks, I accordingly had a Dep^y appointed me there, with a Salary of 2^{sh}:6 a day; And thereupon I fixd my resolution not to return to the University, but in this way of Publick Business (which was always my own inclination, tho' in duty to my Father, if he had lived, I should have taken Orders) to begin the World; accordingly Sent word to my Chum Rich^d. Chambre[33] *at*

---

[32] This sequence of events is corroborated in Samuel Lynn's own account '*A Short Narrative of the case of Samuel Lynn …*'. He fails, however, to mention his brother Francis's help in this respect.

[33] The Rev. Richard Chambre, an Old Pauline (i.e. a former pupil at St Paul's School), was at Trinity as a Pauline Exhibitioner from 1692 to 1698. Later a Fellow of Sidney Sussex College, and afterwards Vicar of Loppington in Shropshire. He died in February 1752 aged, according to '*The Gentleman's Magazine*', 70, which seems likely to have been a mistake for 80.

Cambridge, to dispose of my Bed, & other things to the best advantage for paying what remain due to my Tutor &c.

November 7.ᵗʰ following, My Bro: Samˡˡ returnd from his Expedition, and took his place again with Mʳ. Blathwayt, and I continued with Mʳ: Clarke.

We now come to what in Francis Lynn's life were to prove pivotal meetings – one of them in particular:

About this time, Mʳ Tho: Thompson, who was Lieutᵗ. of a Company of Invalids³⁴ at Upnor-Castle³⁵ in Kent, happened to have some matters before the Board of Genˡˡ. Officers, and applying to me to assist him, & putt him right in his proceedings, he invited me to dinner to his Lodgings, at Mʳ Morlands his Brother in Law, in Sᵗ Margarets Church Yard Westminster where at Table I the first time saw Mʳˢ Mary Thompson his Neice, and fell in Love with her, which after some time I made known to her, & courted her accordingly.

'Mrs' Mary Thompson was in fact unmarried; 'Mistress', abbreviated to 'Mrs', was then commonly used to refer to both married and single women. "*Mr Morland*" (or Moreland) was the second husband of Mary's mother, the former Elizabeth Thompson,³⁶ whose first husband Lt. Robert Thompson, eldest brother of Thomas Thompson, had died violently in 1678.

---

³⁴ Such companies were formed from those who had become unfit for military service due to wounds or disabilities sustained on active duty, or were retired without a pension.

³⁵ Upnor Castle was, and is, an Elizabethan artillery fort on the banks of the River Medway in Kent.

³⁶ Not to be confused with her mother-in-law Mrs Elizabeth Thompson, the wife (and soon to be the widow) of Robert Thompson senior.

To find out who these people were, and the extraordinary circumstances and consequences of Lt. Thompson's death, we need to go back more than forty-five years – to the village of Dulwich, five miles or so south of the city of London, and to a substantial property there called Hall Place.

CHAPTER 2

Hall Place, Dulwich

Until it was demolished in 1882, Hall Place lay at the northern end of a 32-acre estate which stretched from what is now Park Hall Road, London SE21, to Paxton Green SE19, bounded on the west by Hall Lane, which ran behind what are now the rear boundaries of the houses on the west side of South Croxted Road, and marked the south-west boundary of Dulwich. To the east of the Hall Place estate was Dulwich Common, essentially almost the whole of Dulwich south of what is now the South Circular road. That eastern boundary now approximates to Alleyn Road.

By 1619 the house was wholly or partly surrounded by a moat – unique in Dulwich, and certainly rare in that part of what is now London's southern suburbia and was then the north-east corner of Surrey – although that had gone by 1810. Renamed 'The Manor House' by its occupant in the 1850s, Hall Place never was the manor house of Dulwich – that was Dulwich Court, also demolished in the 1880s, which lay near the present Court Lane entrance to

Dulwich Park, and there is no evidence (despite persistent claims to the contrary) that Hall Place was ever the residence of Edward Alleyn, Founder of Dulwich College. Nevertheless, Hall Place was by all accounts an imposing house – Dulwich's second most important, at least.

The history of Hall Place and the 26 acres originally farmed with it (not necessarily the same land farmed with it from the mid-17th-century onwards) can be traced back to an early 13th-century clearing at the northern end of the 1,600-acre Great North Wood that stretched from Croydon almost as far as the present South Circular. That part of Dulwich Common on which Dulwich College presently stands was by 1400 no longer dense woodland, but rather scrubby pasture for the local inhabitants to graze their sheep and cattle on, so from Hall Place, looking in any direction but south and west, one would have had an uninterrupted view of fields and common land with, in the distance, the five or six houses along the north side of Dulwich Common and, beyond them, the hamlet at the centre of the 1,200-acre manor of Dulwich, home to some two hundred souls. (By the 1660s the inhabitants would have numbered about three hundred, which increased slowly until the population explosion triggered by the coming of the railways in the 19th century.) The view to the west would have been similarly rural, although partly obstructed by one house, which may also have dated from medieval times, on the west side of Hall Lane, in the adjoining manor of Levehurst. The name given to that house in the early 19th century was 'The Cottage', belying what was in fact quite a grand structure, and in the late 14th century it may have been known as 'Calverleys'.[37] Levehurst lay at the southern end of the parish of St Mary, Lambeth; Dulwich was part (until 1894) of the parish of St Giles, Camberwell, and is now in the London Borough of Southwark.

The clearing which became Hall Place was made by someone called Gerard (possibly William Gerard who in 1235 looked after the Dulwich woods for Bermondsey Priory),[38] and in 1404[39] was referred to as "*a messuage formerly called Gerardes, now Kinolles*". From 1376 to 1398 this freehold property, which either had never formed part of Dulwich manor or had been sold off or given away by Bermondsey Priory at some time prior to 1290,[40] was owned by a famous and fearsome English warrior called Sir Robert Knolles, or rather by trustees on his behalf.

We know of owners before Knolles – from 1329 they were, in order, Henry Horpol, John le Herde, Thomas de Hockele, Richard de Bailey, Laurence de Merkyngfeld, Robert de Boxford, Gilbert de Meldeborne, and John Pere – and we know of owners after Knolles – Sir Robert Denny, William Weston,

---

[37] It appears to be so marked on a map of Levehurst manor dated 1563 (on which Hall Place is also marked, on the periphery). Coincidentally, or not, Sir Robert Knolles (mentioned below) and Sir Hugh Calverley, both renowned soldiers, were close friends, if not related.

[38] '*The 1235 Surrey Eyre*', vol. 2 (ed. D. Crook), Surrey Record Society 1983.

[39] Dulwich College Archives, Court Rolls, CR B8(r), ll. 47-50.

[40] Although freehold, 40*d* p.a. rent was payable for it, so that there was a 'superior' freehold above it in the feudal 'ladder'. Such sub-infeudations were banned by the Statute of *Quia Emptores* in 1290.

John Wynter, and Nicholas Molyneux – up to about 1460, but there is then a gap of 70 years when we have no information at all. We know almost nothing about some of these owners, and a very great deal about others – de Boxford, Knolles, Denny, Weston, Wynter and Molyneux in particular. (The latter two were 'brothers-in-arms', who in 1421 had pledged to each other that any property either acquired in England with profits they made in France – which included 'the manor of Knolles' – would belong to the survivor, an agreement which Wynter broke by the terms of his Will prior to his death in 1445, and which Molyneux spent most of the following eight years seeking to enforce, with eventual success.)[41]

We have no physical description of the original building, so I have to apply some educated guesswork. The mansion, or manor house, would in medieval times have been at least two storeys high, and almost certainly constructed principally of wooden beams, probably local oak – oak trees were predominant in the Great North Wood. Typically it would have contained a great hall, a solar (the family's private living and sleeping quarters, generally on an upper floor), a kitchen, storerooms, and quarters for servants and (if the owner kept one, which Sir Robert Knolles certainly did, and Sir Robert Denny may have done) a personal force of men-at-arms, to guard him when he was in residence and the premises when he was not. It might also have been protected by the moat previously mentioned. If there is any surviving archaeological evidence of any of this, it is now buried

---

[41] '*A Business-Partnership in War and Administration*', part of '*England in the Fifteenth Century*', by Dr. K. B. McFarlane, 1983.

under No's 1 to 7 South Croxted Road and 64 to 74 Park Hall Road.

The story of the house resumes in 1530, by which date – no-one knows when, how, or why – the freehold had been re-acquired by Bermondsey Abbey (as it now was), which granted to John Scott of Camberwell a 50-year lease of Dulwich manor, including "*a Manor or Tenement called Knowlys now held and occupied by John Wylcokkes*", and apparently used by Wylcokkes as a lodging house called "*a blynde ostery*" (i.e. a blind hostelry, whatever that was) containing "*unruly men and women*" (on second thoughts, one can guess what it probably was).[42] John Wylcokkes had gone by 1534, and by 1542 someone had renamed the house Hall Place, although there are some later references[43] to "*Hall Place alias Knowles*".

After the dissolution of Bermondsey Abbey the eventual buyers of the manor of Dulwich from Henry VIII were a London goldsmith, Thomas Calton, and his wife Margaret, and the Letters Patent[44] granted to them in 1544 referred to "*the messuage or mansion house called the Hall Place (now or late in the tenure or occupation of Thomas Henley) and all and singular houses buildings, structures, barns, stables, dovecotes, lands, tenements, fields, meadows, pastures, rents, reversions, services, woods, underwoods, &c., ... and demised or let to the said Thomas Henley*". I believe that the lands farmed with Hall Place at this time (apart from its immediate 'curtilege') were exclusively to the north, and not (as later) to the

---

[42] Dulwich College Archives (DCA), Court Roll for 27/2/1522, CR E2(verso), ll.27-29.

[43] DCA, Warner's Catalogue (WC), Muns. 581, 586/587.

[44] DCA, WC, Mun. 331.

south, of it, as that was still woodland.

Thomas Henley's leasehold "*farme called knowles*" o1
Hall Place passed by his Will in 1544 to his wife
Elisabeth for her life, then to his son William. In May
1597 the then lord of the manor of Dulwich, Thomas
Calton's grandson Francis, granted to a Camberwell
yeoman, John Bone, a 21-year lease of the "*messuage or
tenement comonlie called or knowne by the name of Hall place
… in Upper Dullwich*" with about 12 acres adjoining,
lately occupied by Edmond Curson and formerly by
his father Christopher Curson, and another 33 acres
(some of the parcels now forming part of 'Belair')
lying north of Hall Place, all for £20 a year.

John Bone was gone from Dulwich by the Spring
of 1619, and on 22nd June 1619 (the day after Edward
Alleyn's new foundation of Dulwich College received
its Letters Patent from James I) Alleyn – the retired
Elizabethan actor/impresario who had bought the
manor of Dulwich from Sir Francis Calton in 1605 –
granted a new lease[45] of Hall Place and its barns,
stables, outbuildings, orchards, etc. – 2 acres in all –
and the moat (its first recorded mention) around the
house, and six acres called the homefield adjoining
south of the house (but none of the other lands which
Bone had farmed, for which Alleyn had other plans),
to William Lawton, a London haberdasher. Hall
Place's relatively brief interlude as the abode of
yeoman-farmers was over, and for the rest of its
existence it was to revert to being the residence of
wealthy men of business, of one sort or another.

Lawton's was one of the last Dulwich leases to be

---

[45] DCA, WC, Muns 582 and (for counterpart) 583.

term of more than 21 years – the
h the College, after Edward Alleyn's
was allowed by its Statutes to grant,
anged by private Act of Parliament in
_. in addition, College leases had to be granted at
a 'rack rent', in other words the full annual market
rent, and without charging a 'fine', or premium, or
capital sum, at the start of the lease. Lawton had paid
Alleyn a premium of £40 for his lease.

Unlike some if not most of his predecessors,
William Lawton actually lived at Hall Place. His
haberdashery business may have failed, as after March
1628 his rent remained unpaid, and by March 1633
the lessee of Hall Place and its 8 acres was Arthur
Rawthmell, a lawyer with offices in Chancery Lane.
However, the centre of gravity of the Hall Place estate
was shifted south, towards the woodlands, and to add
to his lease of the house and its 8 acres, Rawthmell
was granted another of 20 acres (actually about 23
acres, in five fields) lying southward of Hall Place and
its 'homefield', at an additional rent of £6 p.a., to
make a total of £14. We learn nearly thirty years later
that those '20 acres' were formerly called Lings
Coppice,[46] woodland cleared by Edward Alleyn's
direction, and were to remain part of the Hall Place
estate for the rest of its existence.

After Arthur Rawthmell died in June 1644, his two
sons Robert and John became embroiled in a legal
dispute[47] with an uncle of Robert's wife, Robert
Ballett, into whose possession Rawthmell's Will and

---

[46] The modern housing development called Lings Coppice is
some distance to the north, along Croxted Road.
[47] TNA, Pleadings Bundles C 2/ChasI/R1/71, and C 10/10/21.

deeds had come. The matter was settled on the basis that Ballett handed over the Will[48] to Robert Rawthmell (who had borrowed substantial sums from him) in return for having the leases of Hall Place and other Dulwich lands assigned to him. Robert Ballett remained as tenant of all these properties (although they were temporarily forfeited to the Commonwealth on account of his support of the Royalist cause) until March 1652. He then assigned his leases to a Mr St. John Gwilliams (or Gwylliams), of Grays Inn, of whom I know only that he subsequently succeeded to a baronetcy and that in 1683 he was thought[49] to bear a striking resemblance to Richard Cromwell, Lord Protector for nine months in 1658, then living incognito. St. John Gwilliams was succeeded to Hall Place (and Lings) by John Cutter, late in 1656.

The Dulwich manor court rolls for 1656 record a presentation by the manor jury regarding "*A Cottage lately erected by Arthur Rothmeale upon the waste of the said Mannor, which said Cottage togeather with some land lying between the Moate and the said Cottage belong unto the Common or waste of the said Mannor from the hedge at the south end of the Barne to the Orchard at the north end of the house commonly called Hall Place*". Rawthmell had indeed been 'presented' in 1641, and he and his successors several times since, for encroaching on the west part of the Common (owned by Dulwich College) by building a 'Court House' and a brick bridge with a gate, and in 1656 the Jurors asked the College, as Lord of the Manor, to arrange for its removal and for the land to

---

[48] TNA, ref: PROB 11/193/12.
[49] State Papers Domestic, Car.II: 420, No. 721.

be restored as Common. This never happened.

Early in the Interregnum, Parliament had sacked the College's four Fellows and replaced them with two ineffectual substitutes. This insufficiency of Officers prevented the College from enforcing its legal rights and granting new leases – none of any Dulwich properties was granted between the end of April 1644 and the restoration of the monarchy in March 1660. As the old leases expired, the tenants simply 'held over' at their old rents. The College fought back as best it could. Soon after John Cutter took over Hall Place, it authorised one Harris, representing the College's interests, to issue ejectment proceedings against Cutter. Harris claimed that the College had in November 1656 granted him a lease of the premises, from which Cutter had ejected him. "*The Founder and his successors have let leases of the lands in question which are out divers years. And the defendant hath noe title to them, but will kepe them at the old rent which are worth three times the value … And the Cottage is built upon the waste of the Common there and the defendant was presented for erecting it.*"

The College did not pursue the matter – indeed, it may have been too late to do so, as Rawthmell and his successors had effectively acquired 'squatters' rights' over the land he had commandeered, which remained part of the Hall Place estate. There are no contemporaneous maps or plans of Hall Place, but I have shown what I think was the extent of the encroachment by edging on the plan reproduced below.

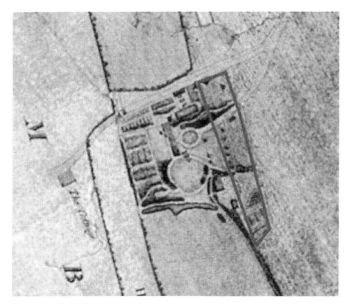

An extract from a map of Dulwich c.1806, showing Hall Place (but not its estate, to the south), with the approximate extent of Arthur Rawthmell's 1641 'encroachment' edged.

It is possible that the '*moate*' mentioned in the 1656 court roll had been constructed not long before it was first referred to in William Lawton's 1619 lease, but for most of the preceding century Hall Place had been occupied by yeoman-farmers who would have been unlikely to have been able to afford such an extravagance, or wanted it, so I think it more likely that it dated from Sir Robert Knolles' time. By 1656 the moat must have been principally ornamental, whatever its original purpose.

John Cutter reached some sort of compromise with the College, as his name appears in the rent table for Lady Day[50] 1657 at £20 (instead of the previous £14) a year, far short of the 'three times' claimed by the College's attorney Mr Harris. On 20th September 1661 the College granted Cutter a lease[51] of "*All that messuage or Mansion howse called Hall place, with all Barnes Stables out howses Orchards yards Gardens backsides with the moat round about the said Messuage*" (c.2 acres), and a parcel of pasture called Homefield (6 acres) lying south of the messuage, and four closes or fields of pasture (c.20 acres) called Lyngs lying southwards of the former, for 21 years at a rent of £20 p.a. and two capons, "*sweet and good*", annually on 29th June.

Despite being granted his new lease of Hall Place in September 1661, John Cutter had decided to sell anyway, and he or his agent furnished a 'particular' of the property to, no doubt amongst others, Nicholas Thurman, a London merchant. On 3rd May 1662 Thurman called to view the premises and to inspect the new lease. Having done so (perhaps, in the case of the lease, too cursorily), he agreed to buy Cutter's leasehold interest for £520 (less an apportionment for rent due) and (so Cutter later alleged) to pay another £15 for a piece of plate, a marble dial, and some other chattels which Cutter said he was happy to leave behind.

---

[50] March 25th, when until 1752 (the year when Britain switched from the Julian to the Gregorian calendar, and lost eleven days in the process) the legal year started. In this book, all dates between 1st January and 24th March inclusive, up to 1752, are given 'Old Style', with the 'New Style' date indicated in brackets. Francis Lynn himself, in his 'diary', employed the convention of referring to dates between January 1st and March 24th as, e.g., "15 March 1694/5".

[51] DCA, Bickley's Catalogue (BC), 100-92.

The deal, however it was interpreted by each of the parties, was struck, and on 26th May 1662 Dulwich College granted Cutter licence[52] to assign the lease to Nicholas Thurman. Thurman later claimed[53] that Cutter had given him to understand that the land was worth £60 a year (Thurman thought, after a few years' experience of it, that it was worth no more than £40 a year), that the annual rent was £20 and no more, and that when the lease expired the College would automatically renew it at the old rent. Furthermore Cutter had (so Thurman said, although Cutter denied it) promised to repair the barn which had partially collapsed, and to provide four hundred loads of London dung, each load to be as much as four horses could draw, before the sale was completed. Cutter declined to provide Thurman with a receipt for the £520 until the £15 for the plate (and dial etc.) had also been paid. He also denied that the barn had fallen down while he was owner. However, in the spirit of compromise, he agreed to leave 100 loads of dung "*in a place very neere and convenient to bee laid on the premisses*". He conceded that "*the glass windowes*[54] *of the dwelling house on the premisses*" were "*somewhat broken*", and had replaced them, with which Thurman, he claimed, had "*declared himselfe well pleased*".

The reference to broken windows suggests that the house may have been unoccupied for some time. Thurman's request for 400 cart-loads of dung – a very large quantity of fertiliser on any reckoning – suggests

---

[52] DCA, WC, MS VI/24c.

[53] *Thiruman [sic, Thurman] v. Cutter*, 1664-67, TNA refs: C 7/345/70 and C 7/489/54.

[54] Glass windows in residential properties in England were rare prior to the 17th century.

that his intention was to convert to arable use the fields of pasture which Lings had been since it ceased to be woodland, and to make the "*farme*" (which is how he consistently refers to the Hall Place estate) pay for itself rather better than it had previously.

How these proceedings, which seem to have gone on fitfully until 1667, were resolved is unknown, but on 1st November 1662, on surrendering John Cutter's lease, Nicholas Thurman, merchant, of Sherborne Lane in the parish of St Mary Woolnoth, London, was granted a lease of "*a messuage or Mansion House called Hall Place*" of which he was already in occupation, and the lands that went with it (using exactly the same description as in Cutter's 1661 lease), for 19 (not 21) years from Michaelmas 1662, at £20 and "*a couple of fat capons, sweet and good*", on June 29th every year.[55]

Of Nicholas Thurman's origins I can say nothing for certain. The surname 'Thurman' had been known in England since the Middle Ages, but originated in Scandinavia, and Nicholas Thurman may have been born there, or in Germany, or in the Low Countries. There is no record of his birth in England, at least none that I have encountered. At any rate, by 1657 Nicholas had married Elizabeth, daughter of James Vickers, a prosperous 68-year-old merchant and former Alderman of London, and she is referred to in Vickers' Will[56] of 8th October that year only as "*my daughter Thurman*".

---

[55] DCA, BC, 100-106 (dated 17/7/1662); Env. 19/1 (dated 1/11/1662). It must have been the capons that Cutter forgot to tell Thurman about. Easily done.
[56] TNA, ref: PROB/11/269/289.

The probate court transcription of Vickers' Will covers nine sheets of parchment. Much of it is given over to scathing criticism of Vickers' other son-in-law John Hackett (who had fled to Ireland, leaving his wife and three children destitute) and of his own eldest son, John, whom Vickers had sent to trade in Russia "*which was my former Life*", but who had proved to be (in his father's opinion) a disobedient wastrel. Nevertheless, Vickers provided legacies for him and his three minor children, as well as for Vickers' wife, Mary, other sons Edward and William, and daughters Anne Hackett and Elizabeth Thurman, totalling in excess of £14,000, an enormous sum for the time. John's infant children were, at 21, to receive between them half of a £5,000 debt (which John and his father each claimed as due to him), and John himself, "*to satisfie his covetous wicked desire*", was to get the other half.

Nicholas Thurman, James Vickers' son-in-law, was appointed "*Executor with my wife for the better Carying on the busines*", by which Vickers could have meant either the business of administering his estate or the mercantile business in which he and Thurman were partners. Either way, this shows that Nicholas Thurman was someone whom his father-in-law trusted, and who after Alderman Vickers' death was to be the *paterfamilias* of his somewhat dysfunctional family, some of whom came to live with Thurman and his wife. (Two of Edward's daughters, Rebeckah and Abigale, were still living with their aunt Elizabeth and her second husband in 1697.) The executors were, "*for theire paines and Care*", to share one-quarter of residue (which eventually proved to be £552 4s 1d), and the other three quarters were to be divided in specified shares between members of Vickers' family.

Vickers died shortly after making his Will, and was buried at St. Augustine's, Watling Street, on 6th November 1657.

Nicholas Thurman dealt, amongst other commodities, in wine[57], brandy[58], and raisins[59], and would, like his father-in-law, have plied his trade in Russia and all points between there and England. He owned a 3/16ths share in a 90-ton ship called '*The James of London*' that frequently sailed between the ports of London and Malaga[60] and further afield. He was active in commerce at a time when England and the United Provinces (the Netherlands) were vying for control of trade in the East Indies, the Baltic, and elsewhere in the world, even though throughout the 17th century strong cultural, social, and political links developed between the two powers.[61] These Anglo-Dutch trading disputes sometimes descended into war, first between 1652 and 1654, again between 1665 and 1667, and again later in that century and in the next. In between these wars were occasional skirmishes, such as when in October 1661 the Privy Council resolved[62] that the Dutch ambassadors should be approached about making reparation to Nicholas Thurman, Edward Vickers (Thurman's

---

[57] TNA, State Papers Domestic, Charles II, 1666-67.

[58] TNA, Treasury Books 1679-80[*sic,* the entry, relating to brandy being imported by Thurman and others, relates to 1668], *Out Letters* (*Customs*) VI, pp 59-60.]

[59] *Bands v. Norman & others* (1673), TNA C6/52/8.

[60] *Ibid.*

[61] Lisa Jardine's '*Going Dutch*' (2012) explains the origins and development of these links, culminating in the 'Glorious Revolution' of 1688 which in all but name was a successful invasion of England by the Dutch.

[62] TNA ref: SP 84/164/83, folio 126.

brother-in-law) and Edward Adams, for the seizure of a ship called '*The John Baptist*', from which one can at least infer that the three men owned its cargo, if not the ship itself. In January 1667[8] a House of Lords sub-committee heard the evidence of Nicholas Thurman and fourteen other merchants, claiming that the goods aboard several French merchant ships seized *en route* had been bought with the proceeds of English commodities, and were not French goods (the importing of which had been banned by Royal Proclamation).[63]

Once the broken windows of Hall Place were replaced, and other repairs carried out, Nicholas Thurman, his wife Elizabeth, and their three-year-old daughter Mary (born on 10th June 1659, and baptised eleven days later at St. Mary Woolnoth Church[64]), could have moved in, with their servants (including Hannah Pratt) and some or all of Elizabeth's indigent relatives, and probably did so. Nicholas and Elizabeth had no other children who survived infancy, so their daughter Mary might have been expected to inherit considerable wealth.

As well as making the land attached to Hall Place more profitable by growing crops, Nicholas Thurman had the bright idea of setting up a tile kiln, using some of the rich brown Dulwich clay lying not more than a few inches below the surface of his fields, to take advantage of the high demand for bricks and tiles after the city of London was all but destroyed by the

---

[63] *House of Lords Journal*, vol. 12. France was, temporarily, siding with the Dutch, who had recently sacked the fort at Sheerness and briefly occupied the Isle of Sheppey.

[64] Ancestry.co.uk, FHL Film number 897089.

Great Fire of September 1666.[65] He applied for the necessary licence from Dulwich College, which was duly granted on 6th November 1667.[66] Thurman was to be allowed to open up a quarter acre of one of the fields "*called Lings*", in order to extract clay "*for the making of Tiles, and to build and set up a Kilne for the burning of them, and two workhouses*", but for a period of seven years only.

When Nicholas Thurman made his last Will[67] on 27th March 1671, he left his houses and lands in Sutton, Wildherne and Charleton (all in Hampshire) and a house in Dukes Place, London, to his daughter Mary. Evidently he had second thoughts, and in a Codicil dated 15th May gave that house to his sole Executrix (his wife Elizabeth) instead, for the payment of his debts, legacies and funeral expenses, if the proceeds of two other houses in Philpott Lane[68], mentioned in the Will, proved insufficient for the purpose. If Mary – who was not yet 12 – died without issue, the properties left to her were by the Will to go to his wife Elizabeth, who in any case was to receive "*All that Colledge Lease of Gods guift Colledge of Dullwich And the Messuage or Tenement grounds and premises thereby granted for and during the remainder of the terme therein unexpired And alsoe all other the Coppyhold lands in*

---

65 Between 1668 and the end of 1672 at least 9,450 new brick houses were built in the city, to replace the previous wooden structures which had burned down.

66 DCA. The licence has been inserted at the end of the second 'Register Book of Accomptes', 1652-1678 (BC:28).

67 TNA ref: PROB 11/336/93.

68 The properties in Philpot Lane were to involve Elizabeth, and her then husband Robert Thompson, in litigation in 1685, when they were sued by one Sydrach Denham. [TNA ref: C 7/91/24]

Dullwich aforesaid lately taken up by me of the Colledge", an annuity (or "*Rent Charge lately Purchased of Sr Edmo: Bowyer*") of £30 p.a., a house in St. Helen's (in Bishopsgate, leased from the Leathersellers Company), another house in Bishopsgate, another (leasehold) house in Winchester Street, and "*my Jewells Plate and houshould Stuffe And all other things not herein bequeathed*".

Since there was no clause specifically disposing of residue, those last seven words would have deprived Mary Thurman of everything other than the properties in Hampshire, although they may well have produced a substantial income for her in later life.

The Will and Codicil were not particularly well-drafted, and several points – particularly the issue of how many properties would have to be sold to cover any debts, and who was to be entitled to any excess proceeds – could later have led to argument, if not litigation. The "*Colledge Lease*" clearly refers to Hall Place and its estate, and "*the Coppyhold lands in Dullwich*" referred to 6 copyhold acres in Napps (in three parcels, lying together east of Croxted Lane) which Thurman had bought from Richard Dawlman (son and heir of Robert Dawlman, a London publisher of Puritan tracts) in 1669, but Thurman seems to have forgotten that only the previous year he had also acquired from Dawlman another 5 acres (although under-estimated at the time as $4a.1r.0p.$)[69] adjoining south of the 6 copyhold acres, and this was leasehold (held of Dulwich College), not copyhold. Not being specifically mentioned, it arguably formed

---

[69] There were 40 perches ('*p.*') to the rood ('*r.*'), and 4 roods to the acre ('*a.*'), which was 4,840 square yards (about 0.4 hectares).

part of residue, disposed of by those words "*and all other things not herein bequeathed*", in which case Elizabeth Thurman would have been entitled to it anyway. That, as we shall learn, could not necessarily be said for the copyhold.

CHAPTER 3

Dulwich and Sheerness

Copyhold was an ancient form of tenure, quite possibly pre-dating the Norman Conquest. The imposition of the feudal system after 1066 moulded it into a form which lasted virtually unchanged until its abolition by statute in 1922, leaving only the tenures more familiar to us, namely freehold and leasehold. The essential feature of copyhold was that land could only be sold, given, or passed to an heir, by being 'surrendered' to the lord of the manor in question (or, more usually, his steward), to the use of a specified person (or persons). The lord (or his steward) would then, after the completion by the new tenant of certain formalities such as making 'fealty' to the lord, paying an entry fine, and, if the previous copyholder had died, giving a 'heriot' of the deceased's 'best beast' (or its equivalent value), admit the new tenant to hold the property "at the will of the lord". The tenant would then be given a copy of the relevant entry made by the steward on the manor court roll – hence the term 'copyholder'.

In practice, the lord's will could be fettered by the

established customs of the manor in question, so that his tenants could hold their lands for life, or for a number of lives, or, like a freehold, in perpetuity. In Dulwich the latter was invariably the case.

With the passage of time, the tendency was for copyholds to be converted into more lucrative – for the manor's lord – leaseholds, and in Dulwich this process was certainly hastened by Edward Alleyn, who not only purchased the lordship of the manor from Sir Francis Calton in 1606, but at about that time also acquired as tenant most of the copyholds, which thus merged with the manor freehold. After 1626 only three were left in Dulwich, two of them in College Road (one opposite the Dulwich Picture Gallery, the other comprising the site of 'Oakfield' and Allison Grove), the third near the Turney Road junction with Croxted Road, where the railway lines now intersect. (A fourth copyhold would be created out of former common land between Acacia Grove and Park Hall Road when Dulwich Common was enclosed after 1805, and was allocated amongst the remaining copyholders.) From the 17th century onwards, the copyholders, unlike most of their medieval predecessors, were generally wealthy absentee landlords.

There were strict rules of copyhold inheritance to be followed. These did not necessarily conform to common law (which generally followed the rule of primogeniture, but after the Wills Act of 1540 could be varied by the testator's wishes). In Dulwich, in common with some manors in Kent, the custom was that when a copyholder died it was – as in the old folk or 'fairy' tales – his *youngest* son, not the eldest, who inherited, and if there were daughters they inherited equally (or alone, if there was only one). Surviving spouses did not come into it, unless they were already a joint owner.

Therefore for Elizabeth Thurman, and not her daughter Mary (who according to manorial custom was the sole heir), to have been admitted to the copyhold which Nicholas Thurman purported to leave Elizabeth in his Will would, in the absence of any previous surrender of the property by him to the uses declared in his last Will (a device being used increasingly often), have required two reputable Dulwich tenants to declare on oath (perhaps perjuring themselves in the process) that, immediately before his death, Thurman had surrendered the copyhold to the use of his wife. Although there is no evidence that that happened, Elizabeth Thurman somehow managed to be recognised as the heir.

Almost immediately after signing (and sealing) his Codicil, in the presence of the same three persons who witnessed his Will, Nicholas Thurman died. His widow Elizabeth wasted no time obtaining probate, which she did with perhaps indecent haste on 17th May 1671, before Nicholas was even cold in his grave – his burial at St Giles, Camberwell, did not take place until five days later. Nor does she seem to have lost much time in finding a second husband, Robert Thompson, who may have been a friend of her late husband Nicholas – and of herself. Thompson already had children of his own – sons Robert, Levet, and Thomas, and a daughter, Elizabeth.

I have not traced where or when Mrs Elizabeth Thurman and Mr Robert Thompson were married, but it must have been between September 1671 (when Mrs Thurman is briefly recorded in the College rent tables as tenant) and March 1672. Thereafter Robert Thompson is recorded as responsible for the rents payable on his wife's leaseholds (£20 p.a. for Hall Place, £3 5s p.a. for the 4a.1r.0p. in Napps), and on her copyhold (a mere 1s 3d a year for the 6 acres in Napps). Before her marriage to Thompson, Elizabeth Thurman took the relatively unusual precaution of insisting on a pre-nuptial agreement, whereby whatever property she owned would remain hers to dispose of after the marriage. This stipulation was to have a crucial impact on the future of Hall Place. Whether the Thompsons continued to use Hall Place as their family home I do not know. It is more likely than not that the property was let to a suitable under-tenant, and the family (including two of Elizabeth's Vickers nieces) lived at Robert Thompson's London house.

Where Robert Thompson (or Thomson, or Tompson) came from I have been unable to discover. A Major (later Colonel) Robert Thompson figures fairly regularly as a person of some authority in Parliamentary proceedings during the Interregnum, and later as a major shareholder in, and Director of, the East India Company, but he seems to have been a different Robert Thompson from ours, as was the Robert Thompson who was a Clerk of Writs in 1690,[70] the Robert Thompson whose daughter Elizabeth married William Ashurst, Lord Mayor of London 1692-94,[71] and the Robert Thompson who

---

[70] TNA, State Papers Domestic, William & Mary, *S.P. Dom. Warrant Book* 35, *p.* 416.
[71] *Survey of London*, vol.17, St Pancras part I, Highgate Village.

on 25th July 1649 was approved[72] by the House of Commons as a Commissioner for the Navy.

Whatever his origins and previous history, in 1660 our Robert Thompson was a convinced monarchist, for one of Charles II's first acts on ascending the throne after the Restoration was, in June 1660, to appoint Thompson as one of his six Grooms of the Privy Chamber in Ordinary, a post he was to hold (with increasing seniority) until 1694. The Grooms *"received salaries of £73 consisting of wages of £20 and board wages of £53. ... they were also entitled to diet and lodging when in attendance, candle ends, livery worth £40, riding wages and fees of honor which averaged about £30."*[73] This influential position involved personal contact with the king, and guarding the doors to his private apartments.

In March 1663 Thompson was joined by his barely-teenage son Robert, appointed a Supernumerary Assistant Groom of the Privy Chamber, no doubt on his father's recommendation. However, either from choice or necessity (if he was sacked) Robert junior soon exchanged his royal livery for naval uniform, and by 1672 was in the navy garrison at the rebuilt fort, next to the new naval dockyard, at Sheerness. (The fort had been ransacked by the Dutch, whose forces had occupied the Isle of Sheppey for nine days in 1667.) From there, at the north-west corner of Sheppey, one could see over to The Nore naval base on the Isle of Grain and, on a clear day, across the Thames estuary to Essex.

---

[72] House of Commons *Journal*, vol. 6, pp.269-270.

[73] british-history.ac.uk, *'Office-holders in Modern Britain'*, vol.11 (revised), *'Court Officers 1660-1837'*, pp. 38-42.

As this part of Kent figures prominently in events which were about to unfold, I shall cite two passages, the first written at the end of the 18th century, but which probably applied equally well at this earlier period:

"Some years since the building of a fort here [at Sheerness], a royal dock has been made adjoining to it, intended chiefly for the repairing of ships which may have met with any sudden accident, and for the building of smaller ships of war, such as 5th and 6th rates, small frigates, yachts, and such like vessels, though sometimes ships of a larger size have been built here .... This yard, in time of peace, is under the inspection of the commissioner of the navy residing at Chatham, who has a clerk of the cheque and a storekeeper resident here under him."[74]

For a general description of how dockyards such as that at Sheerness were organised, I turn to the National Archives Guide to Royal Naval Dockyard Staff:

"The senior official of each dockyard was the commissioner, who was supported by senior officers including: clerk of cheque and storekeeper - responsible for finance and administration; shipwright - responsible for building and repairs; [etc., etc.] ... Clerks and foremen, known as inferior officers, supported the senior officers. The senior officers of a victualling yard were the agent victualler (in larger establishments only), the storekeeper or naval officer, and the clerk of the cheque."

A specific example of what went on is provided by young Robert Thompson himself, writing from

---

[74] Edward Hasted, 'The ville of Sheerness', in *The History and Topographical Survey of the County of Kent*, vol. 6 (1798).

Sheerness to a senior Whitehall functionary, Sir Joseph Williamson (M.P.), on 1st September 1672:

"Ships daily come in and out to refit. The St. Michael *and* St. George *came in this afternoon, and there are in harbour near twenty men-of-war and frigates. Several are past being capable of being despatched so quickly as to go out with the fleet again, if they do go, which will not be known till his Majesty comes. ... It will be near a fortnight before they can possibly be ready."*[75]

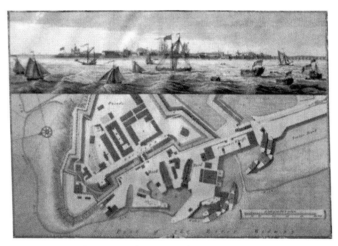

The fort and dockyard at Sheerness, 1676.

Ten days later he reported to Williamson again:

"His Majesty arrived at the fleet about four yesterday afternoon, and a day or two hence will be resolved on what will be done for this winter expedition."[76]

---

[75] TNA, State Papers Domestic, Charles II, 314, no. 156.
[76] TNA, State Papers Domestic, Charles II, 315, no. 7.

And again two days later:

"This evening's or to-morrow morning's tide, his Majesty sails for London again. It cannot be known what is resolved on board, it being very private, and none but the flag officers at the Council. Prince Rupert's maritime regiment will be raised speedily."[77]

What Robert Thompson's precise role was at Sheerness in 1672, apart from reporting to – or spying for – Sir Joseph Williamson, is unclear, although a clue as to part of his duties is provided by a letter he wrote to the Navy Commissioners from Sheerness on 30th May 1673 (by which date he was a Lieutenant, deputising for the Governor of the garrison):

"The two smacks ordered here being out of victualling I have ordered (the Governor being absent) one of them up to know your commands for to revictual. I thought it necessary to spare but one at a time lest any packets should come in the meantime."[78]

On 28th June 1675 Robert Thompson of Sheerness, Kent, Gent., a Bachelor, aged *"about 24"*, and Elizabeth Newby, of Whitechapel, Middlesex, Spinster, also aged *"about 24"* and *"at [her] own dispose"*, were married by licence at Whitechapel.[79] Actually Elizabeth was nearly 26, having been born to Francis

---

[77] TNA, State Papers Domestic, Charles II, 315, no. 30.

[78] TNA, State Papers Domestic, Charles II, May 1673, 345, no. 144.

[79] Kent: Canterbury – Marriage Licence allegations, Dean of Westminster, 1558-1699 and Vicar-General of the Archbishop of Canterbury, 1660 to 1679 (Marriage)

and Mary Newby (or Newbye) on 2nd August 1649 (which, the parish register tells us, was a Thursday) and baptised at St John's Church, Wapping, three days later.

Thompson seems to have been a somewhat hot-headed, officious and occasionally insubordinate young man, unlikely to have been popular in the Sheerness garrison. In 1674 he wrote to the Navy Commissioners accusing some of his fellow officers of embezzling broom.[80] On 9th November that year Daniel Evans, Porter of the dockyard, reported to the Navy Commissioners that Lt. Thompson, the fort's Commander-in-Chief (presumably only in the absence of the Governor of Sheerness, Maj. Darrell), had refused to allow him to bring his beer into the fort without an order from the Governor, and asked for action on this "*before the beer is spoiled or embezzled*".[81] In August 1677 Thompson's pet monkey – yes, he kept a monkey as a pet – attacked and severely frightened the child of Henry Kidwell, the Blockmaster. "*Yesterday* [wrote Thompson on 12th August] *Kidwell came in a great fury, drew his knife, fell upon the monkey to kill him at which I was forced to prevent him with a good cane*". Thompson claimed that Kidwell then threatened him.[82] Kidwell, hauled off to prison, admitted that he had taken up a lever after Lt. Thompson struck him "*several times*", but he felt that the witnesses, who were soldiers, would say whatever their officer told them to say, and he asked to be

---

80 TNA: ADM 106/298.
81 TNA: ADM 106/305.
82 TNA: ADM 106/324/452.

moved to another Yard.[83] On 5th February 1678 Captain Perryman, Master Attendant at Sheerness, reported that the previous day Captain Godfrey had showed him the Board's letter to have the *Swallow*'s guns put aboard her for ballast, but Lt. Thompson *"would not allow it"*.[84]

While Lt. Thompson was throwing his weight around at Sheerness, countermanding orders from his superiors in the process, another young man had arrived in the area from north-east England and was endeavouring to make his way in the world – Samuel Hunter, who will figure a great deal in what follows. From the fact that when he died fifty years later almost all of his surviving relatives were living in or near Durham, it is highly likely that he was born there. Samuel Hunter, son of Thomas Hunter, born and/or baptised at Bishopwearmouth on 8th June 1651, is the most likely candidate for our Samuel Hunter.[85] When, how, or why he decided to travel to south-east England is not known.

At any rate, by May 1673 Hunter was Clerk of the Cheque at Sheerness.[86] He had not been long at the dockyard when on 29th November that year tragedy struck, and a 60-gun warship, the *Anne*, with a complement (including some wives and children) of 250, blew up off The Nore, on the Isle of Grain opposite Sheerness, and sank. Hunter reported on the following Sunday to the effect that the disaster, which

---

[83] TNA: ADM 106/328/34.

[84] TNA: ADM 106/333/144.

[85] Bishopwearmouth Parish Register, ancestry.co.uk FHL Film Number: 0091083, 0091084

[86] TNA: SP 46/137/437; ADM 106/281/159.

had so far claimed 120 lives, might have been caused by carpenters' candles in the powder room.[87] (Another source attributed it to "*the gunner's negligence, who was disordered with drink*".)[88]

Samuel Hunter was close in age to Robert Thompson junior, and the two were certainly acquainted, if not actually friends, so when in 1676 Lt. Thompson visited, or was visited by, his step-sister, Mary Thurman, whose 17th birthday was rapidly approaching, he must have introduced her to Hunter, perhaps at some assembly or similar event at or near the garrison in Sheerness. Mary may have been chaperoned by her uncle Edward Vickers, who, separated from his wife Petronella,[89] was shortly to be appointed by the Customs Commissioners as Customs Collector at Colchester,[90] a post he was to hold (while continuing his activities as a merchant) until his death there in June 1688.[91] If so, Hunter may have quizzed Mary's 'Uncle Vickers' on how best to seize prohibited or untaxed goods, a subject on which Vickers would have been knowledgeable, and about which Hunter wrote to the Customs Commissioners on 2nd June 1676.[92]

---

[87] TNA: ADM 106/291, folio 234.

[88] TNA, State Papers Domestic, Chas II, December 1673: R. Yard to Sir J. Williamson, 5/12/1673.

[89] When buried in May 1682 at St George's, Southwark, she was referred to in the parish register as "*Petronella Viccars, widow*", suggesting that she at least had regarded the marriage as over.

[90] TNA, Treasury Books, Entry Book September 1676, *Out Letters (Customs)* III. p. 213.

[91] TNA, PROB 11/392/289

[92] TNA, Treasury Book; Entry Book: June 1676, *Out Letters (Customs)* III. p. 159.

Whatever the circumstances, Mary Thurman and Samuel Hunter met and fell for each other, and on 28th October 1676 they were married at Rainham Parish Church[93], about eight miles from Sheerness, on the mainland. Samuel was 25, Mary 17. As a minor, she presumably married with the blessing, or at least the acquiescence, of her mother, Elizabeth Thompson. Who attended the ceremony, apart from the bride and groom, is not known, although the fact that Rainham is on the main road from London to Dover suggests that wedding guests from London were expected, and that a ceremony on Sheppey itself, requiring a crossing of the Swale at Kingsferry, would have been considered too inconvenient for them. There was probably a marriage settlement made immediately before the day of the wedding, transferring ownership to Samuel of property for the eventual benefit of any children of the marriage, failing which for Mary herself, but it has not survived and we do not know its terms. For reasons which emerge later, however, it seems likely to have been of the houses and lands in Sutton, Wildhern and Charleton (all in Hampshire), worth £56 a year, which Nicholas Thurman had intended by his Will to go to his daughter Mary anyway.

Hunter seems to have been a conscientious and generally efficient worker. His duties as Clerk of the Cheque included reporting to the Navy

---

93 Rainham Church parish register. His name is given as 'Sammuel Hunter', hers as 'Mary Thurnman', so tracing the entry was more than usually a matter of luck.

Commissioners[94] on his examination of the books of the dockyard, paying merchants for provisions, victualling vessels, paying workmen, and keeping ships' musters. By December 1674 he had acquired a smack (a traditional fishing boat) to facilitate this, and was obliged to justify to his masters allowing his men to lodge aboard it (*"to ensure its safety"*, so he claimed).[95] In February 1675 he and four other dockyard officers requested *"an allowance for house rent as there are no houses suitable for officers in the yard"*.[96] They would have been hoping for accommodation in one of the 'Mile Houses' (later Mile Town, so called because it was within a mile of the dockyard, where their conditions of employment required them to live, but beyond the less salubrious blue-painted workers' dwellings of Blue Town).

On 30th October 1675, after dealing with a routine matter in the first part of his report, Hunter wrote:

"I hope your Honors will finde by the Accompt you shall receive from Mr Gregory & Mr Kirk of the Musters of the Eagle *& the* Armes of Horne *no grounds to distrust mee or to believe me guilty of the Least Dishonesty; I being satisfied that I dare take my Oath I have not wittingly wrong'd his Majesty of six pence, Since I had ye Honor to serve him in this Employment. I humbly Begg your Honors Pardon for this Digression, & Remaine [etc., etc.]"*.[97]

---

[94] There are 126 such reports written (or subscribed to) by Hunter in the TNA ADM 106 series of Admiralty papers, covering the period 1673 to 1678.
[95] TNA, ADM 106/305, folio 70.
[96] TNA, ADM 106/313, folio 199.
[97] TNA, ADM 106/313, folio 145.

I can find no trace in the Admiralty archives of correspondence from any of Hunter's colleagues suggesting impropriety or dishonesty on his part, so either, expecting such charges to be put, he was getting his defence in early, or he was showing signs of paranoia. There is an endorsed note that the letter was read on 1st November, and then read again two days later, so perhaps their Honours were puzzling, as well they might, over this curious passage.

In January 1676 Hunter requested leave to travel to London[98] (from which he did not return until the end of March), and again on 16th May 1676,[99] no doubt to prepare for his wedding. He stayed away until early July, perhaps on honeymoon. His only other recorded absence from his post had been two weeks' leave granted to him in November 1673.[100] Otherwise he seems to have spent his time in Sheerness and Queenborough. The stratified red clay cliffs at nearby Minster, with their rich fossil deposits, and the stark beauty of the ruined Minster Abbey, may have provided some diversion, but otherwise the landscape was bleak and the locality, apart from north Sheppey, unhealthy marshland.

In December 1676, needing additional income to support his young wife and himself, Samuel Hunter petitioned to be appointed as Waiter and Searcher at Queenborough,[101] and six weeks later the appointment was confirmed by the Commissioners of

---

[98] TNA, ADM 106/319/23

[99] TNA, ADM 106/319/33

[100] TNA, ADM 106/289, folio 294.

[101] TNA, Treasury Book; Entry Book: December 1676, *Out Letters (Customs)* III. p. 253.

Customs,[102] on the basis that he would reside at Queenborough and allow £5 out of his salary for each of three boatmen to be employed under him. The Waiter and Searcher at a port was responsible for examining incoming vessels for goods which might be liable for taxation or duty. Queenborough, a small settlement of mostly fishermen's cottages – until 1650 it had boasted a castle built by Edward III, but this was demolished on Oliver Cromwell's orders – is less than a mile south of Sheerness, so Hunter would have had no difficulty in keeping up his old acquaintance, including that with Lt. Robert Thompson, now his stepbrother-in-law, as his new job was in addition to that of Clerk of the Cheque at Sheerness. In fact, as he later disclosed to the Navy Board, he had "*alwayes a good man upon ye place, who is both knowing and Carefull*"[103] to deputise for him at Queenborough.

On 8th October 1677, "*Having an extraordinary occasion to come to London*", Samuel Hunter requested ten days' leave, promising when it was granted (twelve days later) "*to waite upon your Honors*" while in town.[104] The sad reason for this request becomes clear from his next report on 27th November, apparently written in London. In it he apologised for not being able to wait upon them the following day, "*my wife's extraordinary Ilness occasioning my going out of Towne this Morning*" (which suggests that by now she was with her mother at Hall Place), and he thought that as "*Some false Informacion & Suggestion being made unto you,*

---

[102] TNA, Treasury Book; Entry Book: January 1677, 21-31, pp. 520-534.
[103] TNA, ADM 106/333/86.
[104] TNA, ADM 106/328/72 & ADM 106/328/74

that your Honors believe me worthy of your displeasure, if not a farther Punishment", they should know that for three months past he had been

> *"but twice Absent from Sheerness or Quinbrough where (for want of Conveniency in ye fort) I am forc'd to Lodge. I could heartily wish that by your Honors meanes wee had houses built att Sheerness (though the Aire be ne're so bad) fitt to defend us from ye Cold & bad weather accustomed to that place, that wee might have some better Incouragement to be Continually Resident there, & not be lyable to be expos'd to that Misfortune that I was, that for want of timely Leave from your Honors for my Accompanying my Wife to London, where Lodgings were provided for her Lying in, Shee was unhappily delivered at Quinbrough, which I have Reason to Believe for want of Conveniency & good helpe there, was ye occasion of ye Death of her Childe & extreame Sickness of herselfe, which I am afraid yet will goe nere to Cost her Life.*
>
> *I should be heartily asham'd to trouble your Honors with this so unusuall & unseemly a Narrative, butt to make you sensible, that besides that of being somewhat serviceable to his Majesty, wee have not ye greatest pleasure in our Imployments; However, mine I am sure (what'ever ye Malice of some people would falsely make your Honors believe) hath been manag'd with that Integrity & Circumspection, that his Majesty's service hath not in ye Least suffred or bene neglected ..."*[105]

There are those hints of stress and paranoia again, exacerbated by grief for his dead child and concern for his ailing wife. On 24th December 1677 Hunter reported from London that he had *"Just now Come to Towne with my Sick wife from Sheerness"* (for which

---

[105] TNA, ADM 106/328/76.

absence he begged their Honours' pardon, and asked for leave to remain there until Thursday "*when I will not faile to Return to my Buisiness*"). As there was no house for him at Sheerness (which was why "*I have Removed my Family to London, from when they[106] are not to Returne, till itt shall please his Majesty to build us Houses*"), he asked for permission to live on board his smack ("*seeing ye place cannot afford me better Entertainment*"). He listed several reasons why he thought he should be allowed to keep the smack, which he also needed for mustering ships "*as low as ye Redd sand* [in the Thames Estuary] *& upp ye Two Rivers* [the Thames and the Medway]*, as farr as Holehaven* [on the Isle of Thanet, Essex]", carrying letters to Chatham and books to London, and lending to officers on His Majesty's service. He also hinted heavily that he would prefer to give up his employment at the Custom House in Queenborough, even if it paid "*twice ye Advantage to me as ye other*".[107] He expressed the hope that, in considering his arguments, their Honours would not be influenced "*by some body amongst us, whose Knowne Rashness without any Reason or Consideracion, would Indeavour to make your Honors believe that my Selfe & ye Vessell are misemploy'd upon a small Concerne of ye Custom House my Lord Treasurer was pleas'd to Intrust me with*". One is bound to wonder who that informing "*some body*" was. It may well have been Lt. Robert Thompson.

Six days later, after receiving a negative response

---

[106] This suggests that Hunter and his wife had another undocumented child aside from the one that she had lost in childbirth, but if so that child did not survive infancy either.
[107] TNA, ADM 106/328/86.

and further instructions, Hunter reported that he had returned with the smack to Sheerness and again hoped that he might continue using her. Being ordered to return it, when he had more need of it than ever, "*makes me Suffer in my Reputation (which is as deare to me as my Life, & on which I build all my future hopes)*", but if not, he asked for a four-oared yawl – and for a wooden house "*for want of better, as other of ye Officers have, hoping that What'ever paines ye Malice of some people hath taken to Remove up your Honors' favour from me* …") – to be built for him.[108]

Hunter was now showing signs not only of paranoia, but of severe depression, which may well have contributed to the traumatic events about to unfold.

---

[108] TNA, ADM 106/328/90.

CHAPTER 4

Sheerness and its aftermath

By mid-January 1678 Hunter's relations with his superiors and his colleagues were worsening, as apparently was his own mental health. On 15th January Captain Godfrey, Deputy Master Attendant at Sheerness, reported that the complaints against himself by Mr Daniel and others were prompted by revenge *"because Mr Hunter has said that I am an informer. Mr Hunter says he has more power to command the men there than I do"*.[109] On the same day Hunter, who had evidently been told that he could not keep his smack and that it must be returned to Deptford, reported that he had returned from London in it after the holidays, but bad weather had prevented the Master Attendant and the Clerk of the Survey from surveying it before it was returned to Deptford.[110] (This was independently corroborated by the latter, William Dormer.[111]) He repeated his request for a yawl and lodgings.

---

[109] TNA, ADM 106/333/138.
[110] TNA, ADM 106/333/96.
[111] TNA, ADM 106/333/118.

Nine days later Hunter asked for ten days' leave so that he could "*attend to business in London*".[112] His wife was still not fully recovered from illness, so that he was away longer than intended, as the next report from him was not written until 11th April. On 4th May he reported that he had returned his smack, but again asked, as a matter of urgency, for a four-oared boat, which he wanted so that he could perform his duties (and not, he stressed, for his private ends).[113] Ten days later he somewhat querulously expressed the hope that this request had not been forgotten, as without a suitable boat he could not get to the ships at The Nore, Red Sand and Holeshaven to muster them.[114] Another reminder from him followed after another ten days, but he was able to report that the Governor had at least lent him a small apartment to live in, although it needed a small shed to be built onto it for storing coals and beer.[115] On 6th June, in his last letter as Clerk of the Cheque, Hunter again asked, again without success, for the provision of a boat for himself.[116]

Hunter was by now seriously behind with his administrative work – he had finalised the 'quarter books' only up to the previous Christmas.[117] Not only that, but he and Lt. Robert Thompson had evidently fallen out badly. What caused the rift, and whether it was sudden or had been building for some time, remains a matter of conjecture. It could have been about which of them had precedence when the Navy

---

[112] TNA, ADM 106/333/100.

[113] TNA, ADM 106/333/104.

[114] TNA, ADM 106/333/106.

[115] TNA, ADM 106/333/108.

[116] TNA, ADM 106/333/114.

[117] TNA, ADM 106/330/231.

Commissioner at Chatham (Sir Richard Beach), or the Governor of Sheerness (Major Nathaniel Darrell), or both of them, was absent, or it could have been to do with Hunter's wife (and Thompson's step-sister), or Thompson's wife, or any numbers of issues. We simply do not know.

Elizabeth Thompson had recently given birth, or was soon to do so, to a daughter, named Mary. I can find no record of the baptism of any Mary or Marie Thompson, Thomson, Tompson or Tomson whose father was named Robert and mother Elizabeth, anywhere in the United Kingdom in 1678.[118] There is reliable evidence, cited in the next Chapter, that Mary Thompson was aged 18 at her wedding on 13th April 1697. If so, she must have been born on or after 14th April 1678, at around the time of her father's death.

Perhaps Samuel Hunter was not paranoid, and was genuinely the victim of persecution by the overbearing Lt. Robert Thompson. Whatever the reason for their falling-out, on 11th June 1678 Hunter's assistant, Richard Cheyney,[119] was obliged to

---

[118] A Mary Thomson, daughter of Robert and Elizabeth Thomson, was baptised (ancestry.co.uk, FHL file no. 91131) in September 1677 in South Shields, about six miles from where most of Samuel Hunter's family still lived, but that must be coincidence, as there was no reason for the Thompsons to be in that vicinity, and indeed Lt. Thompson's duties in Sheerness and his wife's advanced pregnancy would have prevented such a journey. Besides, that would have made Mary Thompson 19, not 18, when she married, and one assumes that her husband would at least have been sure of her age.

[119] There is a local landmark east of Sheerness called Cheyney's Rock, but this was named long before Richard Cheyney's brief time at Sheerness (he had left by 1679), probably after local

report to the Navy Commissioners and "*to give your Honours an Accountt of ye Accident which this Morning happned between Mr Hunter & Lt Thompson of this place (by way of Duell), the Lt receiving a Wound which Mr Hunter fearing to be worse then I hope itt will prove, hath absented himselfe. …*". The duel had been fought with rapiers, and – either from luck or by superior swordsmanship – Hunter's had pierced Thompson's midriff. Cheyney offered to cover Hunter's duties in his continued absence.[120]

The following day Cheyney reported that the wound had proved to be more serious than supposed. Lt. Robert Thompson had died "*yesternight*".[121]

Cheyney's submission was followed on 13th June by one from a number of officers at Sheerness dockyard, who jointly reported that "*A Lieutenant from the garrison and Mr Hunter challenged each other to a duel on the 11th when Mr Hunter mortally wounded the other and immediately fled. Last night the Lieutenant died.*"[122] Either Thompson or Hunter must have challenged the other first, but which was the challenger Hunter's colleagues (one of whom would have acted as his 'second') were not saying.

Lt. Robert Thompson was buried that same day at Minster, about a mile east of Sheerness, close to

---

magnate Sir Thomas Cheyne (d.1559), from whom Cheyney may have been descended.

[120] TNA, ADM 106/333/62.

[121] TNA, ADM 106/333/64. Correctly anticipating Hunter's dismissal from his post and, wasting neither time nor opportunity, Cheyney asked in the same letter to be appointed as Hunter's successor (which he duly was).

[122] TNA, ADM 106/333/192.

where the duel had been fought.[123] The vicar at the time, who probably conducted the funeral service, was the Revd. Thomas Brockbank.[124] There may have been few, if any, mourners apart, one supposes, from his young widow Elizabeth (with whom he would have been sharing married quarters near the fort), possibly with her baby daughter Mary. That is assuming that the statement made many years later that Mary's father had been killed "*when she was a child*" is correct, and that Elizabeth was not still pregnant with her unborn child. To have been 18 when she married, Mary would have had to be born before 13th April 1679, which means, assuming a normal-term pregnancy, that she could have been conceived as late as mid-July 1678, after her putative father's death. Perhaps – and I must admit that this is mere speculation, probably unworthy of what aspires to be a serious history – Elizabeth's pregnancy had been discovered very shortly before 11th June 1678, in circumstances where Lt. Robert Thompson knew that he could not have been the father, and that his wife's child's true paternity was the cause of the duel between himself and Samuel Hunter.

Within days, if not hours, of hearing of his son's violent end, even before Richard Cheyney's second letter confirming it reached the Navy Commissioners on 16th June, and probably before he knew anything of the background to the duel, Robert Thompson senior was taking advantage of his privileged access as

---

[123] Ancestry.co.uk, FHL Film number 1751981: Item 2. The fate of Thompson's pet monkey is not known.
[124] '*A History of the Abbey Church of Minster, Isle of Sheppey, Kent*' (W. Bramston, 1896), p.85.

Groom of King Charles II's Privy Chamber, and bending His Majesty's ear about the matter.

On 14th June, the very day after the funeral, King Charles ordered[125] that the estate of Samuel Hunter, Clerk of the Cheque at Sheerness, should be forfeited to Robert Thompson senior. Three days later the king's decision was brought to the attention of the Treasury, and a memorandum was made that, "*Robert Thompson, Groom of the Privy Chamber, alleges that the King has granted him the estate of Samuel Hunter, Thompson's son-in-law, amounting in inheritances and leases to about £56 p.a., being forfeited by Hunter killing his brother-in-law, Robert Thompson's son Robert, who has begged it for ~~his daughter, the wife of him slain~~ himself. He therefore desires that no grant of it may pass to any other.*"[126]

Strictly speaking, of course, Samuel Hunter was not Robert Thompson's son-in-law, but his wife's, and by "*his daughter*" Thompson, according to the still-prevailing convention, meant his now-widowed daughter-in-law (Elizabeth Thompson, *née* Newby). He evidently decided, on reflection, that he himself would be a more deserving recipient than she, hence the contemporaneous deletion above. That, I suggest, gives some idea of Thompson senior's character.

This action was hardly likely to have had the support of Thompson's wife, the former Mrs Elizabeth Thurman, if as I suspect the "*inheritances and leases*" amounting to "*about £56 p.a.*" were the Hampshire properties which had previously been left by Nicholas Thurman to his (and Elizabeth's)

125 TNA, State Papers Domestic: Charles II, June 1678, p. 51.
126 TNA, Treasury Books, vol.5, Entry Book for June 1678, Caveat Book, p.34.

daughter Mary, now Samuel Hunter's wife, and which Hunter had acquired only by virtue of Mary's marriage settlement.

Samuel Hunter may have made his escape overland *via* Queenborough (to bid goodbye to his sick young wife Mary, if she was not still in London), taking the ferry to cross the Swale at Kingsferry and thence to the Dover-London road. He did not use his own vessel to escape. (A few months later Richard Cheyney reported to his masters that he had fixed up the old smack that Hunter had left behind, although it was "*so decayed*" as to be hardly worth it.[127]) He may, on the other hand, have stowed aboard one of the ships then in port at Sheerness or The Nore, perhaps bound for the West Indies, which would explain connections which Hunter made and which feature in his later life.

As it turned out, Hunter did not need to lie low for long, and indeed there is evidence that he did not do so, as the Clerk of Control at Sheerness (William Dormer, promoted from Clerk of Survey) reported on 25th June that Hunter was refusing, without an account, to hand over money that had been paid to him in respect of a deceased seaman's wages, despite the widow now having obtained letters of administration (and appointed Dormer as her attorney), which suggests that Dormer and Hunter must have been in contact since the duel.

We learn a little more of the circumstances of the duel from the report of the Inquest held at Minster on 22nd June 1678, when a jury of twelve local men

---

[127] TNA, ADM 106/333/76

reported to the Coroner (Robert Thomas) that on 10th June, at Minster, Samuel Hunter, labourer – he would have objected strenuously to that description – attacked Robert Thompson Esq. *"with a rapier ([valued at] 2s. 6d.)*[128] *and ran him through the navel, inflicting a wound from which he died on 11th June. The jury found this to be murder."*[129] (According to Richard Cheyney's reports at the time, corroborated by his dockyard colleagues, the duel took place on 11th June, and Thompson died on 12th June; Cheyney's account is more likely to be accurate.) At Maidstone Assizes, on 1st April 1679, Samuel Hunter was indicted for the murder of *"Robert Thompson, Gent."* The Indictment is endorsed *"Elizabeth Thompson. True Bill. At large."*[130] Thus we may deduce that an Elizabeth Thompson attended the Inquest, but this seems much more likely to have been Lt. Thompson's young widow than his step-mother.

There is no report of Hunter turning himself in or being arrested, and no extant report of any trial, although there must have been one of some sort. The only penalty imposed upon Samuel Hunter for the killing of Lt. Robert Thompson was that of having his (actually his wife's) property forfeited, and he seems to have avoided any criminal conviction. Whatever the law may have said, the death in a duel of either or both combatants was often not regarded as murder, nor apparently even as manslaughter, if the authorities were satisfied that the duel was fought over 'a matter of honour'. What that 'matter of honour' might have

---

[128] A quaint feature of criminal law reports of the time was the practice of attributing an estimated value to any weapon used.

[129] TNA, Assizes 35/119/7, m. 56.

[130] TNA, Assizes 35/120/5, m. 71.

been in this case is something we can, sadly, only guess at. It must have been enough to persuade the court to overturn the Minster jury's finding of murder.

The senior Elizabeth Thompson's view of her son-in-law's conduct seems to have been more sanguine than that of her husband Robert, which suggests to me that she regarded Samuel Hunter as the more innocent party to the duel, and perhaps had no great opinion of her deceased stepson Lt. Robert Thompson. She soon had an opportunity to demonstrate her feelings, for at the College Audit Meeting in March 1680[1][131] it was ordered that a lease be granted *"for the Seperate use of Mrs Elizabeth Thompson of the Messuage or tenement lands and premises in Dulwich in her occupation to whom shee shall nominate provided it be one as the Corporacon shall approve of; as also the tile Kilne to be pulled down with the appurtenances thereunto belonging before the 4ᵗʰ day of September next."* A £500 bond was required as security for an obligation *"that noe gounds be dugg nor tile made or brick"* being complied with. The lease was to be from the following Michaelmas (29ᵗʰ September), at the old rent of £20, plus a pair of capons (or 10s. in lieu) on 24ᵗʰ June and another pair on 3ʳᵈ September, yearly. (Here is interlineated *"the Tennant to be Mr Page"*, and amongst the deeds which Samuel Hunter left at his death was a 1684 lease of unspecified property to *"Jo. Page"*.[132])

---

[131] Audit Meetings at Dulwich College, attended by the Master, Warden, Fellows, and a 'Court of Assistants', were held twice yearly, on 4ᵗʰ September and 4ᵗʰ March or as near thereto as possible, to consider new grants of leases and other similar matters.

[132] Recited in *Stokoe v Lynn* (1727) – TNA C 11/693/20.

Elizabeth's husband Robert Thompson must have been unhappy about this, as he seems to have gone behind his wife's back, and at the College Audit Meeting in March 1683[4] it was resolved "*Uppon the Applicacion of Mr Robert Thompson for a new Lease It is Ordered; That if hee shall fully performe all former Covenants with the Colledge heretofore made by Nicholas Thurman by or before the fowerth day of September next, That then they will make him offer of their Termes uppon which they Intend to Graunt a new Lease.*" Six months later, and "*It is Ordered, That if Mr Robert Thompson shall fill up and levell all the Pitts dug in ye Field Called Lyngs, and make up the ground of the pitts so to bee Levelled, equall in goodnes with the other parts of the same field by or before the fowerth of March next — That then the Colledge will graunt a Lease to whom Mrs Elizabeth Thompson shall Appoint and the Colledge Approve of of the Lands now in Mr Thompsons Possession for 21 yeares from Michaelmas 1681; under the same Rents and Covenants as are Contained in the old Lease Graunted to her former husband Nicholas Thurman decd Otherwise this order to bee void.*"

Another six months passed, and on 5th March 1684[5] (four weeks after the death of Charles II and the accession to the throne of his Catholic brother James II) we find[133] that "*Mr Robert Thompson having filled up and Leveld all the Pitts in the Field Called Lyngs According to the order of the last Court, therefore on the Mocion of Mrs Thompson to have a Lease graunted to her Sonne* [actually, of course, her son-in-law] *Mr Samuel Hunter, for 21 years from Michaelmas Last, It was Rejected,*

---

133 DCA, BC:29; also Taylor v. Dulwich College, 1719, cited in W. F. Noble's '*Law Suits pro & con Edw. Alleyn of Dulwich*' (1875), p. 423 ff.

and orderd to bee graunted According to the last Order of the 4ᵗʰ of September Last." Eleven days later the lease was duly granted, although for 19 years, not the usual 21. The description of the property in the lease[134] was identical to that in the 1662 lease (and for that matter the 1661 lease), even down to the "*four closes of pasture called Lings*". Either the scrivener who prepared the document had not been told of the change of use, or Nicholas Thurman or his successor had abandoned his crop-growing plans. The Order of a year earlier was conveniently forgotten – perhaps that is what "*It was rejected*" is meant to convey – and Samuel Hunter was from Lady Day 1685, until the end of his life, listed in the Warden's rental accounts as paying the rents for both Hall Place and Napps-at-will, in place of Robert Thompson.

There is some evidence that by 1694 Robert Thompson had established a *rapprochement* of sorts with his son-in-law, for during litigation following his death his daughter Elizabeth gave evidence that in that year he had taken a bond from one Isaac Ragg, as security for a loan of £300, in the name of Samuel Hunter, and he had also lent sums of money to Hunter himself, secured by two bonds.[135] He also paid on Hunter's behalf 5*s* 'capon money' due in September 1687.

Since the tragic event at Sheerness in 1678, Samuel Hunter had managed to rejoin the Admiralty, and by November 1684 was Muster-Master of Lord

---

[134] Surrey Deeds No.64, Minet Library. A very rare instance of a lease from Dulwich College not kept in its own archives.
[135] TNA, *Banks v. Davenport & others*, C 7/21/71.

Dartmouth's fleet.[136] Hunter and a colleague had to petition the Treasury Lords for payment of their outstanding Navy bills (£68 9s 10d in Hunter's case) because they were *"not on the ordinary establishment"*.[137]

Dulwich College, from The European Magazine, 1792.
Shoddily constructed between 1613 and 1619, almost all of it
fell down at different times during the next century or so, and
had to be rebuilt.

The payments were approved and eventually paid.[138] By March 1685 Hunter was living in the parish of St Martin-in-the-Fields.[139] For the next four years we have no definite information on him, but for

---

[136] Lord Dartmouth kept a private fleet of up to 22 ships at this time.
[137] TNA, Treasury Books: Entry Book: November 1684, 1-10, pp.1377-1392.
[138] *Ibid.*: December 1684, 6-10, pp.1435-1443
[139] *Ibid.*

seventeen days in early 1690 he was acting Secretary to the Accounts department of the Commissioners of Transportation, who at the time were dealing with transporting men and provisions to Ireland "*during the late war with France*".[140]

At some time during the 1680s Hunter obtained a position[141] at Trinity House, London (actually based in Deptford), and on 27th February 1692[3] the renowned Samuel Pepys recorded that Hunter and a Mr Mann had dined and discoursed "*at my table*", where they told him of their recent inspection of the relatively minor damage suffered by English warships "*after this last fight*",[142] On 27th April 1694 Pepys hosted a dinner for Lord Clarendon "*with other company*", which must have included Samuel Hunter, for Pepys recorded that "*Mr. Hunter tells me that Trinity House itself complains of Collins's ill performance of his Book of Carts* [i.e. Charts][143]; *and yet he dedicates it to them as well as to the King.*"[144]

In 1693 Hunter is known to have been occupying offices in the Tower Ward of the city with Thomas Baker and two other clerks,[145] but where he was living

---

[140] *Ibid.*, vol. 24, 1710, Warrant Book: May 1710, 6-10, pp. 275-287

[141] Due to the corporation's ancient records being destroyed by fire in 1714, we do not know what position Hunter held, but he was probably a Younger Brother.

[142] Samuel Pepys, Naval Minutes, 289. The sea battle referred to was at Barfleur or La Hogue, where the French fleet was trounced, twice, by an Anglo-Dutch force.

[143] '*Great Britain's Coasting Pilot*' by Capt. Greenvile Collins, 1693.

[144] Samuel Pepys, Naval Minutes, 386.

[145] 'Four Shillings in the Pound Aid' 1693/4 for the Cities of London and Westminster.

is not known. Not, it seems, at Hall Place. A lease granted by the Hunters in June 1700 (of Mary's inherited property in Sutton, Charlton and Wildhern, near Southampton) indicates that the couple was then residing at (or near) Trinity House, Deptford.[146] Hunter certainly retained an affection for Trinity House for the rest of his life, and would include a reference to it in his last Will.

By 1694 Robert Thompson, having served through three reigns (Charles II, James II, and William and Mary) as Groom of the Privy Chamber, and reached the age of 75, had decided to retire. According to the later evidence of his daughter Elizabeth Banks, Thompson sold his office – presumably with the consent of William III, now sole monarch following Mary II's death – for about £800, £300 of which he immediately lent to one Isaac Ragg,[147] a Bellman (i.e. town crier) and later innkeeper, of St Giles-in-the-Fields.

Levet (or Levit, short for Leviticus) Thompson, the elder of Robert Thompson's two surviving sons, must have been a disappointment to his father. The post of Waiter and Searcher (Samuel Hunter's old job at Queenborough) at Whitehaven in what is now Cumbria fell vacant in June 1684, and Levet Thompson (who in 1679 was living in Wokingham, Berkshire, with his wife Mary and new-born daughter Anna Marya) successfully applied for it.[148] Less than

---

[146] TNA, C 11/1171/23, *Hunter v. Carter* (1717), refers.
[147] TNA ref: C 7/21/71, *Banks v. Davenport & others*, 1698.
[148] TNA, Treasury Books, vol. 7, Entry Book: June 1684, 2-5, *Out Letters (Customs)* VIII, pp.280-282: IX, p.1

nine months later he was sacked.[149] However, he stayed in the area, and in July 1696 was living in Kendale.[150] Levet's younger brother Thomas, as we know from Francis Lynn's 'diary', was by 1695 lieutenant of a Company of Invalids stationed at Upnor Castle on the Medway, and seems to have got himself into some unspecified difficulty from which Lynn had to help extricate him. The last we hear both of Levet and of Thomas is in 1697, when they were token beneficiaries of their father's Will. (He left them only twelve pence each, clearly intended to express his disappointment in them.)

Thompson's daughter Elizabeth had married John Banks, gent., on 24th February 1690[91] at St Stephen's Church, Coleman Street. In August 1695 Banks was offered a post as one of the port of London's two wine-tasters, at £80 a year, but for some reason had declined it.[151] Perhaps he was tee-total. By 1698 the young couple had moved to Westminster.

It only remains to account for Lt. Robert Thompson's young widow, Elizabeth. On 14th August 1684, in London, she was married to a Mr Morland or Moreland, whose first name is not given in Francis Lynn's 'diary' or in any of his correspondence, but is

---

[149] *Ibid.*, vol.8, Entry Book: Feb. 1684[5], *Out Letters (Customs)* X, pp. 1-3.
[150] *Records Relating to the Barony of Kendale*: vol.3, pp.54-55. There Thompson joined an association pledging allegiance to William of Orange. With anti-Jacobite feeling running high in the country, many such associations were formed.
[151] TNA, Treasury Books, vol. 10, Entry Book: August 1695, *Out Letters (Customs)* XIII, pp. 206, 207.

known from the marriage licence allegation[152] to have been Christopher. This was the "*Mr Morland*" at whose house in Westminster Francis Lynn met his bride-to-be in 1695, and Christopher Moreland was recorded in the Rate Books for Manchester Court in Westminster between 1695 and 1701 (when, coincidentally or not, the Lynn family moved into Manchester Court). The Morland or Moreland family was prominent in Strood, Kent, where (so Francis Lynn later recorded) 'Mr Morland' was buried in August 1719, and at this time, 1695, Christopher Moreland was the head of that family.[153] The marriage may have been one of convenience, if only to provide young Mary Thompson with a substitute father, as there is no record of Mr and Mrs Moreland living together. After 1700 they certainly lived apart. Morland's death is otherwise unrecorded, and there is no trace of any Will made by him, although it appears[154] that whatever property he owned passed on his death to his widow Elizabeth, and on her death would have passed to her daughter, Mary.

We may now resume with entries in Francis Lynn's

---

[152] London, Calendar of Marriage Licence Allegations 1660-1700, Book 25.

[153] '*The History of Strood*' (Henry Smetham, 1899) includes many references to the Moreland family, and contains the following passage: "*Mr. C. A. Cobb has an old legal document, bearing date April, 1702, in which 'Mr. Christopher Moorland, of Ratcliffe Highway, in the County of Middlesex, gent.', with 'Elizabeth his wife', enters into a bond with Thos. Gibbs, of Strood, in the County of Kent, butcher. … Christopher signs 'Moreland'.*" Intriguingly, one of the three witnesses is 'Fra: Lynn'. The locally-prominent Moreland family owned 'The Gables', St Peter's Place, Strood, until at least the end of the 17th century.

[154] From a reference in Samuel Lynn's 1737 Will.

'diary', which continues:

13.ᵗʰ Aprill 1697, I marry'd Mʳˢ: Mary Thompson beforementioned at St. Allhallows Church upon London Wall, I being 26 Years old and She 18. She was the only daughter of Robert Thompson Esqʳ. some time Dep: Govʳ: of Sheerness, and Lieutᵗ. of a Company in that Garrison, who (whilst she was a child) had the misfortune to be killd in a Duell by Samˡˡ Hunter Esqʳ who was then Clerk of the Cheque there.

This same day fortnight, being the 27.ᵗʰ dyed my Wifes Grandfather Robert Thompson Esqʳ of Dulwich, aged 78 Years, and was buryed in Camberwell Church.

Robert Thompson's last Will,[155] written only two days before his death in April 1697 but not admitted to probate until early December that year, left legacies of £40 to each of his wife Elizabeth and his daughter Elizabeth Banks, and £10 each to his six grandchildren "*Mary Lyn*" (the just-married daughter of his late son Robert, and now the wife of Francis Lynn), Levet's children Robert, John and Elizabeth, and Thomas's children Robert and Catherine. Among the Will's witnesses were Mrs Thompson's nieces Rebeckah and Abigale Vickers. His wife was to receive all personal chattels and "*the bond that is in suite in Scotland*".[156] He appointed his friend Christopher Davenport as sole Executor, and left him a mourning ring and 20*s* for his trouble. He left "*the debt that is due*

---

[155] TNA, PROB 11/442/166. Will proved (by Christopher Davenport) on 3ʳᵈ December 1697.

[156] Thompson is obviously referring to ongoing litigation, but I have not traced it.

to me from Court out of the fee farm rents"[157] to be divided into two parts, half equally between his wife and "*daughter Banks*" (who were also to be the residuary beneficiaries), the other half equally between the six named grandchildren. Perhaps significantly, Robert Thompson left not even a token legacy to his son Robert's widow, now Mrs Elizabeth Moreland.

---

[157] These were in effect freehold reversions, some of them relics of the feudal system, others more recently created in respect of Crown lands – plantations in Ireland, for example – and at times when the monarch was short of funds he had no compunction about selling them off to his subjects. The first such mass sale, at effectively a 50% discount, was under the Commonwealth in 1651. Charles II was constantly in need of funds, and at some point during his reign promised to assign fee farm rents worth £1,046 14s 0d to his (by now senior) Groom of the Privy Chamber, Robert Thompson. Prior to 1692 Thompson sold some of them, worth £246 14s 0d, but in January that year he petitioned the Treasury for the remainder to be assigned to him,[157] and these were the fee farm rents mentioned in his Will.

CHAPTER 5

Mrs Thompson and others

Litigation, as so often throughout this story, followed hard on publication of Robert Thompson's Will, and in 1698 the Executor Christopher Davenport, the widow Elizabeth Thompson, and Samuel Hunter, had to defend an action brought by Elizabeth Banks and her husband John concerning her father's personal estate.[158] Elizabeth complained that she had not received her £40 legacy despite, she said, there being more than enough in the estate to pay it. (Since only ten weeks had passed since Davenport had obtained probate – the delay in obtaining it being probably due to intra-family wrangling – one might have expected her and her husband to be more patient.) She recited the debts owed to her father's estate, totalling £1,000 or thereabouts, or at least those of which she knew, including the £300 lent in 1694 to Isaac Ragg (she didn't know his correct name, and called him "*one* [*blank*] *Cragg*"), the loan to Samuel Hunter previously mentioned, and two other small loans to unrelated

---

158 TNA ref: C 7/21/71, *Banks v. Davenport & others*, 1698.

individuals. Mr and Mrs Banks asked the court to require the three defendants to account for all sums they had received since Robert Thompson's death. The complainants had a particular interest in finding out what rents had been received from "*one* [Anthony] *Allen*" (at £11 p.a.), "*one* [Robert] *Budder*" (at £3 10*s* p.a.), and "*Mr Bower*" (actually Anthony Bowyer, head of an important Camberwell family, at £7 10*s* p.a.).

These were all under-tenants of lands in Dulwich let to the tenant of Hall Place. We learn more about them from litigation following Samuel Hunter's death.[159] Anthony Allen had in 1686 been granted by Hunter a 13-year lease "*of Land*" (probably the 29 acres south of Hall Place and its garden) at £20 a year. When that expired a new 15-year lease at the same rent was granted in late 1699 to a Mr Burges, and when that was surrendered Robert Budder (a Dulwich tenant in his own right) was on 1st October 1710 granted a 21-year lease of the land from the preceding Michaelmas, still at £20 a year. By 1725 his son Henry Budder had taken this over. Hunter's 6-acre copyhold (in Napps, near Herne Hill) was leased from Lady Day 1702 for 12 years, at £11 a year, to James Ireland (another existing Dulwich tenant), who also farmed Hunter's adjoining five acres held 'at will' from Dulwich College, and who by 1725 had been succeeded to both holdings by his son Thomas.

As for Hall Place, the house known by that name was not the only one in the immediate grounds capable of being used as a residence. There were at least two others. One of them, immediately north-east of the main house but separated from it by the

---

[159] *Stokoe v Lynn* (1727), TNA C 11/693/20.

remnants of the moat, was from 1795 to be leased separately from Hall Place, the first of the College's direct tenants of it being Mr George Harris. The others were probably the gate-house referred to in the 1641 court rolls, and possibly one other occupied by a servant of Hunter's. In 1725 a Mr James Causey held from Hunter a 5-year under-lease of "*a House att Dulwich Common*" (probably the house that Harris later leased from the College) at £13 a year, and Mr George Thompson – perhaps a relation of Hunter's predecessor Robert Thompson – held another of a "*House on Dulwich Common*" (also within the Hall Place enclosure) at £7 a year. Although the rents do not tally too well, either Causey or Thompson was probably the successor of Anthony Bowyer (whose immediate successor, Mr Richard Davies, was on 1st December 1699 granted a 15-year lease at £8 a year), and the other probably the successor of Robert Thompson's tenant Robert Budder.

In their joint Answer,[160] Davenport, Hunter and "*Widdow*" Thompson provided a list of the debits and credits relating to Robert Thompson's estate that each of them had dealt with, or which had passed into or through their respective hands, up to 23rd October 1697. This list tells us that Hunter had recovered £275, and interest, on Isaac Ragg's debt, but had recouped for himself £100, and interest, on two £50 loans he had made to his stepfather-in-law in March 1694[5] and June 1696, and paid out £19 6s for the funeral costs and £24 3s 11d for various tradesmen's bills. Davenport had received £40 "*from the [Clerk of the] Wardrobe*", and paid out (presumably after the Bill

---

160 TNA ref: C 7/21/71, *Banks v. Davenport & others*, 1698.

of Complaint was issued) £20 to Elizabeth Banks and another £20 to her and/or her husband. The personal chattels to which Mrs Elizabeth Thompson was entitled had been inventoried and valued at £62 0s 5d. There were unspecified probate costs for which Davenport would have to look for reimbursement to Samuel Hunter, who had over £100 still in hand. Mrs Thompson had received rents of £7 10s from Mr Bowyer and £9 10s from Mr Allen, but had paid £12 10s to Dulwich College in respect of a half-year's rent due to it from her late husband up to his death.

In August 1699 Mrs Elizabeth Thompson travelled down to Hampshire, no doubt to inspect the properties in Sutton, Wildhern, and Charlton (which had belonged to her first husband, been forfeited in 1678 to her second husband, and been inherited by her from him), and to consult with her managing agent there. We learn what happened next from Francis Lynn's 'diary':

> *August 21ˢᵗ: 1699 Mʳˢ Thompson my Wifes Grandmother dyed suddenly on a journey into Hamshire, & was brought up & buryd in Camberwell Church.*

Mrs Elizabeth Thompson had made her last Will many years before, in 1689, "*by virtue of a power reserved to myself before intermarriage with the said Robert Thompson*". In it she left her jewellery to her daughter "*Mrs Mary Hunter*", and "*all my Interest terme and benefitt of and in the Leasehold of the Colledge of Dullidge in Surry*" (i.e. Hall Place *and* the five leasehold acres in Napps) to her husband Robert for life (assuming he survived her, which he didn't), then to "*Mr Samuell Hunter and my said daughter*" for their joint lives and for the lifetime of

80

the survivor, and that in the event that Samuel Hunter was the survivor (which, in the event, he was) he would pay to "*Mary Thomson my grandchild and goddaughter*" (Mary was still single in 1689) £20 on whichever came first of her 21st birthday or day of marriage (both of which events occurred before Elizabeth Thompson's own death), and £10 to Levet Thompson's son Robert at 21. If Mary Hunter died without issue (which, in the event, she did, but not until many years after her stepmother's death) the residue of the lease was to go to Elizabeth's brother William, upon trust to for the three daughters of her brother Edward Vickers and the two daughters of her brother William Vicars, "*share and share alike*". (We should ignore the variant spellings of surnames, as this could be down to the probate clerk who transcribed the Will.) The three witnesses – George Littlefeild, Mary Hodshin, and John Hilton – may have been Elizabeth Thompson's servants.

Since the Will did not appoint an executor, the person entitled to a grant of representation was (and still is in such cases) whoever had the best claim to the residue, which meant Elizabeth's only child Mary Hunter, who obtained such a grant[161] on 20th January 1699[1700].

Apart from the failure to appoint any executors or to dispose of residue, there was – at least on the face of it – one other major problem with Mrs Elizabeth Thompson's Will, in that the major asset of which she sought to dispose, namely the lease of Hall Place, was not hers to give. She seems to have overlooked the fact that, at her own request made to Dulwich

---

[161] TNA: PROB 11/454/136. Modern lawyers would call such a grant 'letters of administration with the Will annexed'.

College, it had in 1684 been taken in the name of her son-in-law, Samuel Hunter. If the terms of her Will had been carried out to the letter, and before the lease existing at her death had expired, we might expect to find that, after the deaths of herself, her husband, her daughter and her son-in-law, without issue of the latter couple, Hall Place would have been sold by her brother William Vickers (or, if he was no longer living, his executors) for the benefit of Elizabeth's nieces and nephews.

However, that did not happen. Samuel Hunter was the official leaseholder and, after his wife Mary's death, acted as if he were the sole beneficial owner of the property. In 1725 he was to dispose of it (by which time the lease subsisting in 1689 had in any case expired and been renewed – twice) by his own Will. Hunter's name is also shown in the Dulwich College rent tables, after his stepfather-in-law's death but before that of his mother-in-law, as entitled to the 6 acres of copyhold land in Napps, at only 1*s* 3*d* a year (usually paid for several years in advance) but that must have been 'in right of' his wife, Mary, at least until he inherited it personally on her death.[162]

The only explanation I can think of for this apparent aberration on Elizabeth Thompson's part was that, as a condition for asking for the leases of Hall Place and land in Napps to be put into Samuel Hunter's name, she must have required him to enter into a private declaration of trust, which has not survived in the archives, with Hunter acknowledging that in equity Mrs Thompson was the true owner and could therefore direct how the property should in

---

[162] DCA, BC:29; BC:30.

future be dealt with. There is evidence[163] of a declaration of trust made by Hunter on 26th December 1694 in respect of the Hall Place lease, with the other parties being Christopher Davenport and William Vickers, "*for the Uses therein menconed*", but no clue as to what those "*Uses*" might have been. Whatever the terms of the deed were, Hunter comprehensively ignored them, and treated the property entirely as his own.

It seems likely that, after the death of his widowed mother-in-law in 1699, Samuel Hunter had intended to make Hall Place the principal residence for his wife Mary and himself. However, he deemed the old Dulwich house uninhabitable and beyond repair. As Hunter later recorded in his Will, the "*cheif Mansion house*", i.e. Hall Place itself, was demolished, and a new one built on the site. The College Audit Meeting on 4th September 1701 recorded that "*Whereas Mr Sam[ue]ll Hunter Ten[an]t to this Colledge has lately taken downe and Rebuilt a Messuage or Tenement & other Apurtenances on the premisses demised to him by this Colledge which hath Cost him the Summe of 500£, or thereabouts, wee therefore Recomend his Case to our Successors to Renew his Lease (at the determinacon thereof) without Advanceing[164] his present Rent*". (The College proved to be as bad at keeping promises as Hunter was himself. When a new 21-year lease of Hall Place was granted to Hunter early in 1703, the annual rent was increased from £20 to £22, contrary to the '*recommendam*' issued only two years before.) At about the same time Hunter arranged for his 6-acre copyhold in Napps to be

---

[163] *Stokoe v Lynn* (1727) – TNA C 11/693/20.
[164] i.e. increasing.

surrendered at the manor court to his wife Mary and himself for the lifetime of the survivor and to the uses declared by the survivor's Will.[165] In the event, Hunter survived his wife. In 1711 he planted six "*Shrubbed trees*", bought from the College for ten shillings. The following year, after Mary Hunter's death, Hunter purchased five hundred surplus bricks from the College for the same amount, probably for the construction of a vault in the Burial Ground in Dulwich Village, intended to house the remains of his wife and, eventually, of himself.

How was Francis Lynn's career progressing? Between meeting Mary Thompson in 1695 and marrying her in 1697, Lynn had been offered the chance to accompany the newly-appointed Envoy to Florence, Harry Killigrew, as his Secretary, leaving on 19th March 1695[6], but Killigrew's appointment was rescinded and Lynn stayed in England. He continued working for George Clarke, the Judge-Advocate to the Board of General Officers of the Army, comprising "*several Blew Garters, Dukes & Earls as well as Gen[ll] Officers*". Clarke's senior clerk, Mr Thurston, was sacked on 9th June after a row with Clarke, and Lynn, not knowing that Thurston had been dismissed, found himself required to attend a Board meeting, and was called on by Clarke to read the 'Papers' to the Board. Lynn describes what happened next:

I had not read six lines before I was struck with that awe, & fell into that confusion, that I lost my breath, and trembled

---

[165] *Stokoe v Lynn* (1727) – TNA C 11/693/20.

like an Aspen Leafe; Which the Board perceiving M^r. Clarke cheared me up, and took ye Papers from me, and read 'em himself; at the same time Duke Schomberg[166] the President, the Duke of Ormond, & Several others spoke very kindly to me to bring me out of my concern, wch in a little time were off, and after that I never had any more of it.

In other words, Lynn, with commendable candour, admits to suffering what we would now call a panic attack. At this point in the proceedings Lynn learned that he had been chosen to replace Thurston, and later on that a Mr Oldner was to become his assistant.

On 30th October 1697 Lynn was appointed Agent of the Companies of Invalids based at Tynemouth and Chester-le-Street (which Lynn refers to as "*Tinmouth and Chester*") under Capt. Thomas Lloyd,[167] and a year later the Governor of Tynemouth Castle (Henry Villiers) appointed Lynn as Agent of the garrison there "*as I was before to Capt. Lloyd for the Invalid Company*". These part-time employments may not have required him to leave London at all. Francis Lynn continued to work for the Army Board of General Purposes, which was not without its excitements:

Some time this Summer [1700] *a great Mob of Common soldiers and their Trulls headed by a Virago, one Mackintosh,*

---

[166] Meinhardt, 3rd Duke of Schomberg, KG (1641-1719). The 2nd Duke, Charles, who had succeeded to the dukedom after his father was killed at the Battle of the Boyne in 1690, was supposedly Meinhardt's younger brother, which seems unlikely, since it would have contravened the well-established rule of primogeniture.
[167] TNA, Treasury Books, vol. 13, 1697-1698, pp. 390-406 – July 1698.

came to the Horse Guards, calling out for Justice against their Officers, in relation to their Accounts, pretending money due to them, and were very clamourous and rude, insomuch that being deneyd admittance to the Board of Gen.^{ll} Officers who were Sitting, they got a Ladder And Mad^m Mackintosh came up to ye Window and insulted Duke Schomberg and the Board upon wch I was Sent to Hicks's Hall for a Warrant from the Bench of Justices to the High Constable and Civil power to come and disperse this Mob, wch the Guards offered to do by force, but the Duke would not permit it. The Constables did accordingly come & disperse 'em, but this insult occasiond, that the Board never mett again.

So that Business being at an end, I was obliged to look out for some other Employment. And just at the end of this Year, the Parliament came to a Resolution of appointing Commissioners to State the Debts of the Army, Navy, Transports & Prizes, … Who meeting at an Office they had taken in York Buildings for the Execution of their Commission, on the 29.th April 1700 made choice of Mr James Craggs to be their Secretary, and my Self their Chief Clerk; but Mr Craggs declining it, … they appointed Me their Secretary, at the salary of £70 p^{er} ann^{um}, and a promise of further consideration at the end of the Year, when they came to wind up bottoms.[168]

Lynn had to work hard for his salary:

In this Office I had my hands full, the Comm^{rs} Meeting every day at 7 a clock in the Summer and 8 in the Winter, and continuing Sitting till between 3 & 4 afternoon, & then Some of them mett again at 6 and Stayd till 8, nor admitted of any Interruption or Holyday except Sunday, & always required me

---

[168] i.e. finish the job.

to be with them.

In May and July 1700 Lynn was given a £3,000 imprest, in two equal instalments, for the payment of clerks and officers of the new Commission, and on account of prizes taken "*during the late war*".[169] The Board's commission, which was for one year only, expired at the end of April 1701 "*occasiond by some dispute between the House of Lords & Commons*" but it was revived the following February "*and an Office taken in Covent-Garden, I was fix'd again as Secretary at the Salary of £100 p^er^ ann^um^ and the like promise as before; which they made good by a present out of the Contingent money of the Same Summ as the Years Salary; and*", he adds wryly, "*very dearly earned it was*".

Lynn received a further £1,500 "*for incidental expenses*" in May 1702.[170] His 'diary' continues:

*I continued Secretary to this Commission till M^r^: Clarke being made Secretary to His Royal Highness Prince George of Denmark[171] Lord High Admiral, Invited me into his Service again in the Admiralty Office, and accordingly the 16:^th^ December 1702, I had a Seat assigned me there, as Second Head Clerke, next to M^r^: Fawler, at the Salary of £150 p^er^ ann^um^, And the Six Marine Regiments being just then putt under the care and direction of the Prince as Lord High Admiral, M^r^: Clarke gave me that particular Branch in ye Office to prepare Establishments, Orders & Commiss^ns^*

---

[169] TNA, Treasury Books, vol. 15, 1699-1700, pp. 351-364, and pp. 411-428.
[170] *Ibid.*, vol. 17, 1702, pp. 208-221.
[171] Husband of Queen Anne.

relating to them, for his Royal Highness's Signing, and to take my Share likewise of the other business of the Office relating to Naval affairs; And that I might be near at hand appointed me a House in yᵉ Admiralty Court Yard to which I removed from Man-chester Court.

In October 1701 Lynn had moved his family to Manchester Court, Westminster, *"having hitherto lodged with Mother Morland"*, his mother-in-law. At both Manchester Court and Admiralty Court Yard Lynn lived rent-free, and was allowed coal and candles, and £10 p.a. for a housekeeper. Substantial sums continued to pass through his hands; £1,500 in April 1703,[172] and another £2,000 the following month.[173] That latter warrant intriguingly referred to him as *"Francis Lynn Esq., goldsmith"*, which one would suppose to be a mistake, as there are no other references to Lynn having any occupation other than civil servant. However, most goldsmiths were bankers, and although it would be a stretch to describe him as a banker, Francis Lynn definitely engaged in money-lending, as we shall see. With so much money passing through his hands he may have been tempted to try and make it work to his personal advantage before he had to account for it. One of Lynn's acquaintances, Col. John Rice, certainly made use of this practice. More about him in Chapter 7.

Lynn's 'diary' reintroduces a familiar character:

August 1704.[174] *This Month Uncle Hunter was made a*

[172] TNA, Treasury Books, vol. 18, 1703, pp. 217-236.
[173] *Ibid.*, pp. 254-270
[174] This appointment as a Commissioner for Victualling the Navy was actually dated 8th September 1704, according to TNA, Calendar of Treasury Books, vol. 20, 1705-1706, pp. 203-240.

Commiss. *of the Victualling, and I passed his Patent, w*^{ch} *cost in the sev*^{ll} *Offices as follows, Vi*z*.*

	£ s d
Attorney Gen^{ll} *Office* … … … … …	7 : 10 : 6
Secr^{ys} *of State* … … … … … … … …	6 : 9 : 0
Signet & Privy Seal … … … … … … …	12 : 9 : 0
Office keeper … … … … … … … …	0 : 2 : 6
Docquet at the Treasury … … … …	1 : 10 : 0
Clerke for Entring it … … … … … …	0 : 5 : 0
Stamps … … … … … … … … … …	4 : 1 : 0
Crown Office … … … … … … … …	16 : 13 : 4
Hannaper Office … … … … … … …	12 : 0 : 0
Private Seal … … … … … … … … …	2 : 0 : 0
Recepi … … … … … … … … … … …	2 : 13 : 0
L^d. *Keepers Porter & Sealers* … … …	0 : 5 : 0
	----------------- £65 : 18 : 4

Samuel Hunter had made a remarkable come-back since the events at Sheerness in 1678 had threatened to end not only his career but his life. The fact that Lynn paid these expenses on Hunter's behalf, and referred to him as "*Uncle Hunter*", is of course very strong evidence that they not only knew each other but by this time had become friends. Whether they had met at Lynn's wedding to Mary Thompson – and it seems from later evidence that they did – they would certainly have met at the baptism of the Lynns' first child, to whom 'Aunt Hunter' was godmother (as she was for another of their children, Mary).

By 1706 Francis and Mary Lynn had had six children. Generally, where parish records are available at all, they give dates of baptism, which would take place when the child was only a few days old (unless it was very sickly, and baptism was deemed even more urgent). They rarely give actual dates of birth. We saw in Chapter 1 how Lynn recorded not only the date, but the time, of his own birth, and he did the same for each of his children. Whether he was prompted to do so by some belief in astrology, which (so I understand) ascribes significance to the subject's exact time of birth, or because he was a slave to detail, is impossible to say, but for the record the children were:

Robert, born 26th January 1697[98] (at 10.45 a.m.), and named "*after my Wifes own Father & Grandfather*". He died on 2nd May 1698, and Lynn noted, as if the two events were related, that the following day "*fell a great Snow above a foot in depth*".

Elizabeth, born 25th August 1700 (at 5.00 a.m.). The next year, when Puddy was in the early stages of another pregnancy, "*our Child being putt out to Nurse at Cur-green, we took the opportunity of going into the Country, during Summer time, to Visit our Friends*".

Mary, born 25th February 1701[02] (at 3.20 p.m.). When she was nearly seven Mary "*had the misfortune to be scalded on her breast, to that degree that her Life was almost despaired of, and it was 8 months before the Wound was cured*". She was known within the family as 'Polly'.

Francis, born 14th August 1703 (at 4.56[!] p.m.), died 8th December 1704.

John, born 21st July 1704 (at 3.00 p.m.), died "*at

Nurse" 5th October 1704.

George, born 12th September 1705 (at 1.30 a.m.), died 28th February 1705[06].

Soon after George Lynn's birth, on 25th October 1705 …

"*Mr Clarke was dismissed from being Secretary of the Admiralty, by Prince George, on occasion of his Voting for a Speaker agst the inclinations of the Court; And Henry St. John*[175] *Esqr. Secr^y at Warr, was made Secr^y to the Prince in his room for the Affairs of the Marines, who accepted of my Service in that province, but at no certain Salary or allowance; however Mr Burchett increased my Salary in ye Adm^{ty} Office to £200 p^{er} ann^{um}*"

of which in 1705 Lynn was paid £150.[176] Two months later …

December 25th: 1705. The General Officers and Colonels of the Marine Regiments made a proposal to the Prince for erecting[177] *a Fund to raise annual Pensions to the Widdows of Marine Officers, in the manner as is practised in the Army, and proposed me to be their Paymaster at the Allowance of 12^d: in the pound out of it, for my care & trouble, Which being agreed to by the Prince, I had His Royal Highnesse's Warrant & Instructions for my guidance therein accordingly.*

As if he were not busy enough, early in 1706 Francis Lynn took on some additional duties:

February 5th: 1705/6. Mr: Clarke procured me to be made Secretary to the Commrs for Sick and Wounded &

---

[175] Later the 1st Viscount Bolingbroke (1678-1751).

[176] TNA, Treasury Books, vol. 20, 1705-1706, pp. 203-240.

[177] i.e. establishing.

Exchange of Prisoners at the Salary of £200 p^{er} ann^{um} and this day I took place at the Board accordingly still continuing an Office at the Admiralty for the Marine affairs at 100£ p^{er} ann^{um}, under Mr Burchett and Mr St John, the former dispatching the Orders, for their Embarking and Coming on shore, and the latter making out their Commissns. And all General Orders relating to their Establishment and Pay.

The 19th: of this Month I removed from my House in Admiralty to the Office of Sick & Wounded in Princes Court, Having the same perquisits here also, of House rent, Coals, Candles &c as before.

Lynn was put in charge of an office comprising a Chief Clerk (at £100 a year), four other clerks (two at £60 p.a. each, two at £50 each), messengers (at £20 p.a. each) and a doorkeeper (at £30 p.a.). The Commissioners and their Treasurer (Capt. Thomas Savery)[178] were all paid £300 a year.[179] By June 1707 the establishment had been joined by an Auditor (Edward Harley, then just 18, later 2nd Earl of Oxford), at £100 p.a.[180]

For the next two years there is no mention in in his 'diary', or in the public records, of Francis Lynn's career, but during 1708 he received an unspecified part of £3,056 12s 1d "*for necessaries, incidents and*

[178] Thomas Savery (c.1650 to 1715) was a remarkable man. As well as his work for the Admiralty, he patented the first working steam engine, albeit a highly inefficient one, used for quenching fires in mines.
[179] TNA, Calendar of Treasury Books, vol. 25, 1711, pp. 213-253.
[180] *Ibid.*, vol. 26, 1712, pp. 181-203.

extraordinary services" relating to the Marines.[181] In October 1709 he was paid £174, again "*for disbursements for the Marine Forces*".[182]

There are a few 'diary' entries unrelated to Francis Lynn's family or career, two of them matters of public record:

January 4ᵗʰ: 1697/8 a Fire happened at Whitehall, which consumed the greatest part of that Palace …

Novr: 27ᵗʰ: 1703, This day happened the most Memorable, the Great Storm.

The 'Great Storm',[183] which would have reached its peak on the date Lynn mentions, actually started on 24ᵗʰ November 1703, and lasted a week. It was "a destructive extra-tropical cyclone" – most Britons now would call it a hurricane – which hit central and southern England, blowing down 2,000 London chimney stacks, and wreaking havoc among ships at sea. Over one thousand seamen drowned on the Goodwin Sands alone.

One other entry in Lynn's 'diary' up to this point must be mentioned. He records that in or about August 1703:

"*I became intimate with Capᵗ: William Morgan, who proved the best Friend I ever had in the World, making my Interest intirely his own, which I studyed to return in the best manner I could*".

---

[181] *Ibid.*, vol. 22, 1708, pp. 445-446.

[182] *Ibid.*, vol. 4, 1708-1714, pp. 135-142.

[183] Wikipedia gives the date of 'the Great Storm' as 26ᵗʰ November 1703, Old Style (7ᵗʰ December 1703 New Style, i.e. according to the Gregorian Calendar in use on the Continent.)

In 1712, apparently thanks to William Morgan's "*interest*", Lynn's son Philip (whose birth I have yet to mention, but will rectify the omission in the next chapter) was commissioned as an Ensign to the Colonel's Company in Lord Slane's Regiment of Foot. Philip thus became eligible for Army pay, just two days shy of his 4th birthday! This is the only recorded favour to Francis Lynn that I can find done by William Morgan, who after 1715 spent the rest of Lynn's life importuning his "*dear Frank*" for favours for himself. Much of the Lynn-Morgan correspondence is taken up with money matters, and money matters, and Morgan's predilection for living dangerously, were ultimately to test their friendship to destruction. Francis Lynn's connection with William Morgan was in the long run to prove very costly, for Lynn and for his family.

CHAPTER 6

Annapolis etc.

Shortly before Christmas 1710 Lynn's old patron and mentor, Judge-Advocate George Clarke, returned to the Admiralty as one of the Lords' Commissioners, "*And I removed my Marine books and Papers to another place to make room for Lodgings for him*". At the beginning of the following February, 1711:

Her Maj^y Queen Anne having thought fitt that a Committee of the Privy-Council should meet at the Warr Office to regulate the Affairs of the Army, And M^r: Granvil afterwards Lord Lansdowne, then Secretary at Warr, being as Such directed to attend them, He did not think fitt so to do, as not being a Privy Councilor himself, for wch reason he could not be permitted to Sitt at the Board; and My Brother Samuel, who was Deputy Secr^y at Warr,[184] *having his hands so full, that he could not be spared from the current business of the Office to do it, recommended Me to M^r: Granvill, as a proper person to attend their Lords^s. having been Secretary to so many Publick Boards already; accordingly M^r: Granvill moved their*

---

[184] On 19th November 1709 Samuel Lynn had also, so his brother records, "*bought the Post of Muster Master Gen^ll. of the Marine Forces.*"

Lords'. therein, and I was appointed to attend them, take their Minutes, & execute their Orders; Which I did at their Several Meetings from April 9th: 1711 to the 1st. of August following; After which day their Lords'. never mett again; having during their sitting made several Regulations for the Army, amongst which one was, That upon Sale of all Commissions both ye Buyer and Seller should each pay 12d: in the pound of all the purchase money, to be applyd to the use of Chelsey-Hospital, and by Warrant under Her Maj^{ts} Royal Sign Manual, I was appointed Receiver of ye said Poundage, With the allowance of 12d. in the pound, out of all money should come to my hands on this Acc^t. for my care & pains therein.

Besides this attendance on the Committee of Lords, having some spare time on my hands from ye business of the Sick & Wounded, and ye Marine affairs, I agreed wth my brother, to spend it in his assistance in the business of the Warr-Office; on condition I should have a settled salary of £100 p^{er} ann^{um}, and free access to the Secretary at Warr at all times, without going thro' him to him; wch was complyd with, and I continued therein, till the Death of the Queen, When we were all turnd out.

Francis Lynn's 'diary' continues:

Her Majty having thought fitt to Establish Four Independent Companys of Foot at Annapolis Royal in Nova Scotia as also a Garrison with proper Officers and Gen^{ll}: Francis Nicholson as Govern^r and Commander in Chief, He recommended Me to be Agent to the same, And I was accordingly appointed Agent by Warrant under _ Maj^{ts} Royal Sign Manual, bearing date Oct^r: 15th: 1712, and I acted as such for the Garrison till the 24th. Decr. 1713, when I resigned the same (at Mr Gwyn's request who was then Sec'ry at Warr) to Mr Geo: Gordon, a Clerke in the Office; having received on Account of that Garrison Subsistence only for 16 Months, *from 25ᵗʰ. Augˢᵗ 1712 the date of their Establishment, to the 24ᵗʰ. Decʳ. 1713 afore mentioned, amounting to £5777: 7: 2. For wᶜʰ I was allowed Agency, & a Man per Company.*

The former French fort of Port Royal in Nova Scotia had been seized by the British in 1710 and renamed Annapolis Royal, after Queen Anne. On 15ᵗʰ June 1713[185] General Nicholson, Governor of New England (who had defeated the French at Port Royal), wrote to Lt.-Governor Moody, from Boston. "*I was very glad to hear of your arrival at Newfoundland … I think you have ye folio works of ye author of* the Whole Duty of Man[186] *given by Mr. Francis Lynn for the Garrison of Annapolis Royall …*". By mid-1713 the Annapolis Royal garrison was in dire straits, requiring funds for repairs and subsistence, unpaid for eight months. After some haggling about what exchange rate to apply between sterling and New England money (£1 equalled about NE£1.50), Treasurer Oxford was recommended to pay six months' subsistence to Francis Lynn, as the garrison's Agent.[187] Lynn seems in turn to have been unconscionably slow in paying this over, and although he says that he "*resigned*", it seems more likely that he was forced to do so. Capt. Lawrence Armstrong and his fellow officers at Annapolis Royal were in the meantime obliged to pay

---

[185] TNA, Calendar of State Papers Colonial, America and West Indies, vol. 28, 1714-1715, August 1715, 1-13, pp. 254-268. The date given in the Calendar is 1711; 1713 is much more likely.

[186] '*The Whole Duty of Man*', first published anonymously in a folio collection in 1684, was a popular and influential 'high church' Anglican devotional work.

[187] TNA, Calendar of Treasury Papers, vol. 4, 1708-1714, June 4-July 15, 1713, pp. 487-496.

their men from their own resources.

February 1712/13 about the latter end of this Month, the Commission for Sick & Wounded Seamen being determined by the Lords of the Admiralty, a New one was constituted, consisting of two Commissioners only Viz.^{t} Coll. Herbert, & D^{r}: Adams; The Treasurer Capt Savery, being likewise layd aside, a Commission was granted to me, dated the 5th March 1712/13 to be Cashier of the Office for Sick & Hurt Seamen in his stead,[188] and to continue Secretary likewise at ye same Salary I received before; And August 13th: 1713 Her Maj^{ty}: having appointed S^{r}: William Gifford K^{t}. & Sam^{ll}. Hunter Esqr Commissioners under the Great Seal for Disbanding the Marine Forces, the Lords of the Admiralty appointed me their Secretary to attend them on this Service to the several Head Quarters, at the Allowance of £1:10:0 per diem, whilst employd thereon; And my absence from my other Offices was ordered to be dispensed with during the time, by particular directions from Her Majesty, Which was from 20th Augst. 1713 to the 27th January following; from which time till the Parliamentary Commiss^{n}. of Acc^{ts} was erected, the said Commissioners (to whom Mr Roope & Mr Layton had been added) held an Office in Scotland Yard, upon those affairs, wch I duly attended as occasion required, and at last got a præmium for the Same, at the rate of £100 p^{er} ann^{um} for my Self and Clerk.

In 1711 the Lord High Treasurer (a precursor to the not-yet-recognised office of Prime Minister), Robert Harley, 1st Earl of Oxford, dissatisfied with the service the government was receiving from the

---

[188] Confirmed by *ibid.*, vol. 27, 1713, pp. 163-185, Declared Accounts re: Navy – Sick & Wounded Seamen, Audit Office: Bundle 1825, Roll 516 (A.O.1/1825/516) and 517 (A.O.1/1825/517).

privately-owned Bank of England, had set about ways of funding the national debt, recently enlarged by the continuing expense of the War of the Spanish Succession. The debt of some £9m, spread across different government departments, was consolidated and invested in the new South Sea Company, which despite its declared object of trading in countries bordering the south Atlantic (particularly South America, then controlled by Spain) became little more than a bank to rival the Bank of England. In return for 'investing' this £9m in the Company, the government received Company stock at par value. However, since the Company as yet had no income, the government undertook to pay £540,000 a year (equivalent to interest at 6%), plus £28,279 10*s* for 'expenses', to the Company, which would then distribute it to the various government departments in agreed proportions. (If this sounds like 'creative accountancy' by the government, we should perhaps not be surprised.) The share allocated to the Navy was £1,421,274 14*s* 4*d*.

In April 1713 Treasurer Oxford instructed the Company to permit Charles Cæsar, Treasurer of the Navy, to transfer a sum not exceeding £3,426 13*s* 0*d* to Francis Lynn, Cashier to the Commissioners for Sick and Hurt Seamen, on account of several bills drawn from Port Mahon for the subsistence of sick seamen in the hospital there.[189] The following month the Company was instructed to transfer to Lynn another £967 2*s* 10½*d* for the same purpose,[190] and

---

[189] *Ibid.*, vol. 27, 1713, *Money Book XXII*, p. 198.
[190] *Ibid.*, Warrant Book for May 1713, 1-15, *Money Book XXII*, p. 226.

on 1ˢᵗ June another £1,773 16s 6d to satisfy several bills of exchange drawn from Lisbon (where coincidentally the same Richard Cheyney we encountered in Sheerness in 1678 was now Clerk of the Cheque) for the subsistence of sick seamen there.[191] Three days later the Company was instructed to assign a further £12,385 1s 6d to Lynn towards answering the demands of £14,770 3s 0d for his Office in all its branches at home and abroad for the nine months to Lady Day 1713.[192] In the same month Cæsar was instructed to pay Lynn £1,501 8s 7d, to satisfy certain bills on account of Her Majesty's service at Barbados, only this time the source was to be funds raised from the 1713 Land Tax.[193] By the end of 1713 Lynn received a further £970 4s 2½d *"for stationery wares, etc. for the use of the Secretary at War's Office for a year to Xmas"*,[194] and £425 7s 3d in settlement of *"an Accompt"* rendered in connection with the Royal Chelsea Hospital.[195] Whatever their source, these were very substantial sums, and Francis Lynn was entrusted to ensure their proper and prompt disbursement.

In Lynn's capacity as Cashier to the Commissioners for Sick and Hurt Seamen, another

---

[191] *Ibid.*, Warrant Books: June 1713, 1-15, *Money Book XXII*, p. 239.
[192] *Ibid.*, Warrant Books: June 1713, 1-15, *Money Book XXII*, p. 242.
[193] *Ibid.*, Warrant Books: June 1713, 16-30, pp. 250-268, *Disposition Book XXII*, pp. 128 and 130.
[194] TNA, Calendar of Treasury Books, vol. 27, 1713, Declared Accounts: Army: Guards & Garrisons: Pipe Office: Roll 100 (E.351/100); Audit Office: Bundle 59, Roll 63 (A.O.1/59/63)
[195] *Ibid.*, Declared Accounts: Army: Chelsea Hospital: Pipe Office: Roll 1781 (E.351/1781); Audit Office: Bundle 1468, Roll 20 (A.O.1/1468/20).

£3,134 13*s* 3¼*d* was authorised to be paid to him on 15th August 1713,[196] another £177 14*s* 0*d* on 12th September,[197] and another £3,600, as imprest and specifically "*to satisfy the bills drawn for building the Hospital at Port Mahon*" on 1st October.[198] As Secretary to the Commissioners for Disbanding the Marine Regiments,[199] he wrote to a Mr Tilson (apparently his own assistant) on 13th August and 3rd September.[200] Those Commissioners were each to be paid at the rate of £3 a day "*for every day each of them shall be abroad on the said service*".[201]

Samuel Hunter was in 1711 still a Commissioner for Victualling the Navy, as he had been since 1704. These Commissioners employed an accountant, cashier, secretary, storekeeper and clerk of the bakehouse, clerks, muster-master, purveyors, and others. Their salaries and expenses from 1st January to 7th June 1711 came to over £6,300, with each of the Commissioners on £400 a year, and four of them, including Hunter, shared a £65 a year housing rental allowance.[202] In July 1712 Hunter was promoted.[203]

---

[196] *Ibid.*, Warrant Books: August 1713, 1-15, *Disposition Book XXII*, p. 150.

[197] *Ibid.*, September 1713, 1-15, pp. 339-351.

[198] *Ibid.*, October 1713, 1-15, *Money Book XXII*, p. 341.

[199] It may be relevant that the Muster-Master of Marines at the time was Samuel Lynn, who was Francis Lynn's brother.

[200] *Ibid.*, September 3-30, 1713, pp. 505-512.

[201] *Ibid.*, September 1713, 1-15, *Money Book XXII*, p. 311.

[202] TNA, Treasury Books, vol. 25, 1711, pp. 213-253.

[203] TNA, Calendar of Treasury Books, vol. 26, 1712, pp. 181-203.

Francis Lynn noted:

July 6th: 1712, My Uncle Hunter was made Commiss^r of the Navy, and I passed his Patent, wch cost much about the same summ as that for the Victualling before mentioned.

At that time the eight Navy Commissioners, based in Seething Lane, employed a Surveyor and, no doubt, many more junior staff.[204] Hunter's salary was £500 a year and a housing allowance of £80.[205] He shared an office with Sir William Gifford and Thomas Layton in Scotland Yard (connecting Northumberland Avenue with Whitehall).

Britain's part in the War of the Spanish Succession had effectively ended by now, and the Marines were – as often happened in times of relative peace – considered surplus to requirements. Their regiments were to be disbanded or converted to regiments of Foot Soldiers. On 7th August 1713 instructions (confirmed by Letters Patent of appointment dated three days later) were sent from Hampton Court to Sir Stafford Fairborne and two of the Navy Commissioners, including Samuel Hunter, to finalise the Marine Accounts and arrange for the disbanding of the Marine regiments.[206]

On 11th November 1713 Lowndes wrote to Samuel Hunter:

---

[204] TNA, Treasury Books, vol. 26, 1712, pp. 181-203.

[205] *Ibid.*, vol. 27, 1713, pp. 163-185, Declared Accounts of C. Caesar, 1/1/1712[13]-31/12/1713, Pipe Office, Roll 2349 [E351/2349], Audit Office: Bundle 1729, Roll 155 (A.O.1/1729/155).

[206] TNA, Treasury Papers, vol. 4, 1708-1714, vol. 163: July 16-August 29, 1713, pp. 496-505.

"My Lord Treasurer has appointed Mr. Roope and Mr. Layton as Commissioners in the new Commission for disbanding the Marine Regiments. They are to set forward immediately for Exeter to reduce Col. [Charles] Churchill's Regiment there. You and Mr. Fra. Lynn are to meet the said Commissioners at Exeter on Saturday next to concert proper measures for the reducement of said Regiment and of Col. [Harry] Goring's at Plymouth. You are to bring with you such ships' books and muster rolls as relate to the former [Commission] and deliver them to [the new Commissioners']."[207]

The old Navy Office in Seething Lane, London, in 1714.

So Francis Lynn travelled down to Exeter with Samuel Hunter, the killer of the father-in-law Lynn had never met. If they had not previously discussed the events at Sheerness of thirty-five years before

---

[207] TNA, Treasury Books: Warrant Book November 1713, 1-15, *Out Letters (General) XXI*, p. 71. The regiments commanded by Churchill and Gore were not actually Marines, but had been employed as Marines.

(and it would have been indelicate to do so either at Lynn's wedding or at the christenings of his children), now – with the journey by coach taking, weather permitting, three days, and otherwise four – was an ideal opportunity to do so.

Hunter and Lynn must have been expected to stay in Exeter and Plymouth for several days, for on 17th November 1713, the day before their first meeting with Churchill and Gore (and with Richard Carter, deputy Muster-Master General, who had been sent to assist them in taking the muster of Churchill's Regiment at the specific request[208] of Lord Treasurer Oxford), Lowndes wrote to the Commissioners for Disbanding the Marine Forces enclosing further instructions for Hunter and his colleagues about settling arrears of sea pay for non-commissioned Officers and men, from Christmas 1708 to Christmas 1710, "*and to see that they be mutually satisfied their just demands upon each other*".[209]

Hunter must have done a good job, for the following March he was, in addition to his settled allowance of £3 a day, awarded a bonus of £40 "*for his extraordinary service and charges in disbanding the supernumerary men of Col. Goring's Regiment at Plymouth, which he performed alone, his fellow Commissioner, Sir William Gifford, being indisposed*",[210] and another £24 bonus for a similar exercise in August 1714.[211]

Richard Carter – of whom, later in this story, you

---

[208] *Ibid.*, November 1713, 1-15, pp. 414-433, *Out Letters (General) XXI*, p. 71.

[209] *Ibid.*: November 1713, 17-30, pp. 434-444.

[210] *Ibid.*, Minute Book: March 1713[14], *Money Book XXIII*, p. 49.

[211] *Ibid.*, Warrant Books: September 1714, 21-30, pp. 89-106.

will hear more – also impressed his superiors. Gifford and Hunter provided the following glowing testimonial:

"Mr. Richard Carter has the management of the Marine Office under Samuel Lynn, Muster Master General. On setting out from London to put in execution our Commission for Disbanding the Marine Regiments we requested Carter's attendance. He was of very great use to us as above and has had no salary or allowance whatsoever for the same. We think him very modest in requesting no more than 10s. a day. He has since been employed by your Lordships' directions as one of our secretaries in paying off Col. Churchill's Regiment at Exeter and disbanding Lord Shannon's [Regiment] at Rochester and has given us entire satisfaction."[212]

The Paymaster of Marines was instructed to pay Carter £35 10*s*, at 10*s* a day for 71 days' work.[213]

Things went a good deal less smoothly in Canterbury. In mid-September Hunter and his fellow Commissioners were obliged to report on events preceding the imprisonment, the previous December, of three serjeants, following the partial disbandment of General Wills' Regiment there. The undisbanded and unpaid part of the regiment, unable to settle their debts with the local tradesmen, had mutinied. The rioting continued for three days, and the Commissioners were obliged to call for reinforcements, in the form of "*a party of Horse sent thither to awe the rest*". The ringleaders were imprisoned, and the disbandment continued to its

---

[212] TNA, Calendar of Treasury Books, vol. 29, 1714-15; Warrant Books: October 1715, 12-20; Money Book XXIV, pp. 168-9.
[213] *Ibid.*

conclusion.[214] It must have been a relief to Hunter to return to the relative tranquillity of Hall Place after this episode.

The flow of money through Francis Lynn's hands had continued apace, and he was now able to invest some of it – one hopes only what was rightfully his, although the sums involved make this seem unlikely – in acquiring assets in his own name, or making loans to friends and acquaintances, at interest. Although I do not know when and how he might have acquired it – it may have been inherited from his brother John, or even from his father – he, or someone of the same name, had become the owner of a copyhold tenement and 16 acres of land called 'Brayes', in Kingston, Hampshire, and at the beginning of October 1713 sold it to a William Brixey, perfecting the sale by the customary method of surrendering it at the manor court to Brixey's use.[215]

By the Autumn of 1714 the disbanding of the Marines had effectively been completed, bar drawing up muster-rolls to ensure that every Marine had been paid what was due to him – a task on which Francis Lynn's brother Samuel was engaged. Francis Lynn was slated to be appointed one of two 'Commissioners to Clear the Officers of the Marine Regiments', but the Attorney-General advised that such a Commission would be in some way unconstitutional, and instead Commissioners of Accounts, whose remit included

---

[214] *Ibid.*, Warrant Books: September 1714, *Disposition Book XXIII*, pp. 9–10.
[215] Court Rolls for the Manor of Brockenhurst, Ringwood, Hampshire: Hampshire Archives & Local Studies, National Archives ref: 6M80/E/T411.

stating the Marine Accounts, were appointed.

On 1ˢᵗ August 1714 Queen Anne, "*of ever blessed and happy Memory*",[216] died. Francis Lynn and his immediate superior at the War Office were "*removed*", the Commission for Sick and Hurt Seamen was terminated, and with the disbandment of the Marine Regiments there was no longer any work for him at the Admiralty, so Lynn found himself unemployed, "*And having the misfortune to be too zealouse a Church of England Man, and my Friends all of the same Stamp,*[217] *so left without hopes of getting any other Employ, especially whilst the Administration continued in Whig hands, I resolved quietly to Retire into yᵉ Country to Dulwich, to wait for a turn of the Tide*".[218]

By now Lynn's 'Uncle', Samuel Hunter, was a widower, with no children. His wife Mary (*née* Thurman) had died early in 1711[12], and on 3ʳᵈ February that year was buried in a vault in the Dulwich village burial ground[219] (at the junction of Court Lane and Dulwich Village). Hunter must have retired in 1714 or soon after, as we hear no more of his career as a Commissioner of the Navy or in any other post. He too may have been a victim of the purge by the new Whig administration of known or suspected Tory supporters.

Of the six children born to Francis and Mary Lynn before March 1706, only two, both girls, were living, all four sons having died in infancy. There were,

---

[216] Francis Lynn's 'diary'.
[217] Not all his friends. At least one of them, his "*best friend*" William Morgan, was or claimed to be a staunch Catholic.
[218] Francis Lynn's 'diary'.
[219] Dulwich Chapel Register 1616-1857, ed. T. L. Ormiston.

however, further additions to the family, for on 4th December 1706 (at 5.20 a.m.) Mary gave birth to another daughter, Sophia. Next came a son, born 1st May 1708 (at 2.00 p.m.), named Philip supposedly because it was Saints "*Philip & Jacobs day*", but perhaps because Col. Philip Herbert[220] was one of the boy's godfathers. Ann was born 1st November 1710 "*between 2 and 3 in the Morning*" (the usually punctilious Lynn must have been too distracted to check the exact time), and finally the Lynns' tenth child, Arabella, was born on 31st May 1715 (at "*past 4 in the morning*"). All of these children were to survive into adulthood, although they were lucky to do so. As Lynn adds to his record of Arabella's birth:

The 3[d]. day of my Wifes lying in, She gott cold by mismanagment of her Midwife, and was so extreamly ill, that D[r]. Plumptre & D[r]. Chamberlayn after a weeks attendance gave her over, & declared She could not live; but it pleased God She recovered; My concern for her, & tending her in her illness gott me a fitt of Sickness, just as she began to recover, which had very near carryd me off, Sophy and Philly too at the Same time were taken very ill, as also the little one, who was sent out to Nurse, without expectation of her Life; but it pleasd God before the end of the Month of June we all recovered.

For those of his children who had died, Francis Lynn recorded where they were buried – variously at St Margaret's Westminster, St Martin-in-the Fields, Camberwell and Lambeth – and for all of his children

---

220 A grandson of the 4th Earl of Pembroke, and M.P. for Rye from 1705 until he resigned in 1707 to become a Commissioner for the Sick and Wounded, which is no doubt how Francis Lynn came to make his acquaintance.

he lists their godparents. No child, obviously, is responsible for the choice of its godparents, and their selection was then, as now, probably more a matter of strengthening social ties than of any real expectation that the godparents would play a part in the child's religious or moral upbringing, but Francis Lynn's choices do throw some light on his connections at the time, so I will merely list the names (some of whom have already been mentioned): Sir Richard Holford, Capt. Graydon, 'Aunt [Mary] Hunter' (twice), Sir William Russell, Mr Brocket, Mrs Morland, Mrs Campbell, Samuel Lynn (twice), 'Aunt [Elizabeth] Banks', George Clarke Esq. and Josiah Burchet Esq. (the two Secretaries of the Admiralty), Mrs Fawler, Col. Evance, Mr John Oldner, Lady Holford (twice), Mr Secretary Ellis, Capt. William Morgan, Mrs Elizabeth Lynn (Sam's wife), Col. John Orfeur, Mrs Carter, Mrs Griffith, Col. Philip Herbert, Mr Anthony Brucer, Mrs Busby, Mr Thomas Jones, Mrs Herbert junior, Mrs Canning (Captain Canning's wife)[221] and Mrs Castle. Each child had at least three godparents.

Francis Lynn also recorded in his 'diary' the marriages and deaths of members of his family in addition to those already mentioned. On 19th December 1699, his brother Samuel married "*Mrs*" (actually Miss) Elizabeth Griffin, whom Lynn intriguingly describes as "*a relation of my Wifes*", although how they were related is unknown to me. On 23rd November 1703 "*We received News of the Death*

---

[221] The Cannings (Richard and Margaret) lived, with their children Elizabeth, Margaret, Harriot and Richard (who became a vicar), in Ipswich. The Lynns' daughter Mary ('Polly') stayed with them for "*some time*" in August/September 1717.

of my Brother John, who went over to Flanders to gain experience in y[f] Hospital there, on prospect of preferment at home, but being taken ill on Shipboard, whilst they lay Windbound, was carry'd ashore, and dyed at [222] *in Holland."* On 5th April 1710, at *"about 5 in ye morning My Mother Susanna Lynn dyed at her House in Westm[r]. aged about 75,*[223] *and was buryd by*[224] *my Father"*.

Francis Lynn spent the Winter of 1715/1716 *"partly in Town, & partly at Dulwich"*, and he gave up his accommodation in Prince's Court at mid-Summer 1716. His 'diary' records that on 1st June 1716 *"I removed with my whole family* [to Dulwich]*, having hired a House of M[r] Vanhattem at 36[£] p[er] ann[um] & quitted the Town."* However, this is not entirely accurate. He and his wife, if not their children, were by April 1716 living in a house on Dulwich Common, possibly in Hall Place itself, and on 16th June he wrote to William Morgan:

"You must know, my next-door Neighbour, whose frequent impertinances has given us no little disturbance ever since we have liv'd upon the Common, took occasion about 2 months since to be very inquisitive about You, saying she knew you, who you was, and what You was, with a great deal of female Sawciness thereto relating, which so provoked Your Mistress,[225] *that a terrible Quarrell ensued, wherein Madam acted the Billingsgate to the greatest Degree, and thought she could not*

---

[222] Lynn left a blank space for the place-name, but never filled it in.

[223] Apparently the convention of a lady not admitting to her precise age, even to her children, had already begun.

[224] i.e. with.

[225] i.e. Mrs Lynn.

say anything vile enough of Puddy,[226] who was weak enough to make her some returns which prevent my taking such Measures with her as otherwise I would have done. This has occasioned Our removal from the House to that of Mr Vanhattons at the other end of ye Town[227] nearer the College, but something further from Our Friend ye Commoner,[228] which removal, since it contracts me alltogether into one place (for I quitt my Townhouse[229] now at Midsummer) has and will give me a full imploy for a time till we come to be a little settled."[230]

John Vanhattem (or Van Hattem, but not 'Vanhatton') had recently inherited from his father of the same name the leases of two Dulwich properties: one on the site of 'Brightlands', now in Gallery Road, which I think he occupied himself;[231] the other – which must be the one Lynn means, as the rent for the other, which was leased from the College with 36 acres attached to it, would have given Vanhattem almost no profit[232] – being next to the village burial ground, on the site of 57-59 Dulwich Village. "*Madam*", the fishwife-like neighbour (although, as we

---

[226] 'Puddy', meaning 'short and stout' was Lynn's somewhat unflattering pet-name for his wife, Mary.

[227] i.e. Dulwich village.

[228] Because Hall Place overlooked Dulwich Common, 'The Commoner' was Lynn's usual mode of referring to Samuel Hunter in correspondence. Not once does Lynn refer to him by name.

[229] in Princes Court, Duke Street, St James's.

[230] TNA, C 111/207 ('Master Brougham's exhibits').

[231] until Abraham Jordan, the celebrated organ-builder and inventor of the swell-box, took it over in 1722.

[232] Vanhattem paid only £13 a year for his lease of 57/59 Dulwich Village, so the £36 p.a. rent he received from Francis Lynn would have given him a handsome profit.

shall see, she had a point about Capt. Morgan), was probably Sarah, widow of Richard Dekins, living in a cottage adjoining Samuel Hunter's barn. She may have been a retired servant of his.

Lynn had chosen Dulwich in order, so he later claimed, to be close to his 'Uncle Hunter', who so far as Lynn knew had no living relatives.

How wrong he was!

CHAPTER 7

Debtors and Creditors

Francis Lynn's "*best Friend*" William Morgan was an Irish Catholic, born in Bantry, Co. Cork, southern Ireland, the son of Dennis Morgan Esq. and his wife Christina, *née* Galway. He had a married sister, referred to frequently in correspondence between Morgan and Lynn, but never by name. I do not know when William Morgan was born, but from his later referring to Frank Lynn as acting "*like a father*" to him, I would guess that when they first met in mid-1703, when Lynn was 31, Morgan was a few years younger. Their surviving letters to each other include many expressions of mutual admiration, respect, friendship and love, and I suspect that on Lynn's part at least there was what today we would probably call a 'bromance', although Lynn seems to have had little doubt as to where Morgan's tastes lay. As he wrote to him in France in June 1716, "*How far the Civilitys of the French Ladys may work upon Your virtue I can't tell, but … I always lookt upon You to be flesh and blood*". I imagine William Morgan to have been a young, handsome, charming, plausible chancer. One knows the type.

Lynn's extensive correspondence with William Morgan is littered with abbreviated or altered names, nicknames, and pseudonyms. I initially thought that the 'letter book' containing copies of Lynn's letters to Morgan (and others) might have been a transcript, made in preparation for the 1747-56 case of *Galway v Lynn*, by a clerk who had redacted or abbreviated some of the names in order to protect the reputations of persons who were not party to those proceedings. However, I now think that the 'letter book' is Francis Lynn's own record of what he regarded as his more important private correspondence, and that the abbreviations, alterations, etc. were made at the time by Lynn himself. Such devices also appear in the original letters written by Morgan to Lynn, also submitted in evidence in the *Galway v Lynn* case as originals, not copies. Morgan's situation was – for reasons which will later become clearer – sensitive, and either Lynn, or Morgan, or both, must have been concerned that their correspondence might fall into the wrong hands, so they resorted to using names and descriptions which the other would recognise but which would hopefully signify little or nothing to anyone who might intercept them. They even used pseudonyms for each other: Lynn, at least in his first letter, was "*F. Leenig*" (and "*F. Leeney*" in Morgan's reply), and he consistently addressed Morgan as "*Mr Williams*".

There are some pseudonyms too obscure for us to know whose identities they were intended to mask, but "*Samick*" is Francis Lynn's brother, Samuel; "*Mr Mah---*" or "*M-h-y*" is Francis Lynn's lawyer, Mr

Florence[233] Mahony; "*Mr Pryssian*" was another lawyer, Walter Pryse; "*Mr Genero*" was Lt.-Gen. Robert Echlin, a Jacobite supporter living in exile in France; "*The Commoner*" was Samuel Hunter (whose house, Hall Place, bordered Dulwich Common); "*Jo. K-----*" or "*Capt. Jo.*" was Joseph Knight; and "*the (Old) Colonel*" was Col. John Rice, in whose convoluted financial affairs Morgan and to a lesser extent Lynn both became embroiled.

I do not know precisely when, or under what circumstances, Rice and William Morgan first met, but it must have been at about the time that Morgan became acquainted with Francis Lynn, in 1703. Rice himself later stated that by 1705 he and Morgan were already "*well Acquainted and Intimate*".[234] In 1705 Parliament granted to Col. Rice the sum of £11,420 17*s* 6*d*, payable in Army Debentures, "*for Horses, Arms, and Accoutrements, and Arrears of Pay due to him*". Rice had procured releases from the officers of his Regiment, on the strength of his promise that when he received payment from the government he would pay whatever was owing to them and to their men. In the event, having received the debentures on 19th April 1706, and in possession of the signed releases, he paid the officers nothing, and instead sold all but £1,700 of the debentures (heavily discounted by up to 50%, so Rice was even then not regarded as a good credit risk) to various friends and acquaintances in return for payments in money or its equivalent

---

[233] Florence was then not an uncommon name given to Irish boys, such as Mahony was; it was commonly abbreviated to 'Flurrie'.

[234] *Rice v Lynn* (1719), TNA C 11/1789/28 & C 11/1172/39.

totalling £7,130. £1,750 was used by Capt. Joseph Knight and Mr Charles O'Hara to buy woodland in Ireland (from John Asgill, for £1,500) and other land (from Anthony Hammond, for £1,000), which was "*sold*" to Messrs Mathews and Wetton, apparently in trust for Knight and O'Hara (although as part of these labyrinthine financial dealings there may well have been another declaration of trust, by Knight and O'Hara, in favour of Rice). For their debentures Lord Fitzwilliams paid Rice £2,800, Sir Stephen Evance (the founder of the Hollow Sword Blades Company, an early national bank) £1,000, a Mr Taylor "*upon a Commission of Bankrupt*" £312,[235] a Mr Decloseaux £148, and Capt. William Morgan £1,120 for debentures with a face value of £1,600 (i.e. discounted by 30%).[236] Morgan then sold the debentures to Anthony Hammond at a further 10% discount. Rice and Morgan were still in dispute about them (and other debts) as late as 1719.[237]

It soon became apparent that Rice had kept the money for his own purposes, and in 1706 Parliament, instead of arranging for Rice to be prosecuted for fraud or theft as one might have expected, simply passed "*An Act for obliging Colonel John Rice to account for Debentures granted to him*". The Act provided that anyone who could prove by 1st August 1707 that prior to 1st March 1706 they had in good faith paid Rice on the strength of debentures bought by them in which Rice still had an equity of redemption would be entitled to

---

[235] The figure is not specifically mentioned, but must have been £312 if the total of £5,380 given as received by Rice in money is correct.

[236] *Journals of the House of Commons*, vol. 17 (1712), pp 153-4.

[237] *Rice v Lynn* (1719), TNA C 11/1789/28 & C 11/1172/39.

repayment and interest. Among the claims submitted was one from a widow, Anne Trant, whose attorney (since deceased) had taken an assignment of Rice's equity of redemption in two of the debentures in return for a loan to Rice which had not been repaid.

Still Col. Rice paid nothing to his men, and in May 1708 the Solicitor-General, Sir James Mountague, was asked to look into the affair.[238] He ended his 10-page report to the Treasury at the end of that month as follows: "*I doe humbly conceive that it may be advisable to cause as many of the said debentures, and as much of the produce thereof, as can be mett with in the hands of Coll. Rice, or any of his agents & trustees, to be seised into the Queen's hands as soon as may be, to prevent any further wast and imbezlement thereof.*" Rice, Joseph Knight and John Asgill were summoned to attend a hearing, to which Mountague was also invited.[239]

The *Journal of the House of Commons*[240] for 25th March 1712 records that, prompted by Mrs Trant's claim, a Committee had been set up to look into the Rice affair, and it reported to the House that day. The House agreed with the Committee's findings, and Mrs Trant's claim was allowed, with interest.[241]

What seems remarkable is that Col. Rice faced no criminal sanction for his outrageous conduct, perhaps

---

[238] Calendar of Treasury Books, vol. 22; Warrant Books May 1708, 1-10, pp. 224-233, *Out Letters* (*General*) *XVIII*, p. 415.

[239] Calendar of Treasury Books, vol. 22; Minute Book June 1708, pp. 22-30.

[240] Vol. 17, p. 153.

[241] Sir Stephen Evance, assignee of one of Rice's debentures, committed suicide in March 1712, at about the time the House of Commons was deliberating the affair, which may or may not be coincidental.

because he was regarded as 'an Officer and a Gentleman', although defrauding one's own subordinates is hardly gentlemanly conduct. Whether Joseph Knight and William Morgan were unaware that Rice was a crook is open to doubt. Francis Lynn certainly came to have few illusions about Rice. Against the record of a small debt due to Morgan in 1719, he recorded that the Note given as security was *"in Rice's hands – might as well be in ye Devills"*.[242]

Morgan, who was to become no stranger to litigation in the years to come, was in 1713 one of ten defendants in a case[243] brought by Capt. Joseph Knight, a name familiar from 'the Rice Affair' of 1705-12. Indeed, most of his co-defendants Anthony Hammond, Charles O'Hara, Richard Hedges, Montagu Griffin, Viscount Kenmare, Valentine Brown, John Asgill, Thomas Mathews, and Col. John Rice himself, were also involved in that case. With O'Hara substituted as plaintiff, and Knight joining the defendants, the same individuals (with the addition of John Wetton, but without Hedges and Mathews) were party to another similar action in 1715.[244] When the lawyer Walter Pryse submitted a Stated Account to Morgan in February 1719, it included among the receipts at the beginning of September 1715 *"Costs of Serjt at Armes in Cause Knight v. O Hara … £1:9:0"*; *"What the sd Walter Pryse reced from Regr in Knight con. O Hara it being in Bill Charged to be paid to Regr … £4:15:0"*; and *"Costs of Contempt in Knight c. O Hara … £30:4:9"*, so, as 'costs follow the event', Morgan and

---

[242] TNA, C 111/207, packet 1, item G28.

[243] *Knight v Hammond* (1713), TNA C 11/1228/42.

[244] *O'Hara v Knight* (1715), TNA C 11/1777/9.

his co-defendants must have won the case.

William Morgan's chief occupation was that of Regimental Agent, whose role at this time is explained thus:

"*In many instances it was* [the regimental agent] *who arranged for subsistence to be remitted to regimental headquarters and digested information sent by the regimental paymaster (who was not necessarily very professional in his accounting technique, a fault often shared by the captains with whom he dealt); he drew up regimental accounts for the information of the War Office and his colonel; he attended the War and Pay Offices to resolve any difficulties; he dealt on the colonel's behalf with clothiers, sword cutlers, gunsmiths, insurance agents and other contractors; he acted for the colonel and the other officers in numerous regimental and private concerns …*".[245]

Morgan, then living in St Giles-in-the-Fields, had been employed in that capacity in Col. Edward Jones's regiment from April 1712 – he was obliged to sue his predecessor over funds unaccounted for,[246] and was awarded damages and costs (and interest) of £117 14*s* 5*d*[247] – but was also Agent for at least one other regiment, that of Lt.-Gen. Henry Holt. Among Morgan's papers found after his death in 1744 was an Account Book "*intitled Holts Leidger*", covering the years 1709 to 1713.[248] Morgan had started working for Holt

---

[245] '*Oeconomy and Discipline: Officership and Administration in the British Army 1714-63*' by Alan J. Guy (M.U.P., 1985), p.59.
[246] *Morgan v Beachcroft* (1713), TNA, C 5/257/12.
[247] Morgan's 1720 account with his lawyer, Walter Pryse – TNA, C 111/207, packet 1, item D4.
[248] TNA, C 111/207, Packet 1, Galway's List, unnumbered item. Unfortunately the item is now missing.

several years before that, and in 1707 brought
proceedings relating to the Regimental Accounts
against his predecessor as Holt's agent, Christopher
Broughton.[249] Morgan seems to have purchased from
an Anthony Luker and a Robert Gardner £1,597-
worth and £2,753-worth respectively of uniforms and
'accoutrements' for the Regiment in 1711 and 1712, or
at any rate nearly ten years later, as part of an on-going
dispute, he produced promissory notes addressed to
them, dated April and May 1712 respectively, to repay
them *"out of the first money either Clearings or offreconings that
shall come into my hands for the said Regimt"*.[250] In 1714
Constancia Rodney, widow and executrix of Col.
Anthony Rodney, sued Lt.-Gen. Holt and Morgan
jointly,[251] and after Holt's death sued Morgan alone.[252]
Mrs Rodney must have died soon after, and later in the
year Morgan and Holt's widow and executrix, Lucy,
were sued in 1714 by Capt. Henry Rodney.[253] After
William Morgan's departure for France, Francis Lynn
wrote in May 1716 to Mr Henry Hare, whom he took
to be Lt.-Gen. Holt's executor:

*"Sir, Understanding that money has been issued on Acct
of the Offreckoning of the Marine Regiments, and being fully
empowered by my Friend W:M to transact his affairs in his*

---

[249] *Morgan v. Broughton* (1707), TNA C 6/350/23.

[250] TNA C 111/207, packet 2, items (2) and (3). They were
apparently needed to show that Morgan's profits from acting as
Holt's agent were not as great as they might have seemed. How
these items were still in Morgan's possession, and how he was
able to send them to Francis Lynn apparently at Lynn's request,
is not explained, and I would not be at all surprised if Morgan
had not simply created them himself *ex post facto*.

[251] *Rodney v Holt* (1714), C 11/2341/43.

[252] *Rodney v Morgan* (1714), TNA C 11/2341/37.

[253] *Rodney v Morgan* (1714), TNA C 11/2253/7.

absence, I take the liberty to trouble you herewith and desire, that ye Accts between him and You as Executor to ye late General Holt touching the Clothing furnished the Regiment by the Captain may be adjusted; I am sensible it has been a dispute of some standing, and was once referrd, but not brought to a conclusion; If therefore you please to lett me know when and where I may meet you, that we may agree upon two or more Referrees, to putt an end to this affair, I shall think myself very much obliged to You, being under Ingagements on ye Captains Accts for severall Summs, which I have discharged, and would therefore be very glad to settle, such of his affairs as possibly may be done, in order to my being reimbursed. I have frequently heard ye Capt say, he should be very well pleased to putt it to such an issue, & doubted not of your justice as well as friendship. Being mostly out of town, I pray you please to send your answer directed to Mr Mahony in Princes Court, Dukestreet, St James's, who will be ready to wayt on you at any time …"

As Holt's sole executrix was actually his widow, Lucy,[254] and Mr Hare was merely one of the two Overseers of Holt's Will, Hare may well have decided to ignore Lynn's letter. It may have been to this dispute that Morgan was alluding when he wrote to Francis Lynn in October 1717:

"I must tell you my dear Frank that my great loss will be on account of ye recrutes of ye Regiment on which I laid out all my substance thinking I should get considerable by them, and I neglected getting warrants for that Money because I thought I had you and him[255] at my beck (as indeed I had) in points of

---

[254] She had obtained probate on 6th February 1714[15] – TNA, PROB 11/544/295.

[255] Morgan is referring to Frank's brother, Samuel Lynn.

Justice, but time as you know put it out of our powers. This will be my great loss unless he and you can retrive it".[256] The case was still rumbling on when Morgan wrote to Lynn in June 1718, mentioning that "*He*[257] *sayes Capt Rod[ney] plagues him for the Accts what wee made up 18 year agoe. I canot help him, I think the Law must decide it for had I been at home I could not doe it*". Over a year later Lynn wrote to Morgan, enclosing "*a Copy of a Letter from Capt R-dny to Sam, with his answer to the Same, by wch yuil see how that Mole works underground. We can't understand what he Means by Saying Mr Holt is resolved to be no longer made a fool of*".

I have found no direct evidence that at any time during his career in the English (subsequently British) army William Morgan did any actual fighting, and certainly when Holt's Regiment of Marines arrived back in England in August 1715 (without Holt, who had died at the beginning of that year) Morgan, who had kept long-term lodgings in Piccadilly, had retired to France (*via* Chiswick). Indeed, apart from occasional trips to France on 'private business' – the most momentous of which I will describe in the next Chapter – he may never have left England at all, despite being nominally the captain of a Company in Holt's Regiment.[258]

For several years before 1715 Francis Lynn, his

---

[256] TNA C 111/207. I have corrected most of Morgan's spelling and punctuation.

[257] As the immediately preceding sentence refers to Morgan's sister, I think his chain of thought must have reverted to a letter he had received from the lawyer, Walter Pryse.

[258] Wills of Dennis Riordan made 1713 (TNA PROB 11/534/282) and of Evan Thomas made 20/2/1707[08] (TNA PROB 11/571/148] both refer to him as such.

brother Samuel, and William Morgan had effectively all been acting as bankers, paying bills and lending sums of money – often substantial sums – to each other. The earliest extant set of accounts between Francis Lynn and Morgan starts in July 1705, but even these are not the first, as they show a balance brought forward from a previous set of accounts of £8 8s owed by Morgan to Lynn. Up to Christmas 1715 Lynn received on Morgan's behalf, or made payments to him, totalling £1,895 15s 5d, and paid out on his behalf sums totalling £1,564 14s 7d, making a balance due to Lynn of £331 0s 8d, to which he added four years interest of £58 (equivalent to around 4.5% p.a.) when the 'Stated' accounts were finally agreed at Dulwich on Christmas Day 1715 and Morgan signed a promise to pay the balance of £389 0s 8d to Francis Lynn "*on demand*". The sums credited to Morgan (and therefore shown in the Debit column) included "*A Guinea lent my Wife & another to Mrs Morland*" on 3rd November 1707 and "*Lent to Sarah at home … 11s 3d*" on 16th October 1706. Sarah was Morgan's maidservant, and in February 1716 Florence Mahony "*pd Sarah your Maid she laid out for yow .. £1:2:8*".[259] After Morgan went abroad in mid-1715, leaving Sarah's wages unpaid, she went to work for his sister, but by July 1719 when Francis Lynn wrote to Morgan on various matters she had left that employment too. "*I don't know if Yr Sister has wrote to you about Sarah, She is marryd & gone from them, and has Sett up a Chandlers Shop at ye Entrance into Princes Court, & t'other day mett me going in there, & beggd I would write to you, abt her money*

---

259 F. Mahony's stated account with W. Morgan, TNA ref. C 111/207, packet 1, item D-6.

due from You, she having occasion to lay in Stock for Trade; I promisd her I would, & shall wayt your answer", which, if it ever came, has not survived. Most of the payments made by Francis Lynn on Morgan's behalf are to Army (or Marine) officers, at rates of £7 2s 6d, £4 12s 2d or £2 16s 2d, depending on their seniority. There are also one or two payments to "*the Widdows Fund*".

From at least 1709 until 1721 Francis Lynn' brother Samuel was also financially linked to William Morgan. A set of Stated Accounts up to May 1721 agreed by Samuel Lynn and Morgan's wife (as Morgan's attorney) on 6th November 1725[260] begin with £150 paid to Morgan by Samuel's "*Deputies*" on 13th December 1709 as some sort of start-up fund. The Debits column totals £1,175 3s 10d, and includes such items as payments for State Lottery tickets, of merchants' bills (particularly wine merchants), for uniforms and other military equipment and commissions, for pictures and picture frames, for legal bills and on personal notes and bills, and of cash. The Credits column totals £1,618 18s 3d, including "*Cash rec'd for Mr Lynn's Use from Qu[arte]r Ma[ste]r Gallway*[261] *2 Summs of 43£ & 34£ as per Gallway's Accot in Mr Lynn's hands*", and various commissions from Army officers and others, leaving a balance "*due to Mr Lynne*" at 6th May 1721 of £443 14s 5d.

It is difficult, if not impossible, to fathom what is going on with these inter-connected Accounts. One suspects that the obfuscation was deliberate, and that what we are seeing is some form of money-laundering. Without examining all the relevant accounts of all the

---

[260] TNA, C 111/207, packet 2, item 9.
[261] This was Capt. Andrew Galway, a relation of Morgan's.

parties concerned, one cannot be sure. Hopefully each of them was fully aware of how his affairs stood with the others at any given time. On more than one occasion Francis Lynn had to impress upon William Morgan the need to have some written evidence of particular transactions "*as we are all Mortall*".

Their relationship of debtor and creditor, with the roles occasionally reversed, may have been the cause of ill-feeling between Samuel Lynn and William Morgan. In April 1716 Lynn's brother Francis wrote to Morgan in France:

"*I paid Coz. Samick on Your Acct to make up his 1500£, … I am unwilling to committ to writing the behaviour of Samick, but if there be no hopes of seeing you soon,*[262] *I may in a Post or two say something of it, tho it will not be surprising after what is past*". Morgan replied "*As to Our Co.ⁿ Samick truly I shall not be surprized at any attempts of his. I vow to God I am more concernd for him than I am for any of his behaviors to me … I hear he presses to state an Acc#. on which head I will write a leter to him …*".

In June Lynn wrote somewhat disparagingly of his brother: "*Cos Samicks professions of Friendship cannot be otherwise than dark and close, for I am sure he loves himself the best of all his Mothers Children*", but in November was able to report to Morgan that "*Your Letter to Samick has been very kindly received & he resolves to bury in oblivion all that has passed*", to which Morgan retorted a month later, "*Yow say Samick is well satisfied with my leter. If he can best lay by Intrest*[263] *(which I never thought any parte of*

---

[262] There weren't.
[263] i.e. set aside self-interest.

freindship) he will alwayes finde me sencere".

Thereafter relations between Samuel Lynn and William Morgan seem to have settled down. It may be that the cause of the rift – on which the correspondence does not elaborate – was nothing to do with finance and everything to do with events that occurred at the end of March 1715, to which I will return in the next chapter.

In 1712 Morgan was involved in another dispute. He and Edward Herbert issued proceedings[264] that year against James Cardonnel[265] (or Cardonell, de Cardonnell, etc.) and others, including John Asgill, but they seem to have been unsuccessful. In 1714 Cardonnel counter-claimed[266], and won. Consequently Morgan, Francis Lynn, and a merchant in wine and other commodities, Stephen Creagh, entered into a recognisance with Cardonnel in the court of Chancery to pay Cardonnel £1,500. In August 1715 Morgan wrote to Lynn: "*Before I came out of Towne I left A bond wth Mr Mahoney to endemnifie y^ow and Mr Creagh against that affaire of De Cardonells, And I have left Effects in his hands that in case I should be cast. Neither of y^ow should come to ye least trouble*".[267] Lynn recorded in his letter-book[268] that on 18th February 1715[16] "*I received the Order of Court*

---

[264] TNA C 10/544/55.

[265] Cardonnel had, between 1691 and 1699, been Secretary to successive Dukes of Schomberg, but in 1713 was obliged to petition the Treasury for £2,000 arrears of pay, having been paid for only eight months' work during that time. ('Volume 161: May 1-26, 1713', in *Calendar of Treasury Papers, Vol. 4, 1708-1714*, pp. 480-487.)

[266] TNA C 22/234/21.

[267] TNA, C 111/207.

[268] *Ibid.*

directing the payment of Mr Cardonnels money the 8th of March next', and he paid the debt on Morgan's behalf, by instalments. The first was of £500 (£250 of which was a bill drawn by Lord Barrymore,[269] the rest in banknotes)[270] on 19th March 1716, with Cardonnel agreeing[271] that if the balance, plus interest, were paid by 1st May he would vacate the recognisance. The second instalment of £600,[272] in banknotes (one of £200), including £250 paid by Lynn's Irish lawyer Florence Mahony,[273] followed on 25th April, bringing the total so far to £1,100, with £400 plus interest outstanding. Francis Lynn was therefore not being entirely truthful when on 23rd April he had written to Morgan "*I have payd Mr Card[onne]ll the 1500£*". The deadline came and went, and James Cardonnel was impatient for his money. He sent a servant to Lynn's Dulwich home, with instructions which the servant, finding Lynn away on business but Mrs Lynn at home, may have exceeded. As Lynn wrote to Cardonnel on 31st May:

> "*I have been acquainted with the Message you was pleased to allarm my Spouse with by Your Footman which I cannot but think Something Extraordinary: as to ye Matter as well as the Manner … My affairs at present require my almost*

---

[269] James Barry, 4th Earl of Barrymore (1667-1748), Irish soldier and (towards the end of his life) Jacobite politician. In 1702 he had purchased the 13th Regiment of Foot for 1,400 guineas, but was forced, as a Tory, to sell it in 1715 (after the accession of George I).

[270] TNA, C 111/207, Packet 1, item D(2), DR entry.

[271] TNA, C 111/207, packet 2, item (3). Cardonnel's receipt even records the number of each banknote.

[272] TNA, C 111/207, Packet 1, item D(2), DR entry.

[273] F. Mahony's stated account with W. Morgan, TNA ref. C 111/207, packet 1, item D6.

constant attendance in ye Country for which reason I have lodged the money in Mr Pryses[274] hands, which will be payd You the Moment that Instrument is perfected & executed,"

Lynn said that that would happen in a day or so, and as Cardonnel had had *"above 2/3ds of the Money, I think Your Suspicions are as groundless, as Your uneasiness is unreasonable …"*.[275] Nevertheless, Lynn had got the message, and paid Cardonnel £10 *"for forbearance"* on 26th June,[276] and the balance of £400 (actually paid on his and Morgan's behalf, to Cardonnel's attorney Mr Mowbray, by Walter Pryse)[277] on 2nd July 1716, when Mowbray supplied Lynn with a final receipt.[278]

I have supplied details for almost every aspect of this transaction to demonstrate how difficult it is to make coherent sense of them all. That complexity is repeated time and again with other financial transactions involving William Morgan, Francis Lynn, and Samuel Lynn. Another example is to be found in a letter from Lynn to Morgan of February 1720:

"You wrote over once … about a Warrant for £45 in Sizers hands wᶜʰ had been made out in Sams name & endorsed to You; I find it is in that Office, but with a Caveat or Stop upon it by Mr Herbert in behalf of Arthur Swift[279] (who by

---

[274] Walter Pryse was another of Lynn's lawyers.

[275] C 111/207, Packet 2, Letter book of Francis Lynn, 1715-1720.

[276] TNA, C 111/207, Packet 1, item D(2), DR entry

[277] TNA, C 111/207, Packet 1, item D(2), DR entry.

[278] TNA, C 111/207, packet 2, item (3).

[279] Clerk in the Marines Pay Office 1706 to 1713. Died 1720. His correspondence and papers are filed at TNA under ref. NRA 41370.

the way is reduced to an Idiot, having lost all his Senses &
Memory, & is a Prisoner still in the Kings Bench) to whom he
alledges a balance due of £39 upon an Account between you; of
wch I gott a Copy and send it inclosed, that you may as soon as
possible return me yr answer, and directions what is to be done
in it; for time must not be lost in making a demand of the
Warrant before the Commiss^{rs} rise."

And another example, from a letter of Lynn's to
Morgan of 3rd September 1717, relating to the O'Hara
case, in which Col. John Rice and Capt. Joseph
Knight were involved:

"You have heard I doubt not of the Commission of
Sequestration against O'Hara, by virtue of which Several
things have been seized & sold, amongst the rest there is a
Lease, which answers for 2000 Guineas (as they tell me), this
is sequesterd & putt into J Ks hands (as it ought) and he has
lodgd it with ye Colonel. Now Jo wants to go to Bristoll to be
some time with his Brother, & … they have been with me for
money; I shall never deney my Assistance, whilst it is in my
power, or I have a penny left, but as we are all mortall, I
thought it proper to move before Jo goes away, that the Lease
might be lodged in some other hand, … or that he should make
some bill of Sale to you, or Execute a Deed of Trust, And that
we might take up a small Summ upon it, … to all wch the Col.
as usuall full of blind expressions & riddles answered in the
Negative, taking no notice of Your Wants, but pressing for
money to carry Jo away, tho at the same time he seemd to be
well assured that O'neal, who is to redeem ye Lease would be in
town to do it within a fortnight or very little time, Which seems
to me extraord., that he shd be so hasty for sending Jo K. to
Bristoll, who is to be the receiver of the money, & to deliver up
ye Lease. He allegd Jo had made a Will to You – This I know

*he has, but You and all the World know that Jo may make another, and that the last Will takes place; And who knows what his Brother may prevail on him to do, if the Col. has not done it already. ... I still retain the thought that the Col. has his designs. ... All this I urged, and ... askd him how they came to pay me any of that without such Special Order from You. This extorted some confused bliytings from y*e* Col, but nothing more. Upon this We parted ..."*

We have not heard the last of Col. Rice or of Capt. Knight, or of Francis Lynn's brother Samuel, the subject of the next chapter.

CHAPTER 8

'Samick'

In 1720 Francis Lynn's brother Samuel – *'Samick'* – produced a 34-page booklet entitled *'A Short Narrative of the Case of Samuel Lynn, Esq; late Muster Master General of the late Marine Forces, etc., humbly offer'd to Consideration'*. It deals with his career in public service from 1692, as a 17-year-old clerk in the office of George Clarke, Queen Mary's 'Secretary at War' and Judge-Advocate General of the Forces. Much of the booklet is devoted to what Samuel Lynn regarded as his shabby treatment by his superiors, and whilst not without interest, is not strictly relevant to my story. For those who may wish to learn even more about Samuel Lynn's career, his *"Short Narrative"* is accessible on several Internet websites.[280]

Shortly before the end of the Nine Years' War in 1697, Samuel Lynn went over to Flanders and Holland on the staff of William Blathwayt, then Secretary of State and of War. Peace with France lasted for only five years, until May 1702, shortly after

---

[280] books.google.co.uk has a complete facsimile of it.

the accession of Queen Anne, when England joined the War of the Spanish Succession, and Samuel was promoted to Deputy Secretary at War, again under Blaythwayt.

On 19th December 1699, at the church of St Martin in the Fields, Samuel Lynn married[281] Elizabeth Griffen or Griffin, who was afterwards known to her intimates as 'Goody'. She was the only child of Thomas Griffin, an apothecary who had died in 1683,[282] having survived his wife Elizabeth (sister of Sir Richard Holford, a senior lawyer) whom he married in April 1674 and who may have died in childbirth. The day before their nuptials Samuel and Elizabeth had entered into a marriage settlement, the terms of which are known only from one of the documents submitted in the case of *Lynn v. Cotman* (1739).[283] The parties to it were (1) Lynn, (2) his bride (then of St Martin-in-the-Fields, Middlesex), (3) Sir Richard Holford (her mother's brother) and Thomas Sysum, gentleman, and (4) Thomas Beach of West Ashton, Wiltshire (the need for whose involvement is not explained). A typical marriage settlement comprised two property elements: the '*dowry*', which was brought into the marriage by the bride (or more often by her parents) and settled on the groom and bride for life (but under the groom's control), with remainder to the issue of the marriage, and the '*bride price*' or '*dower*' (confusingly, also sometimes erroneously referred to as a '*dowry*') which was paid to

---

[281] 'London: - Calendar of Marriage Licence Allegations, 1660-1700 (Marriage)', Book 25.
[282] TNA, PROB 11/673/75.
[283] TNA C 11/784/44.

the bride's parents by the groom (or sometimes by his parents) on the basis that it would remain under her control even if she survived her husband. At the time of his marriage, Samuel Lynn evidently had no property of his own to bring to the marriage, and his father, John Lynn, who might otherwise have been expected to provide the required funds, had been dead for eight years. Elizabeth, on the other hand, was the current owner (*"in tail general"*) of some already-settled property, a house *"in Villars* [Villiers] *Street in York buildings"*,[284] let to an apothecary, Francis Bennington (and probably the late Thomas Griffin's former premises). Samuel was content *"that the portion fortune or Estate of the said Elizabeth might be preserved for her and her Children"*, so that henceforth this property would be held in trust for Samuel and Elizabeth for their joint lives and for the lifetime of the survivor, then *"to the first and other sons of that Marriage in Tail Male with remainder to the Daughter and Daughters of that Marriage in Tail with remainder to the heires of the body of the said Elizabeth* [which could only mean any issue by a later marriage] *with remainder to the said Sir Richard Holford and his heires"*. One may infer from this that Sir Richard was the next in line under the existing settlement, and his being a party to the marriage settlement signified his consent to it.

---

[284] In documents of the time Villiers Street is invariably referred to as "in York Buildings" and not, as one might have expected, the other way around. York Buildings, like the modern Barbican, was a large complex (including a concert hall), built in 1675, which spread across three or more streets, straddling Buckingham Street, with Villiers Street on the Charing Cross side and the present street known as York Buildings on the Covent Garden side.

133

Elizabeth had other property: a leasehold house in Great Russell Street, Bloomsbury, a £150 mortgage on property in East Knowle, Wiltshire, and a £65 Bond, and it was agreed that these should henceforth be held by Sir Richard Holford and Thomas Sysum as trustees, upon trust to sell the same as soon as convenient and to invest the proceeds (together with £500 which Samuel Lynn promised to provide "*of his own proper Money*") within five years in buying some suitable trust property within 100 miles of London, to be held for Samuel and Elizabeth for life and thereafter for Samuel's "*right heirs*". (In the event, Samuel Lynn failed to keep that promise.) The trustees were to pay the income – or "*product*" – of the trust property, both before and after such conversion and re-investment, to Samuel Lynn, or "*as he should direct*".

I have traced the baptisms of five of Samuel and Elizabeth Lynn's children: Samuel (17th February 1700[01]),[285] Thomas (18th March 1701[02]), Richard (20th or 26th June 1706), John (27th August 1707), and Henrietta (15th June 1710). Samuel and Thomas were both christened at St Margaret's, Westminster, the others all at St Martin-in-the-Fields. There was another daughter, Elizabeth, who survived to adulthood but predeceased her sister and father without issue.[286] John and Henrietta also both predeceased their father, John probably in infancy. (I can trace no record of his death.)

The defeat of the English-led forces at the Battle

---

[285] According to ancestry.co.uk, the parish register entry incorrectly gives the names of Samuel's parents as Samuel and *Mary* Lynn (FHL Film No. 560372).

[286] *Lynn v Cotman* (1739), TNA C 11/784/44 refers.

of Almanza in April 1707, with an estimated 5,000 killed, led to Samuel being commissioned to devise a plan for providing the widows of officers – but not of rank-and-file soldiers – with pensions which would not be a burden on the Treasury or on the Civil List. His plan involved creating a fund "*by the Allowance of a Man per Troop and Company on the Musters of the Forces (a Method thought more eligible than by deductions from the Officers Pay as had been practised in Flanders)*". The plan was approved by Parliament, and "*in consideration of the great Trouble he*[287] *had been at in first forming and regulating that Affair*", Samuel was appointed Receiver and Paymaster of the new pension fund. By then he was living in Scotland Yard.

William Blaythwayt had been replaced by Henry St. John (later Lord Bolingbroke) in 1704, and on the latter's resignation in 1708 Samuel found himself "*removed from his Employment without any Crime or Reason assign'd*". His office as Receiver and Paymaster of the War Widows' Pension Fund was annexed by the new Secretary at War. This clearly, twelve years later, still rankled with Samuel Lynn.

After a short spell of unemployment, Samuel was offered the posts of Secretary and *aide-de-camp* to General Erle, and of "*Commissary of the Musters of the Forces under his Command*", and sailed with Erle to the Normandy coast. Towards the end of 1708 Erle was ordered to sail for Ostend, land his forces, set camp at Leffinghen, and create a diversion to enable Marlborough to take Lille, which the Duke had been besieging since 12th August. The French garrison

---

[287] Throughout his '*Short Narrative*' Samuel Lynn refers to himself in the third person.

surrendered on 10th December, and Marlborough immediately conveyed the news to Erle. The General, regarding this as *"a piece of News of Importance to the English Nation"*, chose Lynn to carry Marlborough's letter to London, *via* Ostend. Samuel therefore *"embark'd the next day, after a violent Storm over night, which had swell'd the Sea and rais'd such a Surff upon the Coast, that the People of Ostend got out upon the Ramparts expecting to see him cast away,*[288] *but tho' he had the good fortune to get safe out to Sea, he did not land (by reason of the Privateers from Dunkirk which chased him) 'till next morning eight of the clock at Deal, when taking Post-Horses he arrived at four in the afternoon at St. James's, where and in the Town the News was joyfully receiv'd"*.

For this modest service, of which he seems to have been inordinately proud, Samuel Lynn received a £100 bonus. It seems not to have occurred to him that he may have been chosen as being the most dispensable member of Erle's staff. Samuel continued to serve as Secretary both to General Erle and to his successor General Webb, at 10*s* a day,[289] until 1714, when on Queen Anne's death the job was *"taken from him … and given to his Clerk"*. Another long-remembered insult.

In 1709 the then Muster-Master General of the Marine Forces was *"permitted to surrender the said Office"* to Samuel Lynn, and Lynn's appointment as such was confirmed by the Admiralty on 19th November.

---

[288] It is doubtful that the *"People of Ostend"* had any interest in Samuel Lynn's fate.

[289] TNA, Calendar of Treasury Books, vol. 29, 1714-15: Declared Accounts: Army: Guards, Garrisons and Land Forces, Pipe Office Roll 102 [E351/102].

According to his brother Francis, Samuel Lynn "*bought*" the office, a fact he understandably failed to mention in his '*Short Narrative*'.

In 1710 Samuel Lynn was invited to be deputy Secretary at War, and was reappointed Receiver and Paymaster of the War Widows' Pensions. By the time Queen Anne died in August 1714, when he was dismissed from all his offices (as was his brother Francis, amongst many others), there were "*upwards of 200,000 Men in English Pay by Establishment and Subsidies*", so he must have been kept busy.

Just as Francis Lynn had obtained a commission in the Army for his son Philip, so did Samuel Lynn obtain commissions as Ensigns for two of his young sons. Lynn took pride in not using his influence to protect his elder son's fledgling army career when, as a minor, he was reduced to half-pay and then struck off the pay list altogether.

The disbanding of Marine Regiments was begun towards the end of 1713. The Admiralty decided to terminate Samuel's full pay from the end of January 1713[14], "*although the Service was not then half completed*", but despite them agreeing that to the extent that his office would have to continue to operate he should be paid on a *quantum meruit* basis, Lynn was reduced to half pay, at the rate of ten shillings a day.

Wartime conditions had hampered the updating of the muster rolls of the Marine Regiments, what with ships' books being kept at sea and returns being awaited from agents at foreign hospitals where sick and wounded Marines had been treated. In March 1714 Secretary Lowndes wrote to Samuel Lynn, directing him "*with all convenient speed, to make up entire general Rolls for each of the six Regiments of Marines from the 25th of December 1710, to the times they were respectively pay'd or disbanded, and transmit the same to the proper Pay-master*", so that the Treasury might have an exact account of the pay outstanding. Lynn's response was to assure Lowndes that he would comply with his directions as soon as possible, and to ask for an allowance for the clerks necessary for the work, which he estimated would take twelve months to complete.[290]

Late in August 1714 Josiah Burchett of the Admiralty instructed Lynn to employ one of his clerks in transcribing and certifying entries from such of the muster books as had found their way to the Navy Office. At the beginning of 1715 Lynn reported the '*Respits*'[291] to the end of 1711, which was as much as his staff had so far accomplished. Two days later, on 6th January, the Commissioners for Disbanding the Marine Regiments wrote to Lynn, telling him that they needed Accounts for 1712 and 1713 as well, and to know the individual names "*of the Officers on whom the Respits fall*", and that if Lynn's office could not carry out both tasks together he should concentrate for the time being on the latter. "*We have wrote to the several Colonels, to desire they would give you all the assistance that is in their power towards expediting this Work ….*" But on 15th March 1714[15] Lynn's instructions were again

---

[290] TNA, Calendar of Treasury Papers, vol. 4, 1708-1714, pp.553-563.

[291] 'Respites' were the accumulated days of leave to which officers were entitled but had been unable to take during mobilisation, but later references suggest that 'respites' in the sense used here were in some way a source of income for the government, so I think it more likely that they refer to the 12d in the £ deducted from the sales of Army (and Marine) commissions.

countermanded by Josiah Burchett, telling him that the Admiralty had now decided that he should drop his enquiries into the '*respits*' which might be attributable to particular officers, and revert to making up the general Muster Rolls "*with all the dispatch that may be*", returning to the other task when circumstances permitted.

This confusion in his instructions occurred at a time when Samuel Lynn was engaged on important business of his own. He had contracted to purchase the Manor, Rectory and advowson[292] of Tidmarsh in Berkshire, with all the houses and land that went with it. These comprised a 'capital messuage' and seven other dwellings (and ancillary buildings, including a mill and malthouses) and 539½ acres of land (including 80 acres of woodland), then or formerly severally occupied by Thomas Cresswell, James Strode, Martha Strode, Grace Bilson, George Lovegrove, Anthony Dickman, John Rowe senior and junior, Henry Smith, Richard Choak, William Shortlands, Mary Buckall, Joseph Piper, and John Smith, all in Tidmarsh. Part of this was held on a 500-year lease (originally granted by Edward Strode to a John Duncomb) acquired by Francis Lynn and assigned by him to his brother Samuel, and part was an estate which had been acquired fourteen months before from George and Ann Kemble by William Morgan, who had likewise assigned his interest to Samuel Lynn. If the land was even reasonably productive and the rents at market rates, it should have provided Samuel Lynn with a yearly net income of not less than £400.

---

[292] The right to present an incumbent vicar.

However, Samuel was £3,000 short of the full purchase money. His brother Francis agreed to lend him £1,500, and Francis' friend William Morgan the other £1,500. They took a joint mortgage on the property. As security Samuel and Elizabeth Lynn, with Francis Lynn, William Morgan and two other individuals (Richard Carter[293] and James Fury), granted a 1,000-year lease of the Manor, advowson, capital house and other lands in Tidmarsh, and assigned a house in Villiers Street (York Buildings) and the remaining 8-year lease of a house in Great Russell Street (which must be two of the properties mentioned in the 1699 marriage settlement), and a lease of a house and garden in St James's Park (which must be Lynn's own residence/office in Spring Garden), to Carter and Fury as trustees for Francis Lynn and Capt. William Morgan, who were themselves nominees for Samuel Hunter and Capt. Joseph Knight (presumably also as tenants-in-common rather than as joint tenants).[294] On repayment of the £3,000 and interest at 5% p.a., Francis Lynn and William Morgan undertook to reassign the premises, free of encumbrances, to Samuel Lynn.

These deeds were finalised, in triplicate, on 14th and 15th March 1714[15].[295] What should have happened, but did not, was for the Tidmarsh estate to be put into the names of the trustees of Samuel and Elizabeth Lynn's 1699 marriage settlement, Sir Richard Holford and Thomas Sysum or their successors as such. As Richard Lynn later complained, his father "*did not make*

---

[293] Samuel Lynn's deputy Muster-Master.

[294] The difference was (and is) that a surviving joint tenant inherited the whole asset automatically.

[295] TNA, C 11/1654/3 – *Pryse v. Lynn* (1751), C 11/1622/22 – *Lynn v Cotman* (1739), and C 111/207 – *Galway v Lynn* (1747-56).

any Settlement thereof or of any other Lands or Estates as was intended to be done by him". What is also puzzling is that Samuel Lynn was able to mortgage property – the houses in Villiers Street and Great Russell Street – belonging to his wife, which had been put into trust as part of that marriage settlement, without the trustees raising any objection or apparently even being aware of what he was doing. He must have been selective in what deeds he produced for inspection in support of his title.

The financial arrangements between the parties were far from straightforward, and trying to follow the entries in the various available sets of accounts involving the Lynn brothers and William Morgan, as in this case, is a challenge, to put it mildly. A lends money to B to pay to C in order to settle a debt due to D or E, or even to A. For example, in a letter to William Morgan in April 1716 Francis Lynn told him of a payment to "*Coz Samick*[296] *on your Acct to make up his 1500£*". Since Samuel Lynn should have received Morgan's £1,500 on 15th March the previous year, when the mortgage of Tidmarsh Manor was completed, this makes no sense, unless in the intervening thirteen months their situations had been reversed, and Morgan had needed funds which he was now repaying.

March and April 1715 proved very busy for Samuel Lynn in another respect as well. In the early part of the year he had entertained as a house-guest at his home (and office) in Spring Garden, north of St James's Park, one of the most important men in the

---

[296] 'Samick' was how Francis Lynn almost invariably referred to his brother Samuel in correspondence, but was not necessarily how he addressed him.

land, his former superior Henry St. John, by now created 1st Viscount Bolingbroke. This was at a time *"when his Lordship (having then no house of his own in town) requested the Use of that for his more ready conveniency in attending the Parliament that Session"*. Bolingbroke, who had a reputation as a Francophile and a libertine, had been one of Queen Anne's two chief Ministers,[297] and as such presided over an administration which became notorious for its mismanagement of affairs and lax financial controls. In particular, he was blamed for agreeing to terms of the Treaty of Utrecht which were widely regarded as too favourable to the French. With the accession of George I, whom he had managed personally to offend in correspondence, Bolingbroke realised that his days in power were numbered, particularly when on 21st March 1714[15], at the opening of a new Parliament, his attempts to defend his reputation met with derision. Afterwards claiming that he had feared arrest with no fair trial to follow, Bolingbroke prepared to escape to France where, although not himself a Catholic, he had many friends in positions of importance. It was entirely natural that he should look to his former subordinate and current host, Samuel Lynn, for assistance. Bolingbroke knew that Lynn had some useful contacts, among them Captain William Morgan. Time was of the essence, and a plan was urgently devised.

Morgan's cousin, Capt Andrew Galway, was dispatched to Dover with instructions to hire a vessel on the pretext of going over to Calais to examine the records of a ship which had been 'condemned' (in the sense of being forfeited as a prize). He took with him

---

[297] The other was his fellow Tory Robert Harley, Earl of Oxford.

two cousins, Patrick and James Galway. At least one of the three – as the senior, Capt. Galway would be the obvious choice – would have had to travel on ahead to Calais to warn the Governor there of Bolingbroke's impending arrival, and arrange a suitable escort for him.

Henry St John, 1ˢᵗ Viscount Bolingbroke (1678-1751).[298]

---

[298] Photo credit: Lydiard House.

Having sent the Galways on ahead to make arrangements, Bolingbroke remained in town, acting as normally as possible. On the evening of Friday, March 25th, he attended the theatre in Drury Lane, and booked for a performance the following night. However, on returning to Spring Garden he changed his appearance by donning "*a black bob-wig, a laced hat, and very ordinary clothes*", hoping to pass as valet to one of Louis XV's couriers, a M. La Vigne who – coincidentally or not – was returning to the French court. Bolingbroke and La Vigne then set off in a post-chaise for Dover. They may or may not have been accompanied by Capt. William Morgan – accounts differ.

Morgan's subsequent tale was that, having unspecified "*private business*" in Calais, he had sent Capt. Andrew Galway ahead to hire a vessel from Dover, and travelled from London 'post' to Dover himself – alone – on the Saturday night, booking in at the Dolphin Inn. The inn's proprietor was George Slater, who although only in his twenties was a member of Dover's Common Council. At about 6 a.m. on Sunday two men whom Morgan said he took to be French couriers entered the inn. One of them spoke to him, and "*discovered himself to be Lord Bolingbroke*", whom Morgan later admitted to knowing well, and from whom he "*had formerly received several favours*", so that he "*immediately recognized him*". Bolingbroke asked for passage for himself and La Vigne on the vessel hired for Morgan by Galway, and Morgan agreed. All three went on board the vessel and sailed for Calais, arriving at about 6 p.m. the same day. "*Soon after they had landed, the governor of the city waited on Lord Bolingbroke, and carried him to his house….*"

Bolingbroke was still at the Governor's house when Morgan saw him the next morning. Morgan returned to England the next day, Tuesday 29th March – as indeed he had to, for staying in France would have been a tacit admission of his conspiring with Bolingbroke. On his arrival in Dover, Morgan was arrested by a King's Messenger, taken to London, and brought before the Privy Council for examination on suspicion of involvement in Bolingbroke's flight from what his political opponents considered to be justice. Morgan had his story, as recounted above, ready.

Within days of Morgan's examination, other eye-witness accounts of how Bolingbroke came to take 'French leave' were circulating in London. One of them, in a published letter to an unidentified member of the government, gave a graphic version of events markedly different from, and frankly more plausible than, Morgan's:

'Last Saturday there came to George Slater's the two Galways, who are cousins of Captain Galway, and presently went to the pier, and hired a vessel to go to Calais; pretending[299] *it was to examine the records of condemnation of their ship, which was arrested when you was in town. And about twelve at night there came two gentlemen to them post from London, one of them a lord, and the other their uncle,*[300] *Captain Morgan, expecting to go immediately on board, the tide just then serving; but the weather proving tempestuous, they were forced to stay, though very uneasily, till the next tide. My lord was kept locked*

---

[299] For once, the word may be being used here in its more modern sense, rather than as a synonym for 'claiming'.

[300] Morgan's mother was a Galway, which suggests that Patrick and James Galway were his first cousins, not his nephews, and that Capt. Andrew Galway was first cousin to all of them.

up all the time, and nobody suffered to come near him, except La Vigne, the French courier, who went over with him.

Sunday, after dinner (though I don't hear they ate any), the tide serving, the officers of the port waited on them for fees, &c., amongst whom Mr. William Lambe, being in a double capacity (as proctor for Galway in the cause he was pretending to go about, and also Clerk of the Passage), went abruptly into their chamber, which put them all into the utmost confusion, especially my lord, who changed his colour, and looked as if he thought the devil was come for him: but Mr Galway immediately took Mr Lambe by the hand, and, leading him out of the room, asked his pardon, told him they were busy, and desired him and other officers to go to Mr. Diskald's, at the pier, and they would all come to them and pay the fees, take passes, and also consult farther about the law affair. But no sooner were the officers gone, than they went off in the bay on board the vessel, which was in the Road.[301] And now my lord, whom nobody in the house had seen before, was forced to appear. He had got on a very black wig, and a riding-coat, which he buttoned over his wig, and covered the lower part of his face. He carried on his shoulders a pair of leathern bags, and affected a clownish, country air in his walking; though nobody suspected him till he was gone off, and then some of the seamen fancied they knew him. He arrived at Calais about eight o'clock Sunday night, and there the governor's coach attended him on his arrival; and then the man with the riding-coat and black periwig was known to be the right honourable the Lord Bolingbroke.

Yesterday Captain Morgan and the two Galways returned; and finding it was known they had conveyed over my lord, they grew very insolent, and came to poor George Slater, and bullied him, and told him, had he not been a common-councilman, they

---

[301] 'Road' in the naval sense.

would have whipped him round the market for an informing rogue."[302]

William Morgan should have been greatly embarrassed by the publication of this letter, but he was soon to come under public scrutiny for another reason. In May 1713 Morgan and one Nicholas Philpott had jointly been appointed as Receivers and Paymasters for the Reformed Officers. These were Officers in the former Marine Regiments who were being reassigned to other Regiments and put on half-pay. Philpott and Morgan were each required to enter into a bond for £1,000 as a guarantee of the proper performance of their duties,[303] as very large sums were to be entrusted to them. Up to Christmas 1713 they received between them a total of £24,937 9*s* 11*d*.[304]

Something must have alerted the authorities to problems with the payments-out, as in January 1714 Philpott and Morgan were summoned to appear before the Lord Treasurer (the Earl of Oxford), who ordered that "*all the papers be transmitted to the Auditors of Imprests to consider and report what method is proper to pass the accounts of the money already imprested for half pay and what [fees are fit] to be allowed*".[305] Philpott, for all I know, discharged his duties conscientiously. William

---

[302] '*Memoirs of Lord Bolingbroke*' by George Wingrove Cooke (1835), pp. 306-8.
[303] 'Volume 161: May 1-26, 1713', item 32, in *Calendar of Treasury Papers, Vol. 4, 1708-1714*, pp. 480-487.
[304] 'Declared Accounts: Army', in *Calendar of Treasury Books, Vol. 27, 1713*, pp. cix-clxii.
[305] 'Minute Book: January 1714', in *Calendar of Treasury Books, Vol. 28, 1714*, pp. 1-10.

Morgan almost certainly did not.

Whether as a consequence of the report he received from the Auditors of Imprest, or as part of a general intention to 'clean house' following the death of Queen Anne and the change of administration, on 23rd July 1715 the Secretary to the Treasury – our old friend William Lowndes – wrote separately to Lord Carnarvon (as former Paymaster to the Forces Abroad), John How (as former Paymaster of Guards and Garrisons), Thomas Moor (as Deputy Paymaster in Flanders) and William Morgan and Nicholas Philpott (as Paymasters of the Reformed Officers), requiring each of them to "*send to the Treasury Lords speedily a state of all the money received by you for half pay and the poundage deducted [from payments] for that use and of all the payments made by you or your agents out of the same: and how much (if any) doth still remain in your hands or the hands of your agent*".[306]

It can hardly be coincidence that within two weeks of receiving this order William Morgan left for the Continent, where he remained for the rest of his life, leaving Francis and Samuel Lynn and others to face the music.

---

[306] 'Warrant Books: July 1715, 21-31', in *Calendar of Treasury Books, Vol. 29, 1714-1715*, pp. 647-660, *Out Letters (General) XXI*, p. 396.

CHAPTER 9

Mr Hunter's retirement

William Morgan wrote to his *"Dear Frank"* on 5th August 1715, shortly after his arrival in Paris: *"Y^{ow} were not in Towne when I came thence or else I had not missed the Satisfaction of Embraceing y^{ow}; … I hope in God I shall not leave this World till I see y^{or} Meritts rewarded … As the friends[hi]p twixt y^{ow} and I have been these 20 Years past without designe or Intrest, soe I hope wee shall never suffer of neither side by it"*.

"The perplexity of Your affairs", Lynn wrote to Morgan on 23rd April 1716, *"are more than I can at present describe to you, but as I have sett my hand to the plough, and am so farr engaged, I will not look back as long as I am able, since I am sure you will not let me be a sufferer. … I have payd Mr Card[onne]ll the 1500£,*[307] *You know the balance of Acct settled between Us at Xmas was between 4 & 500£, more. I paid Coz. Samick on Your Acct to make up his 1500£, all which put together is too great a summ for me to*

---

[307] This was not strictly true. The payments (of £500, £600 and £400) were made between 19/11/1715 and 2/7/1716 – Lynn's Letter-book, pp.2-3, in *Lynn v Galway* exhibits, TNA C 111/207, so states.

be in advance, without the Securitys which you will herewith receive by Mr Pigou's approbation, not only for mine, & my familys but all our sakes, considering that We are all mortall."

Morgan replied on 12th May 1716: "*I can onely wish it may fall in my reach. to shew y[ow] that I have gratitude suficient to answer the troubles I give my friends. … As to my coming home soone I realy can not fix a time, but it cannot be very long … I am full of truth, and sencerely yo[rs]."*

He was full of something, but not of truth, and I do not think that Morgan ever left the Continent again. All his business in England was done through powers of attorney granted to his wife and others. How Morgan earned a living in France (and subsequently Spain) is unclear, but there are references in his letters suggesting that he was involved in wheeling and dealing of some sort, probably involving smuggling, and not on a small scale. Large profits were needed to fund his other activities, which I will describe in a later chapter.

<hr>

Living at Hall Place with Samuel Hunter (and, at least until June 1716, with Francis Lynn and his family) was a maidservant or housekeeper, Eleanor Farmer. There were no doubt other servants as well, one of whom was John Woodruff, with whom Eleanor Farmer was, or was soon to be, 'walking out'. Hunter resolved to make special provision for Eleanor, and by 28th March 1715 he had prepared, and on that day signed, a 'deed of covenant' in her favour, which was later referred to in his Will and (being 'incorporated by reference') came to be admitted to probate with it. In consideration of her "*long and faithfull service*", Eleanor was at Hunter's death to have a life interest (at a nominal 5*s* a year rent) in "*the little house with the Garden adjoining to my Barn*" currently occupied by Mrs Sarah Dekins "*which is an appurtenance of the Lease I hold of Dulwich Colledge*". Hunter's successor as lessee of Hall Place, whoever that might be, was instructed to grant Eleanor Farmer a renewable 21-year lease of the same[308] after Hunter's death, and to repair the little house by "*flooring the lower Room, railing the Garden and doing what ever else may make her dwelling convenient and comfortable to her*". Eleanor was to have various items of clothes, linen, dishes, plates, cutlery, pots, pans and furniture, including "*the Feather bed, bolster and pillows belonging to the bed in the Garrett where she lyes … one Bible (the largest) and six other Books of Devotion such as she will choose*", i.e. almost all of Hunter's personal chattels, specifically excepting his watch and rings.

The document was duly witnessed and officially stamped. Either Hunter did not regard it as binding – which would be surprising – or he reached a different arrangement with Eleanor Farmer, for when he came to make his last Will several years later he purported to revoke the gift of a life interest in the "*little house next my Stable Yard*" (as he now described it), and replace it with an annuity of £8 a year. From her later actions, Eleanor clearly accepted the change, although had she chosen to (and could have afforded the legal fees required) she might have resisted it successfully. Hunter did at least confirm the gifts to her of his personal chattels (other than those specifically

---

[308] Since the head-lease was not automatically renewable, such a sub-lease would have been invalid.

bequeathed to others), including his "*wearing apparell*".

Hunter's later Will refers to him having "*lately rebuilt two of the said Tenements* [included in the lease of Hall Place] *as I did before the cheif Mansion house*". One can safely assume that the new mansion was built of brick, as probably also were the two tenements. The College records show that new 21-year leases of Hall Place were granted to Hunter early in 1703 (with the annual rent increasing from £20 to £22, contrary to the '*recommendam*' issued only two years before) and again in 1719, following a College Audit order[309] on 4th March 1718[9], at the same rent, but those original leases (and their counterparts) have not survived.

Francis Lynn, now a Dulwich resident, reported in his letter to William Morgan of 16th June 1716: "*My Lady from Barbadoes is come home, and has made one in Our Neighbourhood, having taken a house near where I am at present, so that I have not so much of the Old Gentleman's*[310] *Company as I had*".

By "*My Lady from Barbadoes*" Francis Lynn is referring to Lady (or 'Dame') Rosamund Booth, the widow of Sir William Booth, a Barbadian merchant and plantation owner, who following her husband's death had sold his plantations to her son-in-law Col. Abel Alleyne, and returned to England with her orphaned grandson, William Andrews, taking up residence, on a sub-tenancy, somewhere in Dulwich village. They were to be embroiled in a series of court cases[311] between 1717 and 1720 involving the estates

---

[309] DCA, BC:30.

[310] i.e. Samuel Hunter again.

[311] TNA, ref: C 11/1171/2, *Andrews v. Hunter & others*, 1717; TNA, ref: C 11/1415/33, *Alleyne v. Andrews & others*, 1719; C 11

in Barbados (and to a much lesser extent in England) of William's father, Wardell Andrews, and grandfather George Andrews. Samuel Hunter was unavoidably drawn into the litigation, by virtue of being one (and the sole survivor) of the trustees of Wardell Andrews' 1703 marriage settlement with Mary Booth, a daughter of Sir William and Lady Booth (and a sister of Elizabeth Alleyne). How Wardell Andrews and Samuel Hunter came to be acquainted, and why Andrews had cause to appoint Hunter as a trustee, is a mystery. The trustees were to hold Andrews' Russia (or Rushia) Plantation in Barbados, its buildings and slaves, for Wardell Andrews for life, thereafter for the maintenance of any issue of the intended marriage. In the event there was only one such child, William, born c.1705. Mary Andrews died, and Wardell remarried. When he died shortly after making his last Will in April 1714, his Hill Plantation and its negro slaves, cattle, horses and stock, his dwellinghouse, and most of his personal chattels, passed to his widow for life. William was to get his father's estate in England at 21 or earlier marriage, and until then was to receive generous maintenance. (In the event he died before attaining his majority.) For the English estate the executors and trustees were to include Samuel Hunter, with Col. Abel Alleyne as guardian in respect of the Barbadian property and 'Dame' Rosamund Booth as guardian in respect of the property in England and of young William personally.

The first bout of litigation in 1717 involved an

1418/14, *Hales v. Andrews & others*, 1719; and TNA, ref: C 11/977/2, *Hales v. Hunter & others*, 1720.

allegation by 'Dame' Rosamund Booth of Dulwich,[312] on behalf of her young grandson, that property held in trust by Samuel Hunter and his co-trustees had been misappropriated to their own use. Appearances notwithstanding, I suspect that relations between Lady Booth and Samuel Hunter were in fact perfectly cordial, so much so that in June 1716 Francis Lynn was able to say that *"Many pretend to say 'twill be a Match, but that to me is a meer jest"*. Hunter had to be sued simply to allow Lady Booth to get at his fellow trustees on her grandson's behalf. Evidence for this is that in her last Will[313] made in June 1718, Lady Booth left Samuel Hunter a legacy of £20, which was twice as much as she left her grandson William Andrews. Incidentally, two of the witnesses to her 1718 Will were James Hume, the Schoolmaster Fellow of Dulwich College, and Francis Lynn.

Next to sue was Col. Abel Alleyne, living in 1719 in Westerham, Kent, when he issued proceedings against various persons associated with the Andrews estates, including Samuel Hunter. Again, this may have been mere artifice as far as Hunter was concerned, as he later referred to Alleyne in his Will in friendly terms.

Wardell Andrews' sister, Sarah, had married first John Hallett of Barbados, and following his death her second husband was a Robert Hales who, conveniently for Sarah, was a Clerk to the Privy Council with special responsibility for matters relating

---

[312] Lady Booth, like Francis Lynn, must have been renting a house in Dulwich village from one of the College's lessees, but where exactly, and from whom, is not known.
[313] TNA, PROB 11/565/218.

to the West Indies. In June 1720 they too issued proceedings, on the basis that Sarah had received only three of the annuity payments of £50 p.a. due to her under her father George Andrews' Will, and nothing at all in the last thirteen years. They wanted Wardell Andrews' executors/trustees, including Samuel Hunter and Abel Alleyne, to account for the funds which had passed through their several hands. In Hunter's case, they got nowhere.

In the 1717 and 1719 cases the court ordered that Hunter's co-trustees should account for their dealings with Wardell Andrews' personal estate, but Samuel Hunter was, for some reason, relieved of any such responsibility. When the 1720 case came to court, he was able to point to the two previous decisions, and since he claimed not to have intermeddled in the trusts arising from the Wills of either George Andrews or Wardell Andrews (although, having accepted the original appointments, it is difficult to see how he could have avoided doing so), he asked to be discharged from the office of trustee, and to be indemnified for his costs. It appears that his wishes in these respects were, inexplicably, granted.

Although Hunter was not involved in them, there were at least two other court cases involving Sarah Hales and the Barbadian estates. Her nephew William Andrews died too young to make a Will, and Sarah – as young William's next-of-kin on his intestacy – took possession of the Russia Plantation. In 1727 she successfully defended her title to it against a cousin.[314]

---

[314] *'Engendering Whiteness: White Women and Colonialism in Barbados and North Carolina, 1627-1865'* by Cecily Jones (M.U.P. 2007), pp. 104-5.

We know little more of how Samuel Hunter spent his declining years, apart from occasional clues found in Francis Lynn's correspondence. Hunter was a martyr to gout, and it was probably in search of a cure for the same that early in 1716 he travelled to Bath, to take the waters.[315] However, the cure was evidently unsuccessful, and Lynn refers several times in correspondence to Hunter being laid up with his affliction. Lynn kept Hunter company on many evenings, if not at home then at one of the locality's many drinking and dining establishments. The nearest was *The Gypsy House*, southwards along Hall Lane, but in Dulwich village were, amongst others, *The King's Head* (soon to be renamed *The Greyhound*), *The Bricklayer's Arms* (soon to be *The French Horn*), and *The Bell Inn*. Lynn is known to have visited *The Bell* with friends (although not, on this occasion, with Samuel Hunter) at least once, on 3rd March 1719[20], and since the meeting was on William Morgan's business, for which he looked to Morgan for reimbursement, he kept the receipt. Bread, tongue & sprouts, breast of veal, butter & cheese, oranges, ale and tobacco cost him 9*s* 8*d*, and wine another 13*s* 10*d*, probably for four people.[316]

Lynn introduced Hunter to other members of his circle – his brother Sam, his friends Capt. William Morgan and Capt. Joseph Knight, and his business acquaintance (and Morgan's friend) Lt.-Col. Robert Echlin, amongst others. Hunter had his own friends who may have visited him at Hall Place, including his

---

[315] *"the Commoner is not yet returned from Bath"* – letter from Lynn to Morgan, 23rd April 1716.
[316] TNA, C 111/207, Packet 2.

former colleagues William Lowndes and Kendrick Edisbury, Lady Booth, Col. Abel Alleyne, Richard Lydell, and Thomas Normandy,[317] a 'Colourman' (i.e. paint manufacturer and seller) who lived in one of the two houses on the site of what is now Allison Grove.

Lynn's correspondence with William Morgan – that with his brother Samuel has not, so far as I know, survived – is a rich source of domestic detail. Thus, in June 1716: *"our Friend y[e] Commoner is still the Same, and greets you with great tenderness & affection … Puddy's Mother[318] has taken a house in Southwark Burrough, with intent to be near that Markett to cater for Us, & send it to ye Country by ye Coaches and Carts, that pass, which will be a Service to Us, especially in Winter time. The Girls & Philly (who I believe will never make a soldier) are all well. … And not a day passes but We remember you in Our Cups."* In November 1716 Lynn reported that *"Sam Slater[319] has taken a house at a place called Littleton near Hampton Court & is turned absolute Country Gentleman, as Your humble Servant is Country Farmer"*.

William Morgan's letters, at least until Francis Lynn's death, abound with fulsome flattery of Lynn and his friends. Of Samuel Hunter, Morgan wrote in December 1716: *"As to our friend the Commoner his Merit is beter knowen to Others then himselfe. I could wish to live noe longer then to purchas his Carractor[320] and I hope to live to tell him how much I love and Esteem him"*.

---

[317] Apart from Lady Booth, who had died before Hunter made his last Will, these were all invited to attend Hunter's funeral. Lowndes, however, also predeceased him.

[318] Mrs Elizabeth Moreland.

[319] Francis Lynn's predecessor as Secretary to the Commission for Sick and Wounded Seamen from 23/11/1705 to 4/2/1705[6].

[320] Morgan's attempt at 'character'.

On 15th March 1716[17] Lynn's sister Elizabeth, who on 21st April 1704 had married "*a vile Wretch George Deacon, who afterwards dyed in Newgate [Prison]*", herself died, and was buried next to their parents. Lynn's 'diary' records that on 19th August 1719 "*Father Moreland dyed at Stroud*[321] *in Kent, & was buryd in his Vault there*". This was Lynn's wife's stepfather, evidently long-separated from his wife Elizabeth, the widow of Lt. Robert Thompson. (We are still not told Mr Moreland's first name, but it was Christopher.)

Lynn's 'diary' records other personal misfortunes, such as that on 10th April 1717, when "*Going by Water from Southwark to Whitehall I gott the first Ague I ever had in my Life, w*ᶜʰ *held me till the 21*ˢᵗ *when I gott rid of it by the Discipline ordered me by D*ʳ. *Friend.*" Again, for 12th May 1718: "*This Morning Our House was broken open, & We were robb'd of plate, Linnen, & other Goods to above 70*£. *Value, but never recovered any thing*". (William Morgan, in France, got to hear of this *via* Lynn's friend and lawyer Walter Pryse, and wrote a few weeks later to commiserate: "*God of his great goodness comfort yow and my Dear Puddy, I fear shee lost some things of value tho' Prise tells me the loss was not above 50*£".) On 25th April 1720, "*Coming from Dulwich to town with Capt Canning, I fell in going over a Stile, & bruisd my right Leg, w*ᶜʰ *layd me almost a Month, & I fear will be a Sore Leg during Life*". One suspects that without realising it at the time or even, apparently, later, Lynn must have fractured his leg falling off his horse.

One of Francis Lynn's many roles had been as Agent for the garrison at Annapolis Royal, until Christmas 1713 when he "*resigned*" (or was sacked by

---

[321] actually Strood.

the Secretary at War, Francis Gwyn) and was succeeded by George Gordon. The Governor of the garrison and town of Annapolis Royal until Lynn's removal from post had been Gen. Francis Nicholson, who was also Governor of Nova Scotia until succeeded by Samuel Vetch in 1715. Their Lt.-Governor from 1712 was Thomas Caulfield, who in June 1716 wrote to a friend that "*There never was a Garrison in the British Establishment so hardly used as this has been in all Respects*". Also at Annapolis, until forced to return to England early in 1716 to seek recompense for his expenses in subsidising his troops from his own pocket, was Capt. Lawrence Armstrong, almost the only person to emerge from 'the Annapolis affair' with any credit.

Gen. Nicholson was certainly autocratic, probably paranoid, and possibly insane. Despite the dire conditions in the garrison and the very low morale of the soldiers and their officers, when Nicholson visited in August 1714 he forbad contact with the local Acadian French trappers and the Indian tribes living outside the fort, and the garrison was therefore forced to survive on little more than molasses (which could however be made into rum) and pork. For the sorry state of the garrison Nicholson blamed his former comrade-in-arms Vetch (whom he suspected, on little or no evidence, of embezzlement), Vetch – once he realised that Nicholson was defaming him to his superiors – blamed Nicholson, Caulfield (who died in 1717, aged only 31) blamed Nicholson and Vetch, and no-one had a good word to say of Francis Lynn.

Armstrong presented his case to the Lords of Trade, who asked one John Mulcaster to investigate the available accounts. Meanwhile, Caulfield had written on behalf of the garrison's officers, "*concerning the hardships they have undergone for want of their pay and clothing*". By then, for different reasons, Nicholson and Vetch were also in England – Vetch never left it again, and died in a debtor's prison – and it became clear to the Lords of the Treasury that a major scandal was being uncovered. Lynn and others were summoned by William Lowndes, Treasury Secretary, in Lynn's case to account for all moneys received and paid for the Annapolis garrison "*and by what authority you acted as Agent and under what security for faithful performance*".[322] A hearing, presided over by the Chancellor of the Exchequer, with Nicholson, Vetch, Armstrong, Lynn and Mulcaster present (but not Gordon, although he was summoned), was held on 2nd October 1716,[323] and adjourned pending reports from the Secretary at War, the Paymaster of the Forces and the Comptrollers of Army Accounts, on what had actually been paid to the garrison out of the sums granted by Parliament.

I do not know what precisely was decided as a result of these proceedings, but on 18th November 1716 Francis Lynn mentioned in a letter to William Morgan "*the necessity … that I lay under at present (being called upon to pay in the ballance of my Annapolis Accounts)*" and on 20th December he was ordered to pay £300 to Capt. Lawrence Armstrong, out of sums remaining in his hands as late Agent for the garrison of Annapolis

---

[322] Calendar of Treasury Books, vol. 30, 1716, Treasury Warrants: September 1716, 21-30, pp. 484-497, Out Letters p.121.
[323] *Ibid.*

Royal, on account of Armstrong's pay and that of his Company.[324]

However, Lynn's trials were not quite over. In June 1718 further hearings took place against his successor as Agent at Annapolis Royal, George Gordon. Gordon, Lynn, Mulcaster and Armstrong were summoned to attend another meeting presided over by the Chancellor of the Exchequer, at 11 o'clock on 19th June, and again on 25th June.[325] The upshot was that Lynn's accounts, and those of John Mulcaster (who had now been appointed to succeed Gordon, and was to prove in the 1730s to be a bigger crook than any of the others) were referred to a Col. Gardner (probably 'Robin' Gardner, who fortunately for Lynn was a friend of his) to be audited. Lynn's 'diary' records that on 12th July 1719 "*I settled my Account of Annapolis Agency with Mr Mulcaster, & payd him the balance pursuant to K: George's Warrant in that behalf*".

Lynn was now apparently, like his brother Samuel, out of favour, if not in disgrace. The only employment his former masters were prepared to offer him in 1720 was a court appointment as a 'Messenger in Ordinary' to the Secretaries of State, at £45 a year.[326] (George Gordon was given a similar sinecure.) Francis Lynn did, however, soon find employment in the private sector. As he recorded in his 'diary':

---

[324] *Ibid.*, Dec. 1716, 16-31, pp. 590-616, *Money Book XXV*, p. 128.
[325] Calendar of Treasury Books, vol. 32, 1718, Treasury Minutes: June 1718, 10-27, pp. 61-72, *Appointments Book T* 64/4, pp. 103, 105, and *Out Letters (General) XXII*, p. 307.
[326] '*The Present State of the British Court*' (1720).

May 1720.

This Month, a new Ingraftment[327] being made upon the Old Charter of the Royal Affrican Compa: of England, and a Subscription[328] made for two Millions, to pay the Old Debts, & carry on the said Trade the following persons were chosen of the Court of Assistants, Vizt.

Sr. Wm. Withers Kt Sub Governr.

Humphry Walcot Esqr. Dep:ty Governr.

Fra: Acton Esq	*John Knight Esqr.*
Ld. Bingly	*Richd Lockwood Esqr.*
Martin Bladen Esqr.	*John Lansdell Esqr.*
James Blake Esqr.	*John Mead Esqr.*
Duke Chandos	*Henry Neal Esqr.*
Tho: Cook Esqr.	*Sr. Greg: Page Bart.*
Sr. Math: Dickes Bart.	*John Phillips Esqr.*
Mr. Seth Grosvenor	*Capt. Tho: Panuwell*
Edwd Harrison Esqr.	*Wm. Tryon Esqr.*
John Hanbury Esqr.	*Mr. Jos: Taylor*
Tho: Haws Esqr.	*Edmd. Waller Esqr.*

---

[327] The '*Ingraftment*', the brainchild of Joseph Taylor (listed among the Court of Assistants), was essentially a rights issue designed to raise capital amongst existing (and new) shareholders. It was successful, and initially the Company's share price rose, only to sink back after six months in the wake of the collapse of the South Sea Company share price. It remained in the doldrums thereafter, and the Company became less profitable.

[328] One of the subscribers, according to Dr. David Hunter in '*Musicology Now*' (June 2016 edition), was George Frederic Handel.

Andr: Hopegood Esqr.   Mr Jacob Wachter.

Who at a Meeting at the Affrican House in Leadenhall Street on June 2ᵈ: 1720 did unanimously make choice of me as their Secretary at the Salary of £200 per annum, & all the perquisites belonging to the said Office, as also Apartments in the House for my family, And I was this day Sworn in accordingly.

The Royal African Company, established in 1660 as the Company of Royal Adventurers Trading Africa, had originally been concerned solely with exploiting the mineral deposits – gold in particular – on the west coast of Africa, but soon turned its attention to the more profitable slave trade, which became its chief activity. 50% of the Company's profits went to the Crown. Having fallen into debt, in 1672 it was revitalised and restructured, and granted a new charter as the Royal African Company, with "*the right to set up forts and factories, maintain troops and exercise martial law in West Africa, in pursuit of trade in gold, silver and slaves*",[329] and with James Duke of York (the future James II) as its Governor. Between 1672 and 1689 the Company transported between 90,000 and 100,000 slaves to north America and the West Indies, some of them branded 'DY' (for the Governor), others 'RAC' (for the Company). The Company supposedly abandoned the acquisition and transporting of slaves at about the time of its re-founding in May 1720, in favour of trading in ivory and gold. Gold supplied by it to the Royal Mint was used to produce the 'guinea' (now worth £1 1s, or

---

[329] Wikipedia.

£1.05), so named from the gold's country of origin. In fact the Company's slave trade continued, albeit on a reduced scale.

Lynn's offices and accommodation were at Africa (or 'Affrican') House, at what is now 44-46 Leadenhall Street. The Company continued to do sufficiently well for Lynn to be able to report, with an unusual (for him) degree of immodesty:

Sepf. 29. 1721 The Court [of Assistants of the Royal African Company] *in consideration of my great diligence & application to the business of the Compa. added £100 per ann[um] to my Salary.*

On 25th March 1725 Lynn was joined by his 16-year-old son Philip, as a clerk in his office at £30 a year. However, within twelve months the Company's fortunes had declined, and Lynn was obliged to report that his salary had reverted to £200 p.a. and that Philip's was reduced to £15 p.a. (Lynn had also found work for his nephew Thomas Lynn (b. 1701), and in November 1720 William Morgan wrote "*I hope honest Tom goes on well. I am glad his first setting out is under you*".)

As part of his duties, Francis Lynn had to make representations to the government and others.

"*In early December 1721 James Brydges, 1st Duke of Chandos, requested a meeting with Sir Hans Sloane.*[330] *Brydges ... wished to gain Sloane's scientific expertise and advice on an expedition of the Royal African Company headed by a 'good Botanist' named Mr Hay. Brydges sent Francis*

---

[330] The celebrated naturalist and collector, 1660-1753, after whom Sloane Square was named, and whose collection formed the basis of The British Museum..

Lynn, the company secretary, to Sloane's residence[331] *three days later*[332] *to answer his questions regarding the venture and to inform him of 'the Nature of Drugs, plants, and spices' they were expecting to gather on the expedition".*[333]

On 29th August 1723 Lynn wrote to the then Secretary of the Treasury, Mr Popple, praying "*to be heard against Act of Virginia laying dutys on liquors and slaves imported, whereby not only the trade of Great Brittain in generall, but that of the said Company in particular will be very much affected*".[334] He must have been reassured by Popple's somewhat tardy reply, as on 15th January following he wrote back to Popple, from African House: "*The Court of Assistants of the Royal African Company return you thanks for your letter of 11th inst., and as they entirely depend upon the judgment and justice of the Lords Commissioners in the affair of the Virginia Act, they do not think of giving their Lordships any trouble in that matter*".[335]

That was not the end of the Popple/Lynn correspondence, for on 3rd March 1725[16] Mr Popple wrote to Mr Lynn with a series of questions to which he was anxious to have replies by the following Monday, "*the Board intending to sit that evening to consider thereof, that a state of this matter may be ready to be laid before Parliament this session, in case the same shall be thought necessary*". Four of these related to particular forts and settlements belonging to the Company on Africa's west

---

[331] in Chelsea.
[332] on 10th December, 1721.
[333] *'Missed Opportunities in Early Modern Exploration?' by Matthew De Cloedt*
[334] Calendar of State Papers Colonial, America and West Indies, vol. 33, 1722-1723, August 1723, pp. 318-337, C.O. 5, 1319. No. 28.
[335] *Ibid.*, January 1724; *C.O.* 5, 1319, *ff.* 145, 146*v*.

coast, but the first that preceded them was more general: "*Whether it be for the service of the Publick, that the African Trade should be carried on by a Company, or laid entirely open?*". Lynn's response is not recorded, but the Company's virtual monopoly continued until it was wound up in 1752, so he must have produced some convincing arguments.[336]

Crest of the Royal African Company.[337].

---

[336] *Ibid.*, vol. 35, 1726-1727, March 1726, pp.29-43, C.O. 389, 28. pp. 282, 283.
[337] Image from Wikipedia.

CHAPTER 10

Samuel Lynn's lack of progress

William Morgan's embarrassment over the Bolingbroke affair was more than matched by Samuel Lynn's. As his brother Francis reported to Morgan in June 1716: "*Samicks … affair at Westminster goes still on in ye same Channel, to his Scandal & the Towns Mirth & raillery, being become too publick, but all won't mend it*".

In the meantime Samuel Lynn had received £648 11*s* 5*d* "*for extraordinaries of the Office of the Secretary at War*" for the nine months to Michaelmas (i.e. 29th September) 1714,[338] and £109 12*s* as Paymaster of Pensions for Officers' Widows, for an allowance for subsistence for eight men.[339] Ominously, there is an Auditor's Note: "*There has been issued and paid by this Accomptant within the time of this Accompt, to Samuel Lynn, Paymaster of the Pensions of Officers' Widows, 3,243£ out of deductions from the pay of the Forces, for which he has rendered*

---

[338] TNA, Calendar of Treasury Books, vol. 28, 1714, Declared Accounts, Army, Guards & Garrisons, Pipe Office Roll 101 [E351/101], Audit Office Bundle 59, Roll 64 [A.O.1/59/64].
[339] *Ibid.*

no accompt." [340] Lynn did render an Account, his first, for the period from Christmas 1713 to 24th October 1714,[341] in September 1715. In addition to the £3,246 received from the Paymaster of the Forces Abroad, Lynn received reimbursement of an auditing fee of £68 15*s*, a total of £3,314 15*s*. Out of this he paid pensions to the widows of Lieutenant-Colonels (at £40 p.a.), Majors (at £30 p.a.), Captains (at £26 p.a.), Lieutenants (at £20 p.a.), Ensigns (at £16 p.a.) and Surgeons (also at £16 p.a.) in 45 named regiments, including those of the Earl of Barrymore, Lt.-Gen. Holt, Lord Slane, and Brig. Corbett – four names which appear elsewhere in this book – making his Accounts "*even and Quit*".

Samuel Lynn soon had more than London's "*mirth & raillery*" to cope with. As his brother Francis reported in his 'diary', on 2nd December 1716 "*at 3 a clock in the Morning a Fire happened in the French Chappel in Spring Garden, to w[ch] My Brothers House joyning, was in an hours time burnt to the ground, so that they sav'd very little more than their Lives.*" Not only Samuel's family home – or one of them – but also his office. In Samuel's own words, he "*lost to the value of 4000£, besides Papers both publick and private*". Spring Garden (now Spring Gardens) lay north-east of a part of St James's Park then known as 'the Wilderness', west of Whitehall. It had been developed by Charles, 2nd Earl of Berkeley (1649-1710), who held a 99-year lease from the Crown, and who in January 1701 granted a 96-year

---

[340] *Ibid,* Forces Abroad, Pipe Office Roll 402 [E351/402], Audit Office Bundle 324, Roll 1283 [A.O.1/324/1283].

[341] *Ibid,* Officers' Widows' Pensions, Pipe Office Roll, Audit Office Bundle 233, Rolls 808 & 809 [A.O.1/233/808 & 809].

under-lease to builder John Lacy and others.[342] Out of this a 34½-year sub-underlease was granted from June 1701, assigned to Samuel Lynn (then of Chiswick) on 19th February 1713 for £1,305.[343]

Among the crowd gathered to watch the conflagration[344] was the Prince of Wales, George Augustus (the future George II), who was acting as Regent during the first of his father's many return visits to Hanover. This occasioned a sycophantic 'epigram' by the versifier Nicholas Rowe:

"Thy guardian, blest Britannia, scorns to sleep,

When the sad subjects of his father weep;

Weak princes by their fears increase distress;

He faces danger, and so makes it less.

Tyrants on blazing towns may smile with joy;

He knows, to save, is greater than destroy."

(Others found Prince George Augustus less impressive, and during his father's later absences abroad he was replaced as Regent by a Regency Council.)

Lynn later claimed that some people had, with "*Rancour and Malice*", attributed his misfortune to the fact that the previous year he had "*harbour'd (as they call'd it) the late Lord Bolingbroke in his house … and his Lordship being at that time under no publick Accusation, He*

---

[342] London Metropolitan Archives, ACC/0530/ED/14/001.
[343] LMA, ACC/0530/ED/14/002.
[344] The fire destroyed not only Samuel Lynn's house and office, but the French Chapel Royal (established by Huguenot exiles) and the adjoining *Thatched House Tavern*.

appeals to all the World if such a Request was to be deny'd to such a Gentleman (once esteemed by his Country for his bright Parts and Capacity in Publick Business) by one who had the Honour so long to serve under him". Perhaps Samuel Lynn could simply not resist name-dropping his famous acquaintance,[345] but by continuing, in 1720, to remind his readers of his connection with Bolingbroke he was, and had been, doing himself no favours.

Marine regiments continued to return to England from overseas throughout 1714 and up to the end of August 1715, and were mustered, disbanded and paid off as they arrived, although the Commission for Disbanding the Marines had by then itself been disbanded. The last to arrive from "*Foreign Voyages*" was a detachment of General Holt's Regiment.[346] Despite still not having all the supporting paperwork he required, Samuel and his staff of "*extraordinary Clerks*" (for whose services he was having to pay out of his own pocket) had by the end of April 1716 managed to settle fair drafts of all the general muster rolls of the six Marine Regiments from 1710, engross them on 6,000 rolls of parchment, and deliver them to the Paymaster-General's Office. On 28th April he reported as much to the Treasury, the Admiralty, the Paymaster-General, and the Colonels of the six Marine Regiments, at the same time severally informing them that there was more work to do "*before the Publick Business can be entirely finish'd*".

---

[345] Samuel Lynn's Will gave to his son Richard "*my Writing Candlesticks Snuffers and Stand markt H.St.J.*". These must either have been a gift to Samuel from a grateful Lord Bolingbroke, or were left behind when Bolingbroke fled the country.

[346] TNA, Calendar of Treasury Books, vol. 29, 1714-1715, Warrant Books 22-31, King's Warrant Book XXVII, p.119.

By mid-June 1716 Samuel Lynn had taken his family to their Berkshire home at Tidmarsh, where they stayed until at least September.[347] (They had a third home in Little Sutton near Chiswick.) Francis Lynn reported to William Morgan on 16th June that "*poor Goody* [Samuel's wife Elizabeth] *sheds tears on [another] head, which is the Misfortune attending the little Samuel her Son*". Young Samuel, by now aged 15, was due to undergo an operation that week for "*some inward Impostume*" (i.e. abscess), and his uncle Frank feared for the outcome. In the event Samuel junior survived what must have been the horrific experience of major surgery without anaesthetic (other than the numbness induced by the consumption of a copious quantity of alcohol or of laudanum, which carried dangers of its own), but never fully recovered his health, and died at the age of only 37.

The Commissioners for Putting in Execution the Act for Appointing Commissioners to Take, Examine, and State the Debts due to the Army – the 'quango' was apparently not a 20th-century invention! – were losing patience with Samuel Lynn, and on 22nd August 1716 gave him an ultimatum "*to lay before us at this place[348] on Saturday next at 11 of the Clock in the Morning, all the Muster Rolls belonging to the late Marine Regiments from 25th of December 1708*". Lynn's response six days later was to send the completed muster rolls for one regiment, and to plead for leave to send the others regiment by regiment, "*because my own Duplicates are still in constant use in the Office, and I cannot spare them otherwise, without causing a hindrance to the Business that is*

---

[347] Letter from Francis Lynn to William Morgan, 3rd Sept. 1716.
[348] Dorset Court, Westminster.

still carrying on".

Samuel Lynn carried on the work until the beginning of December, when it was interrupted by the fire at his house in Spring Garden. In January 1717, he petitioned the Treasury to grant an extension to his underlease from the Crown, as an incentive for him to rebuild. This was referred to the Surveyor-General of Crown Lands, Hugh Cholmley, who reported that Lynn's property "... *was granted by Wm. III to George London*[349] *2 June 1701 at 6s. 9d. per an. rent. The house built on part thereof was burnt down by the late fire that happened in the Spring Garden. It has 33 foot front to the Park and is bounded towards the west by the Wilderness; the north east adjoins the wall of the stable yard in the possession of Mr. Davis and south east is limited by the wall dividing this piece from the said way into the Park. It is worth 40£. per an. at a rack rent. For an additional 15½ years to make petitioner's term 50 years I advise a fine*[350] *of 20£. at the old rent.*"[351]

Lynn's petition was accordingly granted.[352] His lease extension was granted by Letters Patent on 30th May 1717.[353] He had insured the premises and its contents with the recently-established Sun Fire Office, and *The London Gazette* and *The Post Boy* both carried an acknowledgement dated 9th January 1716[17] by Lynn and others (most of them the

---

[349] Cholmley is simplifying the title by omitting reference to the head lease and underlease.

[350] i.e. a premium.

[351] TNA, Calendar of Treasury Books, vol. 31, 1717, pp. 126-138, Treasury Warrants: February 1717, 1-10, Warrants not Relating to Money XXIV, p. 79.

[352] *Ibid*, Reference Book IX, p. 302.

[353] LMA, ACC/0530/ED/14/003.

victims of another recent fire, at Limehouse) that they had "*this Day receiv'd our full Claims for the Losses and Damages we have thereby sustain'd*". Some good free publicity for the insurers.

Many months passed, and on 19th November 1717 James Moody, Secretary to the Commissioners of Accounts, wrote to Samuel Lynn, requiring copies of all the Orders and Instructions relating to the Marine Corps he had received since 17th June 1713, which were to be laid before the Commissioners for Stating and Determining the Debts due to the Army. Two days later Lynn sent Moody an abstract of the documents, seeking further directions. Moody's response, if any, is not recorded, but at Christmas 1717 Samuel Lynn was "*struck off the Half-Pay*" on the basis, he claimed, of a mistaken report that he was a Warrant Officer, although he had to admit that, legally, only those who had been on active military service were entitled to half-pay.

His case was referred early in 1718 to King George I by the Board of General Officers, who pointed out that Lynn's Office had been kept open "*without any other Fund than the Half-Pay to support it*". By that time, Lynn, "*having dispatched what publick Business was before him*", was in the process of closing his Office, when he received a letter from Josiah Burchett (of the Admiralty) dated 27th February 1717[18]. Whilst warning that a salary for Lynn "*cannot be regularly paid out of the Naval-Money*", Burchett enclosed a copy of a letter he had written to William Lowndes (of the Treasury), asking "*that some suitable Allowance may be made to you for your Trouble*". In view of this he 'recommended' that Lynn should carry on with "*the adjustment of the said Accounts*", at least until the Treasury Lords had made a decision.

Lynn was copied in with Lowndes' unhelpful response, in the form of a note on the back of Burchett's letter to him:

"The Lords don't know which way to pay him, unless it may be had out of Naval-Money."

Apparently indifferent to Samuel Lynn's predicament, Lowndes wrote on 10th April 1718, "*ordering*" him to provide a Statement of "*the Accompts of the late Marine Regiments*", to be laid before the Treasury Lords. On 26th May Burchett wrote to Robert Pringle at the War Office, explaining Lynn's circumstances and reciting the regulations established for Lynn's predecessor in 1697 to receive half-pay of 10*s* a day, his deputy another 10*s*, and two assistants 5*s* each. However, Burchett did not actually suggest any solution to the problem, assuming he was concerned to find one, and Pringle's response, if any, is not recorded.

The Commissioners continued to press Lynn, and on 13th November 1718 wrote requiring him to compare the lists (which they copied to him) of men who served in the Marines with the general rolls, and to "*report to us, whether the Men appeared on the Rolls preceding, and subsequent to the times of their being omitted, or either of them; and when they do not appear on both, what evidence there is of their having been effective all the time demanded for, or any part thereof. You are to make the utmost dispatch in this Affair, and let us have your Report upon each Regiment as soon as you have gone through the Examination thereof; and at the same time return us the inclosed Lists, &c. thereto belonging*".

Five days later Lynn, by now back in Spring Garden following the fire which destroyed his house and office there two years before, replied acknowledging his orders, which he said he had returned to town expressly to fulfil with "*all possible dispatch*", but "*as the Lists and Numbers of Men to be compared with so many years Muster Rolls, Ships Books, and other Vouchers as are necessary, are very large, they will require a good deal of time to examine with that care, that ought to be had on the part of the Government as well as the Officer*". He again complained of "*the Hardships I lie under, in being obliged to attend the Publick Service, and be at the Charge of keeping a Clerk constantly, and other Incidents of an Office besides, at my own Expence*". He therefore asked for a certificate to cover what was due to him "*for four Years Charge of my Office, ending 31st January last past*", to "*defray the current Charges which I am at in attending the same*". He wrote to James Moody again on 24th November, protesting that he had done all that was asked of him according to his Commission. Everything else for which he was now being asked to keep his Office open, without pay, was "*extra officio*". Nevertheless, he said he would "*be ready to do as far as can be expected of me*".

Samuel Lynn then devoted some time to drawing up an Account of the costs of his Office for the four years to 31st January 1717[18]. It came to £799 13*s* 11*d*, and the Admiralty issued a warrant directing payment of that sum. Lynn supposed that he would be paid in debentures, as Marine pay arrears had been, but in the event nothing happened for nearly two years. Eventually the Commissioners of Accompts expressed the view "*that it was not in their Power to certify that Debt*". This was their parting shot, as their commission expired in March 1720, despite the Accounts of two of the former Marine Regiments remaining unfinalised. Sir Roger Mostyn's Accounts to the end of November 1725[354] include near the end "*money paid to Samuel Lynn, late Muster Master General of the late Marine Regiments, to reimburse his charges from 1 Feb. 1713–14 to 1 Feb. 1717–18*", amounting to £799 13s 11d, so it seems that Mostyn left the payment as late as possible, as on 15th July 1725 Samuel Lynn had had to petition Sir Robert Walpole to compel Mostyn, as Paymaster of Marines, to pay him his money.[355]

Lynn did at least obtain a certificate, if not quite the one he sought, but gratifying to his vanity nonetheless. On 28th December 1719 James Moody sent him the following:

"*These are to Certify, That Samuel Lynn, Esq; late Muster Master General of the Marine Forces, has upon all Occasions, when required, attended the Honourable the Commissioners of the Army Accompts, with the Musters of the said Marine Regiments, and hath hitherto obey'd all the Precepts and Orders of the said Board, and answered every thing on the part of his Office required to be done and performed.*"

However, 'fine words butter no parsnips' as the saying went, and using whatever influence was at his

---

354 TNA Declared Accounts: Marines; Pipe Office: Roll 2573 [E351/2573]; Audit Office: Bundle 1826, Roll 523 [A.O.1/1826/523]; 'Declared Accounts: Navy', in *Calendar of Treasury Books, Volume 26, 1712*, ed. William A Shaw (London, 1954), pp. clxxxi-cciii.
355 TNA, 'Vol. 253: June 1-December 25, 1725', in *Calendar of Treasury Papers, Volume 6, 1720-1728*, ed. Joseph Redington (London, 1889), pp. 342-376.

disposal, Lynn succeeded in having a clause inserted in the Bill going through Parliament to renew the Commission of Accompts, to the effect that "*it shall and may be lawful for the Commissioners, or any [blank] or more of them to state and certify what shall appear to them to be due to Samuel Lynn Esq; late Commissary General of the Marine Regiments, for mustering the said Marines at the several times of their disbanding, as they came home from Sea in the years 1714 and 1715, and for making up afterwards the General Muster Rolls of the said Regiments, and doing the Duty of his Office as Commissary General aforesaid, pursuant to the Orders he received in that behalf, since that time*".

The clause failed (by five votes) to receive the approval of the Commons Committee charged with considering it. Samuel Lynn attributed this to the Committee not knowing the full facts, and to the fact that his supposed friends on the Committee had absented themselves that day. In particular, Lynn resented the contribution to the debate of "*a well known wealthy and worthy Member, who pleaded Riches as a Bar to Justice and Equity, when he was entirely ignorant, not only of the Person he spoke of, but of his Fortune, and his Case*".

One must wonder whether there might not have been something in the imputation of the unnamed "*wealthy and worthy Member*", that Samuel Lynn had profited from his various offices under the Crown more than he should, even in an age when 'perquisites' and bribes were common currency. It does seem that Lynn's attempts to be paid for his work were deliberately frustrated by the authorities, perhaps because the "*wealthy and worthy Member*" was not alone in his views, but perhaps also because

Samuel Lynn had still not been forgiven by the Whig administration, still in power, for his rumoured part in Lord Bolingbroke's flight to France in March 1715.

Samuel Lynn, perhaps rather rashly, had given Capt. William Morgan shelter at his house[356] in Little Sutton, Chiswick, in the Summer of 1715, after the Bolingbroke flight had become public knowledge. Morgan left England in something of a hurry himself in late July or early August 1715, leaving most of his possessions – including his chaise and two horses – behind. Francis Lynn reported to Morgan in June 1716:

"I don't find Chiswick House is yet dispos'd of, tho' Mah[ony] has been obligd to fetch away Your Goods. ... As for Your Chaise, I may have it Samick tells me, if worth fetching but says he had but 2 Horses of Yours; that of ye Chaise I find he does not design to part with, if he can help it, the other has been sold by him. I think he is better able to buy a Chaise Horse than I am, & if you think fitt to write to him to deliver it me, I shall have it, otherwise not; I have now room enough for 'em and they would be of great use to me."

Morgan had also left some small debts, probably Chiswick tradesmen's bills, amounting to £9 11s 7d, and these were paid on his behalf by Capt. Joseph Knight, who in mid-January 1716 was reimbursed by the lawyer Mr Florence Mahony.[357]

---

[356] He apparently called it 'Chiswick House', not to be confused with the more famous one built on a different site nearby in the 1720s.

[357] F. Mahony's stated account with W. Morgan, TNA ref. C 111/207, packet 1, item D6.

Francis Lynn's correspondence with William Morgan, still in France, also recorded mention of several of their mutual acquaintances, including the afore-mentioned Joseph Knight, who had been involved in 'the Rice affair' from its outset in 1705. Francis Lynn reported in mid-June 1716 that "*Capt Jo K is with Us upon the Common,*[358] *and has been so ever since Ash Wednesday*". Ash Wednesday that year fell on 15th February, so Knight's sojourn with the Lynns had lasted four months so far. However, it was not to last much longer, as Knight had willingly fallen under the malign influence of Col. John Rice. Lynn expressed his fears in this respect in a letter to William Morgan of 18th November: "*Capt. Jo (who has left me long since & herds now altogether with him) is become too much a property of the Old Colonels*". He continued the theme in a letter of 3rd September 1717 when, after reporting an argument he had had with Col. Rice concerning the O'Hara case and another debt, and about the Colonel sending Knight to Bristol to see his (Knight's) brother, he commented: "*I can never be perswaded that Jo was forcd away from me, & almost ever since kept in ye Cols Custody, for no purpose or end*".

A month later Morgan wrote:

"*…Jo^s. K. may be prevaild upon or in case of Death a New Will made without his consent, as it has often hapend.*[359] *… You have Inclosed a leter which pray deliver to Jo^s if you and Mr. Pigo thinks it proper. As for the Coll. I hear frequently from him, his Wayes were ever very dark, but I must tell you it can not be in his Intrest to have any assignement from Jo^s Nor*

---

[358] i.e. Dulwich Common.
[359] William Morgan may himself have forged, or arranged the forgery of, at least one Will, that of Brig. John Corbett.

doe I think he would Act soe vile a parte, Not but that I think y^ow are right in y^or caussion … I will not onely write to Jo^s but will write to the Coll on this head".

On 10th June 1719 Francis Lynn had some sad news to report to William Morgan about their mutual friend *"poore Jo"* Knight:

"On Thursday the 2d inst Yor Sister & I went to Chiswick to see Sam, & conferr upon Matters, as soon as We came We sent for Capt: Jo to come & dine with Us, designing to press him to write an answer to Your Letter you sent him … *He sent us word he had been out the day before, and was so fatigued he could not walk so far as from the Packhorse*[360] *where he lodged, & then was, to Sams, nor was he able to gett into the Chariot, which Sam offered to send; Upon this we resolved to go to him after dinner; accordingly She & I were gon half way, when Sam sent after us that that very moment he had received a message that Jo was dead. It seems, as soon as Sams Servant was gon from him, he sayd to the Man of the Packhorse,* "I know what they want, but by G-d they shan't have their Ends", *and immediately crawld out as farr as the upper Packhorse*[361] *right ag[ain]st the Lane leading down to Sams, & called for a dram as soon as he came in, being faint, and soon after another, then desired to lye down a little on their bed, about a quarter of an hour after which, the*

---

[360] Now called *The Packhorse and Talbot* (on the corner of Brackley Road, Chiswick). I am indebted for this and other information on early 18th-century Chiswick to Carolyn Hammond of the Brentford & Chiswick Local History Society.

[361] Carolyn Hammond suggests convincingly that 'Capt. Jo' *"crawled westwards along Chiswick High Road to the pub we now call The Old Packhorse. This was (and is) on the junction of the High Road and Sutton Lane, and Sutton Lane leads straight to Little Sutton where Mr Lynn lived."*

Woman going in to see if he wanted any thing, found him dead. Upon this We went to his Lodging, took an Inventory of his things & lock'd 'em up, & gave directions for his Funeral, which was perform'd on Fryday night[362] *in as decent frugal manner as we could.*

The next day after he dyed, I mett Coll. R---[363] *at Your Sisters house, and talking about Jo's Will, he told Us, the Will did not signify 2 pence, for that some time since Jo had made such Conveyance of Affairs, as rendered that Will of no use, but still that it was done in favour of those it ought; which was all We could gett of him, besides some dark ænigmaticall Expressions, which We could pick nothing out of. I wish what I always feared ever since he drew Jo away from me, & kept him within his own clutches, may not prove too true ... The Col. indeed was pleased to own, when I asked him if Mr Pigou*[364] *or Huford*[365] *were privy to this transaction, that the latter was, from which I hope the best; and Wat*[366] *will see if he can learn from Huford what y*[e] *nature of this Conveyance is & to whom. The Col. came to Chiswick to see Jo: buryed, but because it could not be done by 4 or 5 a clock went away again to London without seeing me, tho he could not but know I was in the Town*".

Alcoholic poisoning may have put Joseph Knight out of the picture, but Col. John Rice still had

---

[362] The Parish Register of St Nicholas Church, Chiswick, includes the burial on 5th June 1719 of Mr Joseph Knight, "*a stranger*". Boyd's London Burials records the surname as Night. [FindMyPast.co.uk.]

[363] i.e. Col. John Rice.

[364] Mr Pigou or Pigot, one of Lynn's lawyers.

[365] Mr Huford or Hurford, yet another of Lynn's lawyers, but in whom he was rapidly losing confidence, suspecting him of siding with his opponents.

[366] Lynn's lawyer Walter Pryse.

unfinished business with Francis Lynn and William Morgan. In 1719 Rice claimed that in about 1705 he loaned £100 to Morgan, with whom he was then "*well Acquainted and Intimate*", at about the time that Morgan, by purchasing £1,600-worth of Rice's Army Debentures, became involved in 'the Rice affair'. Morgan promised – so Rice later improbably claimed – that any profit he made on the Debentures deal would belong to Rice.

Rice subsequently borrowed substantial sums – at least £1,672 4s 11d – from Morgan, giving Morgan his Notes or Bonds to cover the loans. Rice claimed in 1719 that he had paid Morgan all that was due, and so expected his notes and bills to be returned, but Lynn's lawyer Mr Mahony had, he said, avoided doing so. Despite Rice paying him and Francis Lynn further sums, they had endorsed his bills in favour of "*one John Pugh*", a person Rice claimed was "*wholly unknown*" to him, who had sought to have Rice arrested for debt. This, said Rice, was a blatant attempt by Mahony and Lynn to extract more money from him. All his witnesses unfortunately being dead, overseas, or otherwise unavailable – a common excuse used in Chancery cases – Rice asked the court for equitable justice.

The case did not come to trial until late 1719, and on the evidence of Rice's vague and unconvincing Bill of complaint, and Francis Lynn's stone-walling 'Answer' to it – he carefully avoided admitting to knowing John Pugh, a lawyer who had drafted documents for him – it is highly likely that Morgan and Lynn won.[367]

Apart from his involvement in litigation, his work as a civil servant before 1719 and his job with the Royal African Company thereafter, from 1716 Francis Lynn had had conduct of another project, on behalf of his "*best Friend*" William Morgan and of Morgan's colleague Lt.-Gen. Robert Echlin. The scene now shifts to a pair of neighbouring villages in Suffolk – Bacton and Cotton.

---

[367] *Rice v Lynn* (1719), TNA C 11/1789/28 & C 11/1172/39.

CHAPTER 11

'Mr Genero' and the Suffolk Estates

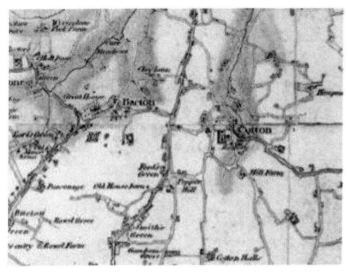

Ordnance Survey Map of Bacton and Cotton, Suffolk, c.1810.

In April 1716 Francis Lynn had, thanks to William Morgan, almost accidentally found himself in possession of substantial property in the villages of Bacton and Cotton, in Suffolk, north of Stowmarket.

It comprised a "*capital messuage*" and farm, partly in Bacton and partly in Cotton, for which widow Rebecca Rodwell paid £120 a year for herself or her under-tenants; another farm in Cotton for which Edmund Beare paid £100 a year; a house and land in Bacton, for which the occupant, widow Balderston, paid £4 5*s* a year, and a tenement and yard in Cotton whose occupant, Gregory Agar, paid £2 10*s* a year. The premises – 28 acres of which were copyhold, the rest (at least 250 acres, and perhaps as much as 400 acres)[368] freehold – therefore produced gross rents of £226 15*s* a year, although out of this the owner would have to pay annual 'quit rents' for the copyhold lands of 15*s* 10*d*, 12*s* 7*d*, 4*d* and 2½*d*, to the lords of the manors of Cotton Hempnalls with Skeith, Cotton Bresworth, Fininghall and Mendlesham respectively.[369]

We have, from a pair of documents dated December 1745, a list of the holdings that then made up the estate, or estates.[370] Although this was thirty years after Lynn's acquisition, they at least partially corroborate the above descriptions. Thus we know that the 'capital messuage' occupied by Mrs Rodwell had previously been the home of a local worthy, Thomas Barnardiston. There was also a cottage lately occupied by Nathaniel Jessup, a home close, Reeves Close, another cottage lately occupied by Henry Hayward, Cooke's Close, four pieces of pasture in the Malt Croft (a common field), the High Park, Black

---

[368] (TNA) Suffolk Record Office, Lowestoft branch, ref. HA12/B4/8/19 & 20.
[369] *Lynn v Galway* exhibit (TNA C 111/207, Packet 1, item D-01.
[370] (TNA) SRO, Lowestoft branch, ref. HA12/B4/8/17 & 18.

Acre, all the barns and buildings on the east side of Calcott Green, etc. etc. Thomas Barnardiston's father, another Thomas Barnardiston, had acquired all these holdings piecemeal, from five named individuals. What is not clear from the 1745 evidence is which named parcels fell within which of the holdings of Rebecca Rodwell, Edmund Beare, widow Balderston and Gregory Agar in 1716.

How Lynn come to acquire these properties is a complicated story, which centres around the retired commander of a Regiment of Dragoons and a former Member of Parliament: Lt.-Gen. Robert Echlin.

Robert Echlin (also spelled Echlyn, Ecklin, etc.) was the third son of an Irish politician and soldier who died shortly after his birth. Echlin served as a captain in Col. Cunningham's Regiment of Foot in 1689, and at the foundation of the 6th (Inniskilling)[371] Dragoons in 1689 became its Lieutenant-Colonel. In 1690 he distinguished himself commanding part of the Regiment at the Siege of Derry and the Battle of the Boyne. He successfully petitioned to be given the Regiment (*"remarking that he knew all the men and was related to all the officers"*)[372] after the killing of its founder (his uncle). By 1707, when the Regiment was sent to Scotland, Echlin was its Lt.-General. The basket-hilted cavalry sword he had made for him at about this time, inscribed '**LT GEN ECHLIN**', now owned (since 2013) by the Royal Dragoon Guards, is possibly the oldest British cavalry sword in existence.

With help from his elder brother, Echlin *"acquired*

---

[371] Now Enniskillen.
[372] Wikipedia.

estates in County Monaghan, but he soon fell into difficulty and suffered years of financial embarrassment. By his own account, the fault … lay entirely with the English Crown which regularly failed to pay his wages or offer him advancement: he claimed that for many years he paid his soldiers out of his own pocket, and was ultimately forced to sell his estates as a result'.[373]

Lt.-Gen. Robert Echlin (c.1657 – 1723).[374]

---

[373] Wikipedia.
[374] Image: Chorley's Auctioneers.

Previously a member of the Irish House of Commons, between 1710 and 1713 Echlin sat in the British House as M.P. for Sudbury in Suffolk. After Queen Anne's death in August 1714 Echlin, as a Tory, was relieved of his command and ownership of the Inniskilling Regiment (and of the Echlin Sword), with *"not a farthing paid"*. *"Embittered by chronic poverty, lack of professional advancement and a failing military career"*,[375] he espoused the Jacobite cause. Echlin is believed to have commanded a Regiment of horse in the taking of Inverness, and may have faced his former Regiment at the battle of Sheriffmuir, which marked the end of the first Jacobite Rebellion in November 1715. After *"running great hazards"*, Echlin reached the Orkneys, seized a vessel, and fled to France. He received a small pension from the Old Pretender, and probably served in Louis XV's army.

According to the Wikipedia entry about Echlin, in 1696 he married Anne Blundell, who survived him. This appears to be incorrect. If Echlin was ever married to Anne Blundell, either she died before August 1713 when he married a Mrs Mary Faussett, or Echlin was a bigamist. Mary was the widow of William Faussett of Dartford, by whom she had had a daughter, Catherine (later Mrs Samuel Buck).[376]

The marriage settlement dated 8th August 1713, to which Mary's father John Bryan (of Rochester) was a party, included a covenant by Echlin that within two years of the marriage he would spend at least £7,000 (of borrowed money, presumably) in buying heritable

---

[375] Wikipedia.

[376] Suffolk Record Office Lowestoft Branch, ref. HA12/B4/8/17 & 18.

land in England, to be held in trust for himself for life, thereafter by Bryan and a co-trustee, or their nominees as trustees, for Mary for life, and thereafter for any male children of the marriage, successively 'in tail'. Three days later the couple married.

On 19th August 1713 Robert Echlin purchased "*diverse Messuages Lands Tenements*" etc. in Bacton and Cotton, in Suffolk, from Thomas Barnardiston. According to Echlin's Will,[377] he bought the estates in Bacton (which he spelled 'Boughton') and Cotton simply "*in order to quallify my self to sit in Parliament*" – he must have failed to get elected on that occasion – but his wife asserted – not unreasonably – that the estates were purchased with the intention that they would be subject to the marriage settlement. The property was conveyed to Echlin at the beginning of September 1713. Barnardiston allowed £1,331 of the £4,331 purchase price to remain outstanding on mortgage (by the usual mechanism of a lease and release), repayable with interest by 1st March 1713[14].

Since it was not then repaid, in theory the premises should have reverted to Barnardiston, but according to the rules of equity (enforceable by the Court of Chancery) Echlin could still keep the property if the mortgage was subsequently paid off, unless the court ordered otherwise. This was, and is, called the 'equity of redemption'. On 22nd January 1714[15] Mary Echlin's father, John Bryan, supposedly as an act of kindness to Robert Echlin and at his request, paid the outstanding amount – £1,508 12*s* with interest – to Barnardiston, expecting Echlin to agree to execute an assignment of the mortgage which Bryan had had

---

[377] TNA PROB 11/607/424.

drawn up. However, Echlin declined to do so. (He was probably already in negotiations for a loan from William Morgan, and preferred owing money to Morgan than to his father-in-law.) Nonetheless Barnardiston, having been paid what was due to him, purported to convey the legal estate to Bryan only three weeks before the latter's death in mid-February 1714[15]. By his Will, Bryan left whatever interest he had in the Suffolk estates to his daughter Mary for life, with remainder upon discretionary trusts for her issue and for others. Francis Lynn later asserted that the terms of the conveyance were that the property was to be held in trust for Robert and Mary Echlin, although I do not know how he could have known that unless Echlin (or Morgan) told him so.

Echlin must have found the other £3,000 from somewhere to complete the purchase in 1713 (so he was not *entirely* destitute), but had evidently stretched his finances to the limit, and on 11th February 1714[15], by the usual deeds of lease and release on consecutive days, he mortgaged the Suffolk properties for £1,000 to William Morgan, who subsequently lent Echlin a further £2,000.[378] Three days later Echlin assigned whatever other interest he had in the properties to one John Corbett, Esq., of St Martin-in-the-Fields, in trust for William Morgan.[379] On 9th March 1715[16] Morgan, who by then owed Francis Lynn various sums totalling £2,350 9s 10d, assigned the mortgage to Lynn, subject to Echlin's

---

[378] TNA: C 11/275/23 refers.
[379] Suffolk Records Office, Lowestoft branch, TNA HA12/B4/7/29. This was Brig. John Corbett, of whom more later.

acknowledged 'equity of redemption'.

On 2nd April 1716 Francis Lynn, accompanied by his wife, one of their daughters, and his lawyer Mr Florence Mahony, set out for Rattlesden in Suffolk, by stages *via* Bishops Stortford, Littlebury, Cambridge, and Bury St. Edmunds, to meet up with the appointed agent for the Bacton and Cotton properties, a Mr Samuel Waller, and "*to take care of ye Estate there*". They were away for eleven days,[380] returning *via* Ipswich, Colchester, Chelmsford and Romford, and the trip cost Lynn £35 17*s* 7*d*, including tips for Waller's servants and servants at Bacton, and half-a-crown spent at *The Pope's Head* tavern with a Mr Gibbons. During the trip he collected rent from Widow Rodwell, and on 9th April she and the other tenants of the Bacton/Cotton properties "*did severally attorn*" to Lynn, i.e. they formally agreed that he was now their landlord (even though, strictly speaking, he wasn't), and he assumed possession of the premises, apart from the copyhold property. That would require Thomas Barnardiston, who was still the registered copyholder, to surrender it (or them) at the appropriate manor court (or courts) to Robert Echlin or as Echlin directed. We know that he did so in at least two cases, for in September and October 1732 Mrs Catherine Buck was admitted as daughter and heir of Marie Ecklyn (the daughter and heir of John Bryan) to copyhold "*lands and tenements of which Francis Lynn died seised and which were formerly held by Thomas Barnardiston*" in Cotton, totalling 22*a*.1*r*.17*p*., of which 19*a*.1*r*.10*p*. was held of the manor of Cotton Hempnalls with

Skeith,[381] and 3*a*.0*r*.7*p*. was held of the manor of Cotton Bresworth.[382] The 1732 copyhold deeds describe the properties in considerable detail.

Shortly after his return, Lynn reported to William Morgan on the visit:

"If I had not gone to Suffolk, that matter had before this taken such a turn, that Madam[383] had been in possession by the tricks she has playd, And my going there was of absolute necessity & with advice both of Mr Pigou & Mr Huford,[384] and what has had its desired Effect. … [P.S.] Pray [give] my most humble service to Mr Generald …"

This is the first mention of '*Mr Generald*', otherwise '*Mr Genero*', etc., and is a coded reference to Lt.-Gen. Robert Echlin who, following his military exploits in 1715, had like William Morgan now separated from his wife and was living in exile in Paris.

A thank-you letter[385] to Mr Waller soon followed, on 24th April, after Lynn's return to London:

"Sir, I received the favour of your Letter of the 18th inst. from Stowmarkett, … I am very much obliged to You for all Your favours, Particularly the kind reception I and my friends found at Your house, for which I don't know how to make amends, as also for your care in my affairs, in getting the Widdow [Rodwell] to Attorn Tenant &c It will be a good thing, if Mr Barnardiston be forced to refund the Summ you

[381] TNA Suffolk Record Office, Lowestoft branch, HA12/B4/8/15.
[382] *Ibid.*, HA12/B4/8/16.
[383] i.e. Mrs Mary Echlin.
[384] Pigou (or Piggot) and Huford were two of Lynn's lawyers.
[385] *Lynn v Galway*, C 111/207, Francis Lynn's letter-book.

mention; I have sent to the Generall and doubt not but that I shall have whatever Orders are necessary, both as to ye Surrender of ye Copyhold, and Your own Proceedings, and such Powers as will be uncontestable, concerning which, I have taken Mr Piggots advice. … My Spouse & daughter joyn with me, in Our hearty respects & Service to Mrs Smith, Mine pray make acceptable to Mr Gibbon, whom I am pleased We have made easy. I am, Sir, Yours &c. FL

P.S. *I intirely leave that affair of Edmd Bears to your discretion, to do as you shall see fitt, & shall be glad to see ye Copy of ye Appraisement at Your leisure.*"

Edmund Bear had been one of the Suffolk tenants, and Waller evicted him. He was soon to be replaced as tenant by Thomas Richer or Ritchie, and eventually, in 1726, Waller provided Lynn with extremely detailed accounts[386] of the income from sales of Bear's livestock and crops distrained "*for Rent due to General Echlin*", and of repairs to Bear's premises and other outgoings. For example, and to give you a flavour of the detail, Waller recorded the following income for May 1716:

By five heifers sold Mr Sparke	*11 0 0*
By three Cowes sold Mr Smith	*10 12 0*
By another Cow sold Mr Smith	*3 5 0*
By a Cow sold John Nun	*3 10 0*
By 3 Cows & a Bull wch were kept upon	

---

[386] TNA C 111/207, packet 1, items C-11 (which runs to 11 pp. up to January 1724) and B-10 (which has many of the same entries, and runs to 20 pp., up to June 1726).

ye farm appraised at	*11 0 0*
By money recd of Harrison for an old Cart	
& other goods	*2 12 0*
By money recd of Edmd Bear for the milk	
of two Cowes untill Mich's 1716	*3 0 0*
Recd by another Cow sold	*3 10 0*
Recd of Sherman for half a Years rent for	
Gipping Lay	*4 5 0*

During the same month Waller incurred the following expenses:

Paid for twelve heifers bought at Thetford	
Fair	*31 10 0*
Paid for Tole & driving to Cotton	*0 1 6*
For my own & man's Journey & expenses	*-- -- --*
Paid more for twenty Scotch steers as they	
were going to Halsworth fair	*41 10 0*
For driving them to Cotton paid	*0 1 0*
Paid Peter Barton for ploughing	*0 13 0*
Paid Mr Punchard for a farrow Cow	*2 10 0*

That same month, May 1716, Lynn wrote to Waller again:

"*Sir, The inclosed Orders I have received this day from the General .... I hoped before this to have seen You in town; at Your Arrival you shall see my Deeds; Mr Goat has been with me from Mr Barnardiston to make proposals, but I referrd him wholly to Mr Pryse and You, which I hope was right; I have not yet received the Copy of the Appraisment of Bear's Goods, but suppose You'l bring it to town with you*".

William Morgan wrote to his "*dear Friend*" Francis Lynn (addressed on the flap by the pseudonym "*Mr F. Leeney*") on 12th May 1716 from his lodgings with Abbé Farley in the College du Plessis, rue St. Jacques, Paris. He expressed surprise that two important deeds for him to sign had not been sent by messenger. "*I have as Near as I can gott the papers from Mr Gen[ll] that our friend Pryssian[387] orderd me, and by degrees I'le send them all to yo[u]*". He did so, and Lynn wrote accordingly to his Suffolk agent Samuel Waller on 6th June: "*I have the favour of your Letter of the 1st inst and am glad to hear you received General Ech---s Letter*". He expressed his confidence that Waller would have dealt appropriately with Barnardiston's surrender of his copyhold and "*the other matter between him and me*", and his approval of Waller's actions regarding "*Mr Bears Farm*".[388] He replied to Morgan's letter on 16th June, explaining "*the absolute necessity of those deeds being executed, together with the Dispatch requisite therein (expecting a Bill to be preferrd against me in Chancery to Shew my Title) occasiond the sending them in the Manner We did, which was with the advice of Mr Templer,[389] and 'tis happy they arrived safe, … for I expect trouble from that Quarter. … I am glad Mr Generalds Letter came to hand, I sent it immediately to Suffolk, it having been reported there that he was dead*".

---

[387] Code for Walter Pryse, Lynn's lawyer.
[388] TNA: C 111/207, Letter-book of Francis Lynn.
[389] Not his actual name, but code for one of the senior lawyers used by Lynn and known to Morgan.

On the grounds that it would be *"very inconvenient"* for him, Lynn resisted a request by Mr Waller that he should visit Suffolk in August 1716[390], but he did pay a return visit in May the following year. Again we have an unusual amount of detail regarding the journey, thanks to the receipts which Lynn kept. This time he took a slightly different route and, since he was travelling without any of his family, only a chaise (with two horses) was necessary. Lynn set off with Mr Mahony from *The Three Nuns* in Aldgate on 17th May, reaching Cotton *via* Ingatestone, Chelmsford, Witham, Colchester, Shalford, Ipswich, and Stowmarket, and returning *via* Bury St. Edmunds, Newmarket, Cambridge, Littlebury, Bishops Stortford, and Epping. Back in Aldgate on 28th May, he paid Mr Richard Burkinshaw £7 10s (for twelve days at 2s 6d a day) for the hire of the chaise and horses. With tips for Mr Waller's servants, and turnpike tolls out of and into London, the whole journey cost Lynn £16 19s 9d.[391]

Having promised in his letter to Morgan of 3rd September 1717 to send him a separate account *"of ye Suffolk affaire"*, Lynn must have done so, although that letter has not survived. William Morgan wrote to him on 5th October:

"As for the Suffolk affaire I am glad yo[w] still Maintain yo[r]. Ground, M[r]. Gennero who is now with me in the Country[392] will send y[ow]. any Orders thats Necessary for calling M[r]. Waler[393] to Account or any Other Writeings that may be

---

[390] TNA, C 111/207, *Lynn v Galway*, Francis Lynn's letter-book.

[391] TNA, C 111/207, *Lynn v Galway*, Packet 2, item A-13.

[392] i.e. somewhere outside Paris.

[393] Samuel Waller, the Suffolk agent.

thought Necessary".

On 27th May 1718 Samuel Waller wrote to Francis Lynn, regretting that he was at present unable to remit any rents for the Suffolk properties. This is the first of a list of eight letters from Waller to Lynn between 1718 and 1725, and three from Lynn to Waller, which are listed and their contents summarised as part of 'Master Brougham's Exhibits' in the National Archives.[394] Unfortunately, none of the originals is now extant.

Morgan had a suggestion for Lynn in his letter of 29th June 1718:

"*Mr Waler will tell y^{ow} that there are wood on the Estate y^{ow} have, which Mr Genero desires y^{ow} will cutt down and Make Money off. Let me tell y^{ow} my dear freind that there shall be alwayes a regard to y^{or} Intrest in the Estate if it be recoverd, and by what Mr Pryse writes it will be worth while. … Mr Gennero & I Drink y^{or} health often, and wee please our Selves with thinking how wee shall live[395] togeather when wee come to y^{ow}.*"

It should by now be apparent that Lt-Gen. Robert Echlin still regarded himself as the beneficial owner of the Bacton and Cotton estates, and William Morgan regarded his own interests as dependant on the General's, and Lynn's interests as subservient to both. Francis Lynn was evidently acquiescing in a legal

---

[394] TNA C 111/207, *Lynn v Galway*, Packet 1, item 27.
[395] Morgan, for whom neither spelling nor grammar were strong points, habitually spells 'live' as 'leive', 'you' as 'yow', and abbreviates 'dear' to 'D^r', which I have corrected to avoid confusion.

charade, in effect acting as trustee or nominee for both Echlin and Morgan, at least one of whom was in no position to assert his right to property in England with any hope of success, or of avoiding arrest.

On 15th December 1718 Robert Echlin, with the consent of William Morgan, acknowledging that neither Morgan's original £1,000 loan nor the subsequent £2,000 had been repaid, released his 'equity of redemption' in the mortgage of the Suffolk properties to Francis Lynn.[396] Lynn afterwards claimed that up to this point he was completely in the dark about the terms of Echlin's purchase from Barnardiston, although it is clear that despite discovering the terms of the marriage settlement, supposedly after Morgan's assignment had been completed, he continued to be on good terms with Echlin, albeit at one remove, when one might have expected them to fall out over Echlin's alleged lack of candour.

The agent Samuel Waller had still not accounted to Lynn for the rents received, but that did not prevent him, on 9th April 1719, sending Lynn an invoice for £30.[397] Lynn continued to encounter difficulties, and anticipated new ones. On 10th June 1719 he wrote to

---

[396] Suffolk Record Office, Lowestoft branch, HA12/B4/8/6. In 1715 William Morgan sued both Thomas Barnardiston (TNA C 11/1969/26) and Robert Echlin (TNA C 11/2211/58), and against the latter obtained judgment in the court of King's Bench for a debt of £600 plus costs of 53s, which on 21st June 1715 he assigned to Francis Lynn (Suffolk Record Office, Lowestoft branch, ref: HA12/B4/8/2). However, the proceedings may not have been as adversarial as they were made to appear, and Echlin may have colluded in them.

[397] TNA C 111/207, *Lynn v. Galway*, Packet 1, item 27.

William Morgan:

"I wish this same fellow[398] *do not find out*[399] *Mrs Trouble*[400] *and create new difficultys there; for she has this term moved the Court that a Receiver may be appointed for the Suffolk Estate, alledging that I only act as Trustee for Monsr Genero,*[401] *which the Court has granted; but I shall be able to sett that aside by producing & making Oath to my Title, & the consideration thereof. Tho' should we but be able to do it, It would be almost the same thing, for as yet I have had little more than the Name of an Estate; nor have I yet been able to gett a stated Account from Mr Wall--."*

No doubt with the getting of proper Accounts in mind, Francis Lynn entertained Samuel Waller to a meal at *The Castle* in Holborn on 26th June 1719, when they consumed bread and ale, rabbit with onions, butter and cheese, and of course wine. The food and ale cost Lynn 3*s* 9*d*, the wine 5*s* 11*d*.[402]

At the beginning of October 1719, later than planned, Francis Lynn again set out for Suffolk to visit the Bacton and Cotton estates. He had warned William Morgan early in July that *"I shall be forc'd to make another trip into Suffolk this Summer, for matters there are but in a bad posture"*. Again, Lynn hired a chaise and

---

[398] Someone, unnamed, who had cast doubts on the validity of a Will that concerned William Morgan, that of Brig. John Corbett, and who apparently knew Robert Echlin.
[399] i.e. contact.
[400] Code for Mrs Mary Echlin.
[401] Code for Lt.-Gen. Robert Echlin. Lynn was indeed merely a trustee or nominee for Echlin, and to have sworn otherwise would have been perjury.
[402] TNA C 111/207, *Lynn v. Galway*, Packet 2, item 4.

two horses from Richard Burkinshaw of *The Three Nuns*, Aldgate, to whom he paid £7 10*s* (as before) at his return on 13th October,[403] but otherwise we have no details of the journey or its precise purpose.

Mrs Mary Echlin's application to the court for a Receiver to be appointed for the Suffolk estates was successful, and on 13th January 1719[20] Waller sent Lynn a copy of the court order to that effect.[404] Mary Echlin remained on the offensive, and on 29th April 1720 Waller wrote to tell Lynn about Mr Goat (on this occasion acting for Mrs Echlin and/or her father's executors) serving ejectment proceedings on the Suffolk tenants.[405] He wrote to him again on 11th June 1720, about the trouble to which the Suffolk estates were putting both of them,[406] although he still failed to supply Lynn with any Accounts. In fairness to Samuel Waller, he may have encountered some difficulty in extracting rents from Widow Rodwell and her fellow tenants. Despite having 'attorned tenant' for Francis Lynn in April 1716, they could hardly have known whether they were coming or going, what with other agents for other principals now asking them for payment and threatening them with eviction.

In fact Mr Waller had collected some rents over the years, and paid them over piecemeal to Francis Lynn. These included, between 10th April 1716 (when Lynn first went up to Suffolk) and 29th June 1725, £567 14*s* 3*d* from Widow Rodwell, £260 from

---

[403] TNA C 111/207, *Lynn v. Galway*, Packet 2, item '(2)'.
[404] TNA C 111/207, *Lynn v. Galway*, Packet 1, item 27.
[405] TNA C 111/207, *Lynn v. Galway*, Packet 1, item 27.
[406] TNA C 111/207, *Lynn v. Galway*, Packet 1, item 27.

Thomas Richer or Ritchie, and £43 12*s* from other tenants, a total of £871 6*s* 3*d* in cash, plus three lots of butter worth £10 13s (of which Lynn sold £2 16*s*-worth to his lawyer Mr Mahony). However, in that time he should have received at least £1,926. No wonder Morgan was urging Lynn in November 1720 to "*Make them bring Waler to An Acctt*".

Lynn wrote to Morgan on 8th February 1719[20], reminding him that "*I wrote you word, the Court of Chancery had Ordered a Receiver for the Rents of the Suffolk Estate; W: Pryse & I have made a state*[ment] *of that whole affair, & taken advice of good Council upon it (Mr Lutwych, for Huford has proved a Villaine, & Pigou is indolent & careless) And doubt not but We shall be able to remove that Order, upon my proving my Title; tho' should the worst come to the worst, I must endeavour to raise money & pay off their Mortgage, & then I shall be quietly possess'd of it. … [P.S.] Pray my most humble service to Mr Genero*".

In 1721 Mrs Echlin and her father's executors jointly brought the first of several unsuccessful actions of ejectment against Francis Lynn himself.[407] Lynn claimed in early 1724 that if there were any legally binding trusts in respect of the land or of the £1,331 'mortgage', which he did not admit to be the case, then as a *bona fide* purchaser for value without notice of it – and how could he have had notice of what was essentially private, or know whether or not the £1,331 had been repaid? – he was not in equity bound by it.[408] Nevertheless, in April 1722 Lynn had taken the precaution of granting a mortgage of the Suffolk estates, by the usual device of a lease and release, to his

---

[407] TNA C 11/1257/28.
[408] TNA: C 11/275/23.

own lawyer Walter Pryse, of Lincoln's Inn.[409]

It was just as well that he did so, because in early September 1723 Lt.-Gen. Robert Echlin died, in France, and Francis Lynn now had to deal with the consequences.

---

[409] (TNA) Suffolk Record Office, Lowestoft branch, HA12/B4/8/8 & 9.

CHAPTER 12

Capt. Morgan's other troubles

William Morgan was always running short of
funds, and importuning his wife and friends for
subsidies. Sometimes these were needed to prosecute
or defend claims for money. There are several
hundred 18th-century court cases to be found in the
National Archives involving someone named William
Morgan, but most of them concern other William
Morgans, and once one has sifted through the brief
descriptions available online, and excluded those
which clearly relate to those others (most of them
Welsh), about three dozen cases, all in the court of
Chancery, remain. A few of these[410] may not directly
or indirectly concern our Capt. William Morgan,
although without examining the original parchments

---

[410] *viz.*, in chronological order, *Morgan v Buckeridge* (1707), C
7/235/7; *Morgan v White* (1713), C 7/239/128; *Miller v Caroll*
(1714), C 11/735/32; *Kyte v King* (1715), C 11/2648/25; *James v
Morgan* (1719), C 11/982/17; *Lewis v Morgan* (1720), C
11/1995/27; *Larimore v Morgan* (1727), C 11/2710/12; *How v Gill*
(1733), C 11/679/31; *Perkins v Morgan* (1739), C 11/534/24;
Morgan v Morgan (1740), C 11/2081/37; and *Hatch v Morgan*
(1742), C 11/625/19.

(which I may someday) I am unable to tell. However, there are enough left to be sure that Capt. Morgan, or his attorneys, spent considerable time and energy both before and after his departure from England in prosecuting or defending multiple cases, all of which concerned money in one form or another.[411] I have already alluded to some of them – the Cardonnel, Holt and O'Hara cases, for example. One other, 'Corbett's affair', took up a disproportionate amount of Francis Lynn's time. Almost all we know of it, apart from the probate records, is from references to it in the Lynn-Morgan series of correspondence, most of them, typically, obscure or oblique.

News of the death in France of Brigadier John Corbett (or Corbet) reached England at the end of August 1717. Corbett had acted on one occasion as trustee or nominee for Lt.-Gen. Robert Echlin in

---

[411] *viz.*, in chronological order, *Morgan v Broughton* (1707), C 6/350/23; *Knight v Hammond* (1713), C 11/1228/42; *Morgan v Barnardiston* (1714), C 11/1969/26; *Rodney v Morgan* (1714), C 11/2253/7; *Rodney v Morgan* (1714), C 11/2341/37; *Rodney v Holt* (1714), *Morgan v Beachcroft* (1715) C 5/257/12; *Ecklyn v Ecklyn* (1715), C 11/1171/15; *Morgan v Echlin* (1715), C 11/2211/58; *O'Hara v Knight* (1715), C 11/1777/9; *Fielding v Morgan* (1716), C 11/1172/8; *Fieldings v Morgan* (1719), C 11/1171/17; *Morgan v Caswell* (1720), C 11/1772/43; *Morgan v Wilson* (1720), C 11/1770/36; *Hammond v Morgan* (1721), C 11/1425/30; *Morgan v Mackean* (1722), C 11/1257/64; *Morgan v Dissideir* (1723), C 11/372/96; *Lynn v Ecklyn* (1723), C 11/275/23; *Morgan v Holt* (1724), C 11/1257/63; *Rodney v Morgan* (1724), C 11/2234/11; *Cole v Rodney* (1724), C 11/247/6; *Rodney v Holt* (1724), C 11/295/23; *Morgan v Wilson* (1725), C 11/1000/7; *Morgan v Fitzgerald* (1725), C 11/280/48; *Morgan v Hall* (1728), C 11/73/39; and *Lynn v Cotman* (1739), C 11/784/44.

respect of the Bacton and Cotton estates,[412] but according to the list of debts[413] due to Morgan as at 15th March 1719[20], prepared for Morgan by Francis Lynn, Brigadier Corbett had owed £438 8s 11d on a Note or Notes held by Lynn, and another £500 due on a Bond. Lord Carnarvon (formerly James Brydges, later the Duke of Chandos), Col. John Rice and Capt. Joseph Knight were also somehow interested in the business, although how is never explained. Corbett left an estranged wife and daughter, and a mistress, Ann Eston *alias* O'Brien. He had made a Will long before, on 7th March 1705[06], which left token sums to his daughter Mary and "*her mother*" (Corbett's wife Ann), and made his "*loving freind Ann Eston* alias *Obryen*" sole residuary beneficiary and executrix.

The news of Corbett's death threw Francis Lynn into something of a panic. On 3rd September 1717 he wrote to Morgan:

"*I was yesterday with Ric---*[414] *J.K.*[415] *& Mah.*[416] *We are like to find opposition in Corbetts affair; they pretend to produce a Will which will create trouble but I hope we shall soon be able to give you some better Account of that matter. In the mean time I assume Mr Mah. will acquaint you what answer my Lord Carnarvon gave.*"

Morgan replied a month later:

---

412 Suffolk Records Office, Lowestoft branch, TNA HA12/B4/7/29.
413 TNA, C 111/207, packet 1, item G-28.
414 Identity unknown, unless Lynn is referring to Col. John Rice.
415 i.e. Joseph Knight.
416 i.e. Mr Florence Mahony, lawyer.

"[Sinc]e I begon this leter I have one from Mah. He gives me noe Acc^t. of w^t. Lord Car: will doe about Corb^ts. Affaires. I have sent him a sorte of a Will^417 that Corb. made a litle before he dyed but I beleive it will onely serve to bring his Mistress to an Agreem^t. I have paid about a 100^£. to Corbet since I have been in this Country".

By mid-April 1719 there had been some further developments, as Lynn reported: *"I doubt not but you have heard of Corbetts affair, of the Whole proceeding whereof you shall in a little time have an Acct from me.".* That 'Account' has not survived, but on 10th June 1719 Lynn replied at length to Morgan's response to it, and to adverse comments made about it by Lynn's brother. Matters had evidently gone seriously wrong:

"I did not doubt but the late miscarriage of Corbetts affair would be wholly layd at my dore, but I thank God I have little regard to the Imputation, because I am satisfyd in my Conscience 'tis unjust, and that I have neither been guilty of Laziness or Forgetfulness in that affair. I must indeed have been strangely stupid & thoughtless of my own Interest (not to mention my Friends) to lett so great a summ of money slip thro' my hands, when I have so great occasion for it, and am so much out of pockett; but without making reflections upon any body, you must give me leave to lay the Saddle upon the right Horse,

---

417 This *"sort of a Will"* was dated 10th June 1717, probably with Mrs Ann Corbett as the main beneficiary, but no doubt with a substantial legacy for Morgan himself. Morgan sought to apply for probate of it, but the Master of the Prerogative Court of Canterbury, Dr. John Bettesworth, threw it out on 9th January 1718[19], the same day that probate was granted of the 1706 Will in favour of Corbett's long-time mistress. TNA PROB 18/35/45 and 11/571/1.

and tell you matter of Fact.

You know Mr Mah[ony] came over to you, not without very great expence, as well as hazard (as it happened) of his Life, more particularly to gett ye Commission executed for proving Corbetts Will.[418] *During his absence ... I did what I could to stave off the determination of Doctors Commons in that affair, in hopes of a return of the Commission, which was done till the Judge was perfectly out of patience; Nor had he at last given Judgment against Us had there been in any Letters of Yours to me, or Your Sisters to her Spouse, any Account of the Commission being executed, or like to be executed, or even the least mention or word in any Letter of such Commission or ye design of Executing it, upon which he lookt upon it to be all Sham & contrivance & admitted Madam to Administer.*[419] *Thus far I think I am not blamable.*

Now as to securing matters with the Commissioners of Accounts I thought we were very safe there, For Mr Bland (whom I believe you may remember at the Horse Guards) who was the person that layd the Accounts before that board, having been fully apprizd of the claim We had, did assure me he would take care that no Debenture should be given out for those Arrears without my knowledge ... Further before Your Sister came over to you, She had ye Assignment from me & putt it into the hands of one whose name I have now forgott, in order to have it entred ... in the Commissioners Office where I have not the least Interest to have any thing done, nor desire ever to appear ... This person dyed suddenly And the Assignment could not be found, or recovered again, nor had I any Sight of it till some time after Your Sister came home again, And after

---

[418] This was the phony Will produced, probably in more ways than one, by Morgan.

[419] Probate granted 9th January 1718[19]. TNA PROB 11/567/50.

Madam had gott Administration & layd her hands upon the Debenture; Which I doubt not she took care to bribe well for the dispatch of. ... Affairs standing thus I advisd with Wat Pr[yse] what was to be done to retrieve if possible this fault pas *... Mr Sayer*[420] *pressed to have an Appeal lodged to bring it before a Court of Delegates, ye Commission being now come over executed, Which he sayd would cost £30 down besides his own Fees, But they were both of Opinion, the money was gott into Hucksters hands, and it would be throwing good after bad, considering the Character of Madam*[421] *and her manner of Life for that being a Foreigner, doubtless she would quitt the Kingdom, and that the proceedings would not only be hazardous, but very chargable. Since this Your Sister & I mett Wat Pr[yse] and he told Us, that here is a Fellow in Town, who has declared the Will was not fairly made nor legally executed, with severall odd Circumstances, which if they should come to appear in the face of a Court, would look with so bad an aspect that I would not for 50 times the money seem to be an accomplice therein ... I shall likewise try what can be done towards stopping the Irish Arrears as you advise."*

In July 1719 Lynn wrote again:

"Sam has communicated to me Yours of the 11th *June G[regorian] stile, Wherein I find that Rice lays the matter at my dore that Sayer does not proceed in Corbetts affair: I do assure you 'tis not £30 nor a far greater summ shd stick with me, were there, either in my own Opinion or in Wat Pryses ... any probability of recovering the money that way; No body can blame Mr Sayer to endeavour to gett the affair again upon the*

---

[420] George Sayer, Proctor in Doctors Commons, where probate cases were dealt with.

[421] This was the lady whom Morgan later ungallantly referred to as *"Corbet's Whore"*.

Wheel in his Office, since he wd on course find his Account in it whether there be success or no, but I must really say, Money is not so flush with me to fling it away upon improbabilitys or rather impossibilitys …"

Lynn did have some positive news to report in his letter to Morgan of 8[th] February 1719[20]:

"Mr Mah: told me he had wrote you word, that I gott 200 & odd pounds of Corbets Arrears perfectly out of the Fire. Madam made a strenous Interest ag[ain]st Me, and trumpt up a Judgment given by that Wretch to Franks for £1000, but by the help of a good Friend I gott thro' it; As for his Irish Arrears, I have heard nothing lately, You know better than I, whom to write to there, to Secure that part."

Morgan mentioned the Corbett case when he wrote to Lynn on 6th November 1720:

"When I was with yow yow tould me of a person yow Mett at Westmenster who offerd to pay yow what money he had in his hands of Corbetts, and yow tould me that the Mrs Corbet offerd to come to an Agreement with yow. I fear there was nothing don in either, for none mentioned it to me …"

Lynn's reply, dated 23rd January 1721, is lost, except for a summary of it made for the 1747-56 *Galway v Lynn* case, which mentions *"shewing his & his Bro's friendly Endeavours to serve Morgan – also abt sd Corbet's Arrears, to be pd into ye Exchequer in Ireland, tho' Frank Lynn offer'd Security for Indemnification but it wou'd not do"*. There is no record of any subsequent letters written by Lynn to Morgan.

Various receipts signed by Morgan's lawyer James Roche show that Lynn had some success in calling in Morgan's debts. On 1ˢᵗ October 1720 Roche acknowledged receipt from Lynn of *"Mr Anthony Hammonds Bond of the penalty of Three thousand pounds ster[ling] Conditioned for paymt of 1500£, whereof there is abt 500£ due, & also Coll James Butlers cash Note of £56 Four shillings ster[ling] with Intrst from the 14ᵗʰ of May 1716. the former payable to Captain Wm Morgan the latter to Mr Lynne"*;[422] on 9ᵗʰ March 1719[20] Lynn obtained a certificate from the Commissioners of Accounts for £847 8s 11½d due to Morgan from the Officers of Lord Slane's Regiment, and handed it to Roche on 6ᵗʰ September 1720;[423] and in May 1721 (or possibly 1725 – the document bears both dates) Lynn delivered to Morgan's lawyer James Roche four documents, described by Roche as follows:

"Received from Francis Lynn Esqr the Four papers Following for the use of Captn Morgan, for which I am accomptable vizt

Bond from John Rice Esqr to John Corbett Esqr

John Rice Esqr Bond to Wm Morgan Esqr for £514:6:2 payable 2d Augt dated the 21th December 1715

Coll'l Rices Bond & Warrant of Attorney to Capt Morgan for 1136:19:4 payable the 10ᵗʰ June 1712. Intrst being included to that day".[424]

---

[422] TNA, C 111/207, packet 2, item P.

[423] TNA, C 111/207, packet 2, item R-2.

[424] TNA, C 111/207, packet 2, item O (in wrapper marked '10'). Although the receipt seems to me to be clearly dated *"May 6ᵗʰ 1725"*, the date given to it in the *Lynn v Galway* case was 6ᵗʰ May 1721.

Unfortunately that tells us almost nothing about the financial arrangements between the parties!

Francis Lynn and his lawyer Mahony had put Col. Rice on the spot in 1719 by endorsing Rice's bills and notes in favour of Lynn's lawyer John Pugh either in retaliation for, or in anticipation of, further underhand dealings on Rice's part.

After reporting the death and funeral of Capt. Joseph Knight to William Morgan in June 1719, Francis Lynn added a postscript to the letter the following day:

"I have this day seen W. Pr.[425] *who tells me Mr Huford hummd & ha'ed upon the questions he putt to him relating to ye Conveyance J: K. made, at last sayd, It would be for yr advantage, but in the close of discourse that you wd be securd what was due to you, but the Estate would be Rices. I … should be very glad of a line or two from You to Signify to me, whether or no I am to have any thing to do with this affair, or to expect any thing from it."*

Col. John Rice's small triumph did not last long, and nor indeed did he, for on 20th April 1720 William Morgan wrote to Francis Lynn:

"Now Coll Rice is dead I beleive yow will not have halfe ye plague yow feard in your Kinde Endevours for me. I beleive it will be Necessary to Administer as a prencipall Creditor in my Name. And if his papers can be found to sease them. I hope in God yow will be Able to bring things to bear without a great Deale of trouble to your Selfe …"

Francis Lynn's final extant letter to William Morgan, of 8th February 1719[20], contains a reminder of his Classical education at Westminster School:

" ... *one had need of Argus's Eyes,*[426] *Briareus's hands*[427] *& Jobs patience*[428] *to have to do with the Rices, the Potts, the Corbets, the Hurfords, & many more Such false Loons I could name, with whom your generous temper & unlimited kindness had led you to be engaged*".

Six days earlier the Lynn brothers had attended an evening meeting at Brown's Coffee House, conveniently close to Samuel Lynn's house in Spring Garden.[429] Present with him, according to the receipt that Francis Lynn kept, were "*Sam, R[obin] Gardner, Dent, Wilson & Young*". The occasion was evidently convivial, with copious quantities of rack[430] in punch, brandy in punch, ale, mutton pie, cheese on toast, bread & cheese, tobacco, and of course coffee, all for £1 6s 4d, not bad for six people.[431] In the course of the evening the party was joined by Morgan's cousin, Capt. Andrew Galway, but he did not stop long. Lynn described the meeting to Morgan:

"... *last Tuesday night We had a Meeting with Friend*

---

[426] Argus Panoptes, or Argos, a hundred-eyed giant in Greek mythology.

[427] Briareus, *alias* Aegaeon, a hundred-handed demigod in Greek mythology.

[428] Job, a character in the Old Testament noted for his stoicism.

[429] Brown's Coffee House later moved to Mitre Court in Fleet Street.

[430] Arrack, or arak, originally from south-east Asia, was a distilled alcohol similar to rum.

[431] *Lynn v Galway* (1747-56), TNA C 111/207, packet 2, item (3).

Robin[432] and two more, the Spending of an Evening with which Company I am perswaded will be of more consequence to the Success of Your Regim[t] Affairs, than any thing We have been able to do for you a good while. It is not proper for me to be very particular at this time (tho' perhaps you may learn something more of it from your Cor: Young, who was with us, and with whom I wish it was in mine & Sams power to Sett you right) but before the 10th of next Month (when that Comm[n] determines if it be not renewed for another Year) I hope to send you such an Acct of Your affairs with them, as may make you easy.

I have the 2 Assignments you sent over, which will or will not be made use of, as occasion may require; Andrew brought them to me, that night we were together, but declined giving us his company, by reason there were some with us to whom he was a stranger, and since that I have not seen him to discourse upon the affair You mention ..."

Lynn could have included other names in his list of "*false Loons*", such as that of William Weldon, who seems to have borrowed substantial sums from Morgan prior to 1716. Francis Lynn tried to get as much of it back as he could without Col. Rice getting his hands on it. £600 of the money was paid to the lawyer Mr Pigot, who accounted to Lynn for £500 of it in June 1716.[433] Ten days later Lynn reported his concerns to Morgan:

---

[432] Since Morgan had supposedly owed Robert Gardner £2,753 since 1712 – see Chapter 7, footnote 250 – it is rather surprising that Lynn should describe him as '*Friend Robin*' – unless he was being ironic, or the supposed debt was a sham, created for their mutual convenience.

[433] TNA, C 111/207, Packet 1, item D(2), CR entry.

" *… I fear there was some leanings, not only in him*[434] *but Mr Huford too, in favour of Wel—n, more than ought to have been, since they were Council for Us, wch I doubt not Rice and Pots have acqu[ainte]d you with*".

Another £700 "*of Weldon's money*", out of £960 or so owed, was received *via* Capt. Joseph Knight in November 1716, and as £600 of that was apparently due to Francis Lynn he kept that and remitted the remaining £100 to Morgan. However, as he reported to Morgan later that month:

"*All the arguments we could use, of the necessity you had for remittances, & that I lay under at present … could not prevail with them, they pretend they have Debts to pay, And that they would not be at the trouble of calling upon Mah--- or me for money when they wanted it for the Law business, And for that reason detain 260 odd pounds of this payment in their hands, as also 100£ of the former payment*".

That seems to have been the end of that.

William Young of Thatcham, Berkshire, the "*Cor: Young*" who had been at Brown's Coffee House, had had dealings with both Morgan and his cousin Capt. Andrew Galway. In January 1715[16] Young had agreed[435] to pay Morgan £1,000 in return for a lifetime 'pension' of £120 a year, and Morgan (or Francis Lynn on his behalf) started paying the annuity. However, over the years Morgan had borrowed money from

---

[434] An unidentified lawyer referred to only as 'the Templar'.
[435] TNA C 111/207, packet 2, Arbitration Award dated 23rd March 1719[20].

Young, and continued to do so, and by Christmas 1715 Morgan owed Young a balance (after subsequent adjustments) of £590 6s 10d. On 15th February 1717[18] Young paid Lynn another £150, which Lynn held on Morgan's account, and on or about midsummer 1718 Young agreed to take a 25% share in 100 hogsheads (about 6,600 gallons) of wine, acquired by Capt. William Morgan and held by Mr Florence Mahony, for £387 3s 8d. £263 13s 4d of this was charged by Mahony to Capt. Morgan, and a further £13 18s 8d was discounted "*being part of Capt. Galways Wines included in sd Account*". I suspect that the wine was acquired through smuggling activities, by Morgan, or Galway, or both, as its original cost is unrecorded.

Lynn reported to Morgan in mid-April 1719:

"*I must acquaint you at the request of Mr Young, that he is very uneasy, that his Accts between him & You is not Signed & his pension settled according to the Articles of Agreement between you, he having as he represents fully complyd on his part; You certainly know how this matter stands, and I must beg You'l send your directions positive what is to be done in it, that he may have an answer*". Two months later he wrote again: "*I am very much at ease by what I saw you wrote Sam in relation to Mr Young, who … I must own till I saw yr Letter, I was inclined to think had hard Measure. I never did rightly understand that affair, but was often pressed to sign ye Account & settle the Pension, but I did not care to do any thing in it till better satisfied, not only in regard to You, but also because I did not care to saddle my self with an annual paymt wch I could not find a Fund for*".

And on 6th July Lynn wrote to Morgan again:

"A day or two ago, I mett Mr Young, who told me Mr Mah: & he had Settled Accts therefore wanted my Signing them, in order to Settle his Pension, but going together to Mahers I did not find it alltogether true, they falling into debates about it; ... I shall do nothing in the Matter without Your positive directions".

On 23rd November 1719 the parties (or their attorneys) agreed to appoint Francis and Samuel Lynn as *"indifferently chosen"* arbitrators.[436] On 23rd March 1719[20] the Lynn brothers settled the accounts between Morgan and Young, allowing Young interest at 12% p.a. on what was owed to him, to bring the total up to £851 11*s* 10*d*, of which £390 12*s* 6*d* was to be paid to Mr Mahony to cover what Young owed him, and £14 10*s* was allowed *"for 300 Livres Capt. Morgan paid to Mr Youngs Order abroad"*.[437] That left £446 9*s* 4*d*. Morgan was to pay £46 9*s* 4*d* of that to Young immediately, and in consideration of being allowed to keep the other £400 was to pay Young an annual pension or annuity of £48 for the rest of Young's life.

Francis Lynn sent a copy of the Award to William Morgan, who wrote on 20th April the following year:

"I have gott the Arbitration yow both Made. I need not tell yow that I am satisfied, but I finde yow have not made mention of ye 40£ bill of Patrick Gallwey as tho' Mr Young Declard that if it was Not a bill Drawen upon me by Gallwey that he would allow it from ye begining. Now this bill being in Britagney I canot come at it till I goe home, but however I hope

---

[436] Since they were both financially involved with Morgan, they were hardly independent, so the description seems an odd one.
[437] That gives an exchange rate of 100 livres = £4 16s 8d.

to avoide future quarles yow will both make Young signe a paper that as the bill be not Drawen upon me he will allow it from ye begining Out of the Annuity, for consider I pay him 12 per Cent. for that bill from Decr 1715 besides 6 per Cent from the beginning. I will write to Roch on this subject. I hope yow will likewise Make him pay Intrest for the 390£, to the time the Annuity Commences, whether at 6: or at 12 per Cent as yow please Gentlemen, these 2 Articles I begg may be sett right, to avoide Any further trouble, for Mr Samick writ word that Young tould yow both that I agreed that noe Intrest should be allowed for the 390£, which is realy wroung in Young. … I begg yow … will assure your selfe and my Dear Sam that your request in favour of Mr Young would serve even for Rice were he alive. I forgive them both and I realy pitty the Dead and recomend repentance to the Leiving. …"

So even after all Francis Lynn's efforts Morgan still expected more work out of him, and on 25th June 1723 Morgan's lawyer James Roche wrote[438] to Lynn about £300-odd still outstanding from Young. That was the last letter to Lynn about that matter, but there were others still to be resolved.

While Morgan was busy on the Continent, he still sought the occasional favour from Francis Lynn. On 4th February 1719[20] he had written to Lynn, from Paris, with a tale of even greater woe than usual:

"It is a great while my d' frind since I have had the pleasure of writeing to y[u], twas my fault, but my d' frank I had nothing to say, I found my selfe as I am and alwayes will be under all the Obligations in the World to y[u] and frind Sam. I found my affaires all sunk to nothing for want of Application, and yet my

---

*frinds did all they could, soe realy in that unhapey state I
resolved to let things take their Course, and endevour to have
patience to see the end of 'em. I have my D^r frank a true sence
of y^{re} sencere Manner, and realy of yor having advanced yor
ready Money to assist me, It is what I should not desire from
soe nomerous a family as yo^{rs}. But I trust in God yo^u will loose
nothing by yor frindly resolutions. ... I begg if any other thing
be necessary that yo^u will ... try if yo^u can save me a little out
of the fiere."*

By March 1720, when Francis Lynn compiled for
William Morgan a list[439] of the debts due to Morgan
of which Lynn was aware, and which were secured,
there was a grand total of £10,291 11s 7d owed to
Morgan by various individuals, of which £2,449 17s
8d was secured by personal Notes, and the rest –
£7,741 13s 11d – by Bonds. The Notes included £181
4s 6d and another £158 19s 11d owed by one Israel
Feilding, whom Walter Pryse was suing on Morgan's
behalf, £590 15s 4d owed by Lord Barrymore, £200
owed by Mr Henry Cairnes, and some smaller debts,
most of which were owed by various Colonels,
Captains, Lieutenants, Majors (including a Maj.
Pursell – £169 17s 6d) and Ensigns. Some of the
debts are marked "*bad*", and there are useful
comments made against others. For example, "*Pryse
knows him*" or "*Mr Pryse knows where he is*" are against
entries for Patrick Gould (£5), Capt. La Forey (£18 1s
5d) and Capt. Douglass (£2 10s), and next to Mrs
Brown's debt of £6 8s 4d is written: "*Lodges over against
the Kings head in Duke Street Lincolns Inn Fields*". Against

---

[439] TNA, C 111/207, packet 1, item G-28.

a £250 Note owed by Col. Edward Jones is "*This putt down by gross being due from his Reg^t & as yet the Agency not computed the Accounts are in Packinghams hands of Jones's Regt who has layd 'em before the Comm^{rs} & lives at ye upper end of Mincing Lane – at a great gate opposite to ye west of ye Monument*".

Lynn ended the document with a written promise to be "*accountable*" to Morgan for the listed debts. One supposes he meant only those debts which he managed to collect, but it was a rash promise, and may have had unfortunate consequences for his heirs.

CHAPTER 13

'Captain Walton'

William Morgan was not planning to come back to England anytime soon, and when at the beginning of 1718 he had heard that Samuel Lynn and a group of Lynn's friends intended to apply for a 'letter of licence' to enable him to return, Morgan wrote hurriedly to his "*dearest friend*" Frank Lynn:

"I hope there is noe step as yet made in it … I w^d not loose the Credit I have gaind amoungst my dealers here for the world. … This onely to y^r selfe and Co^n Sam. to whom Ile writ next post. … Now my d^r freind if it be absolutely necessary for me to come home to setle my affaires Ile run the risk of doeing it privately, and I am sure I can finde out some place either in Town or Country to be in for 2 or 3 Months and keep [my]selfe fro[m] ye knowledge of my Credito^rs, but should the[re] be a proposeall made to get me a leter of Licence all my correspondence^440 w^d know it, and my Credit w^d imediately fall amoungst my Correspondence here; which Ile tell y^w without vanity is pretty tollerable – and indeed I am not without hopes that in some reasonable time the trade I come about may

---

440 He means "*correspondents*".

haperley succeed".

This, I feel sure, was a smokescreen, and the "*trade*" of which Morgan had such high hopes was not commercial in nature, but political. He used a similar expression, and in the same sense, when writing to a Spanish grandee, Don Nicolas, in June 1721: "*In case our home trade should have any delay …*".[441] Morgan, an Irish Catholic, could not safely cross the English Channel without fear of arrest, not least because he was deeply involved in plans to depose the new Protestant Hanoverian dynasty and restore a Catholic Stuart king to the thrones of England-and-Wales, Scotland and Ireland, known since 1707 as Great Britain. This was to be Prince James Francis Edward Stuart, *alias* the Chevalier St George, whose birth in June 1688 as the only legitimate son of James II had precipitated the 'Glorious Revolution' which brought William III and Mary II to the throne the following year. If James Stuart – widely known (after the birth of his son Charles Edward in December 1720) as 'The Old Pretender', and by his adherents as 'James VIII and III' – had agreed to subscribe to the Church of England he might well have become king, but he resolutely refused to abandon his Catholic faith, and on Queen Anne's death in August 1714 the throne was offered, in accordance with a previously passed Act of Succession, to her second cousin once removed, the Elector of Hanover, who became George I.

King George's grasp of English at the beginning of his reign was at best rudimentary, if not non-existent,

---

[441] TNA, SP 35/71/27 – Letter from Morgan to Don Nicolas.

and that and his distant manner – which may have been caused by shyness – did not endear him to his court, to his ministers, or to the wider public. Within less than a year of his accession came the first serious attempt to dislodge him, in the shape of the rebellion of 1715 – 'the Fifteen' – and this was to be followed during the reign of his son George II by the even more serious 'Forty-five', but in between were a number of organised – or in some cases disorganised – insurrections which at the time were perceived as major threats to the stability of the kingdom. The first of these was an abortive attempt by James Stuart's supporters in 1716 to enlist the help of Charles XII of Sweden, then at war with Hanover and other powers over control of the north German port of Bremen, but the Swedish king wanted a great deal of money in return, which James Stuart could ill afford. The second was an abortive invasion of Scotland and the West Country in 1719, which fizzled out due to an insufficiency of troops and resources. The third, and most serious, was the so-called Atterbury Plot of 1720-22, centred around the Bishop of Rochester (and former Dean of Christ Church, Oxford), Bishop Francis Atterbury, although the extent to which he was involved, and whether an insurrection ineptly promoted by one Christopher Layer was part of Atterbury's plot or simply coincided with it, are questions still open to debate. What is known, from correspondence[442] intercepted during these eventful times by Sir Robert Walpole's secret service, is that William Morgan and his cousin Andrew Galway were

---

[442] The SP 35/71 series in the National Archives comprises 145 items, mostly depositions and letters, including seven intercepted letters between Morgan and Galway.

both pivotal figures in several of these plots.

Morgan *"was linked to Ormonde*[443] *both in the 1719 attempt and the Atterbury Plot … and commanded three ships in the Spanish navy.*[444] *He ran many risks for Ormonde who called him 'a very honest gentleman' who had been 'a very great sufferer' for the Stuart cause.*[445] *One of Morgan's extra-curricular activities was to organise the Madagascar pirates under licence from Charles XII, king of Sweden".*[446] Charles offered Morgan the governorship of Madagascar, provided that he could take control of the island – a somewhat remote possibility, one would have thought. Morgan's three ships, all armed, were in 1722 *"cruising in the Bay of Biscay without ever coming to port in Galicia. His base was Morlaix, where Ormonde owned a house. … In 1722, however, Morgan's time was spent on organising James III's fleet. He and other Jacobite naval officers had unlimited leave from the King of Spain to look after James's ships. Morgan was ready to take Ormonde to Bristol …".*[447]

Morgan had been joined in France by his wife Mary, although she returned to London in mid-1723, staying in various lodgings off Red Lion Square, and so far as I know left England again only once, to visit her husband in Seville prior to 1735. He corresponded with her until 1740, but not thereafter until he died in 1744, and she is not mentioned in his Will, so she may have died in the meantime. While

---

[443] The Duke of Ormonde.
[444] HMC, *Stuart MSS*, ii. 158.
[445] *Ibid.*, vii. 665.
[446] *'The Dukes of Ormonde 1610-1745'* (2000), ed. by Toby C. Barnard & Jane Fenlon, p.247.
[447] *'The Atterbury Plot'*, by Evelyn Cruickshanks & H. Erskine Hill (2004), p.149.

they were living in France they were apparently known as 'M. et Mme. Walton',[448] and William Morgan is often referred to in the official files as "*Capt. Morgan* alias *Walton*".

Morgan's Irish cousin Capt. Andrew Galway was also in France, and usually going by the pseudonym of Gardiner. From 1718 to 1722 he commanded the ship '*Revolution*'. In August 1721, when William Morgan wrote to him,[449] it was moored at Cadiz, in Spain, In June 1722 Galway had his "*dear Aunt*" (unnamed, but possibly Morgan's mother Mrs Christine Morgan) aboard,[450] and the ship was headed for Civitavecchia, near Rome, where it arrived on or about 27th June, apparently with the intention of collecting the Young Pretender (Charles Edward Stuart, not yet two years old) and taking him to Scotland. That plan must have been abandoned as being senseless, which it was. By the beginning of November 1722 Galway and the '*Revolution*' were at Genoa,[451] but within a month the '*Revolution*' had been captured in Genoa harbour by Commodore Scott, commander of the '*Leopard*', which prompted Galway to write to Lord Carteret, denying that he was a Jacobite sympathiser, and claiming to be merely a dealer in linen, small arms and gunpowder, trading chiefly in Brazil and Madagascar, who had been duped into dealing with William Morgan over 'the

---

[448] TNA, SP 35/71/21 – Letter to Capt. Andrew Galway.
[449] TNA, SP 35/71/29 – Letter to Capt. Andrew Galway.
[450] TNA, SP 35/71/91 – Letter to Lord Carteret (the courtesy title by which John, 2nd Earl Granville, was usually known).
[451] TNA, SP 35/71/41 – Letter to Capt. Andrew Galway.

Swedish affair'.[452] Galway was, of course, lying.

Francis Lynn had had previous dealings with Galway. His letter to William Morgan of 18th November 1716 mentions what may have been their first meeting:

"The Weather last night preventing my return to Dulwich, I went home with Mr Mah[ony], where he found a Letter from Capt. Andr--- Gal--- advising that he had unlimited Credit upon him, but that he would draw upon very Sparingly; It was not an hour after, but a Bill of his came to be accepted for £500 Sterling payable at 21 days to the Arthurs,[453] Now considering the circumstances Our affairs are in at present You may easily guess the confusion this putt us both into …"

Lynn was obliged to satisfy Capt. Galway's bill, and paid his lawyer Mr Mahony £200 on it on 10th December (by which time it was a week overdue). Galway may have been staying with Lynn, or at least called on him, at the time, as four days later a postscript to one of William Morgan's letters to Lynn asked him that *"If Capt Gallw. comes away soone pray send me my Will that I left with you, for I must think of some alterations in it, Send it Inclosed – without telling him what it is"*.

Morgan's earliest surviving letter to Galway is dated 9th January 1719, and includes a reference to Mr Creagh, who was last mentioned in connection with

---

[452] TNA, SP 35/71/114. Carteret, like Bishop Atterbury (and Francis Lynn), had been educated at Westminster School.

[453] Sir Daniel Arthur, a rich Irish banker, and his wife Lady Arthur, were to become part of the social scene in Spain. Morgan mentions Lady Arthur more than once in correspondence with his wife.

'the Cardonnel affair' of 1715, but whom Morgan now regarded as "*a villain*".[454] Two months later he was writing again, chiefly about his debts of 2,000 livres (about £97) and the possibility of fitting out a Jacobite ship for 50,000 livres (about £2,417).[455] In both those letters, and in his next dated 10th March 1719,[456] Morgan alluded to members of his family whom Galway would have known, namely his brothers James and John, and his father (Dennis), and, in a later letter,[457] to Galway's own relation Patrick Galway. Morgan and Galway apparently had other Irish relatives serving the Jacobite case, and a letter from one John O'Brien to Galway, dated 12th April 1721, mentioned "*our cousin Willm*" and "*cossn Morgan and family*", although it should be borne in mind that 'coz', or its like, was a term used for friends – hence Morgan referring to Samuel Lynn, to whom he was not related, as "*Cos. Samick*".

Morgan's son James, known as 'Jemey', who was also involved in his father's treasonable activities, was apparently a somewhat hot-headed young man. Morgan wrote of him in 1721 that he "*does not know his ignorance*" and "*will not be governed*".[458] In June 1721 he was sent to Spain, to Don Nicolas, who was told by Morgan to "*do what you will with Jemmey*".[459] Unlike his father, James Morgan was able to travel to England without fear of arrest, and on 15th May 1724 brought a note from his mother, intended for Francis Lynn,

---

[454] TNA, SP 35/71/22 – Letter from Morgan to Galway.

[455] TNA, SP 35/71/23 – Letter from Morgan to Galway.

[456] TNA, SP 35/71/24 – Letter from Morgan to Galway.

[457] TNA, SP 35/71/29 – Letter to Capt. Andrew Galway.

[458] TNA, SP 35/71/30 – Undated letter from Morgan to anon.

[459] TNA, SP 35/71/27 – Letter from Morgan to Don Nicolas.

who was not at home at the time, asking for three guineas to bear '*Jemey*'s charges in "*a going to His father*", and to "*place it to my account*". Mrs Mary Lynn duly stumped up the cash.

Morgan's need for money had prompted him to ask his friend Frank Lynn to call in as many debts as he could, and to enforce any securities which remained under the control of Morgan or of his agents and attorneys. Among these were some valuable items of silver, and a diamond necklace. About the former, Lynn wrote in November 1719[460] to the wife of one Col. Carter, in somewhat stern terms:

"*Madam, I find amongst my Friend Morgans papers a bond of One Captain Hanaford for 50£, lent him, Witnessed by one Spencer & Salmon the Scrivener at Charing cross, as also a bill of Sale at the same time made of One large Silver tankard, One large Silver Cup, One large Silver porringer, Six Silver Spoons & 4 Silver Salts Which goods were left in Your hands. I find likewise, that he lent the money at Coll Carters at your request, & that you were both bound to him for the money; I desire the said goods may be delivered to me, & that you will lett me know how I am to come by the remainder of the said 50£, and Interest beyond what those Goods amount to. I desire Your speedy answer to this to be left for me at my Brothers Office in Spring Gardens. The reason I apply to you & not to ye Colonel, is because I find by a Mem'dum of my friends own hand writing, that these things were putt into your hands & not his*".

---

[460] The letter is dated 8th November 1719 on the outside, but has been misdated 8th March 1719[20] when submitted as an exhibit in the *Lynn v Galway* case of 1746-56.

There was also the diamond necklace, which on 6th November 1720 Francis Lynn retrieved from Florence Mahony,[461] his (and Morgan's) lawyer. As Morgan explained in a letter to his wife Mary nearly twenty years later:

"Yow write to me Concerning a Dimond Neclace that M[r] Lynn had from M[r] Mahony for a Pledge for a hundred pounds – in the Year 1720. All I know [is] that Coll Pursell[462] *some years before came to borrow A hundred pounds from me & would give me a Neclace & Cross in Pawn; I did not like the Man, nor would I take Pawn from Any boddy, but I took pitty of him and gave him a letter to my Gould Smyth where I desird him to supley him with that Sume, to take his bond & the Pledge for his Security, which he did. the Other Never paid the Mony, soe I was Obliged to pay my Gould Smyth – And the Necklase & Bond were given up to me, Wheather M[r] Mahony took up a hundred pounds from M[r] Lynn to send to me, Or for his owne use. Or Wheather he gave the Necklase to M[r] Lyn – as he had my Letter of Attorney – all this I can not charge neither my Memory or Conscience with but it will be easeyley knowen by M[r] Lynns receit how he tooke the Necklase … for he was not a Man to geive a receit without being well grounded – Nor would he neglect takeing it up had he given back the Necklase".*

In August 1721 James Roche, the Irish lawyer most closely associated with William Morgan's activities on the Continent, remitted 7,000 livres (equivalent to about £338) either to Mr George Waters (or Walters), the Paris-based banker to

---

[461] TNA, C 111/207, packet 1, Galway's exhibit list, item 29.
[462] Or 'Purcell'; several 'stated accounts' mention *"Maj. Pursell"*, as he presumably then was.

Morgan and several other Jacobites, or to Morgan's banker in Morlaix, "*Monsieur Philibê*". In October Roche wrote to Francis Lynn, telling him that "*our Friend*" – as Lynn would know, he meant Morgan – needed to draw (another) 6,000 livres in Paris "*& desires I may use my Endeavours to raise that Summe or that his Credit's lost. I have his plate weighing 607 ounces*[463] *which I belive I may raise 150£ upon. You have the Necklace, which was pawned already with the plate, if you can be so kind to advance me the £200, on the plate & Necklace you'l very much oblige us, for 'tis better they shoud be in your hands or some Friends of yours … I must find the money for him by Monday, which I can't do without your aid*".

Roche and Lynn met on 2nd November (Francis Lynn's fiftieth birthday), immediately following which Lynn wrote to Roche suggesting that a friend of his (whom he did not name) might be able to help. On the same day Roche, who now had a better idea of the value of the silver, wrote back:

"*The plate at 5s. 6d. [per ounce] which is all that a Gould Smith will lend upon it, amounts to 165£, & no more, & I have no way left to raise the remainder but the dependance I have on your giving me the Necklace to lodge wth the plate for which I'l give you my rec't, & a promisery Note to deliver you as soon Wee redeem. I will lodge them neare you., that your Friend or you may release them at your pleasure, & the better to Enable you so to do, I'l give you the party's rec't for them, twill therefore be proper yt you have the Necklace in your office whean I call at 12 for our time is short, & our poor Friends reputation at stake*".

---

[463] At August 2016 prices, plate weighing this much, assuming it was solid silver, would have a scrap value of over £9,150.

Two days later Francis Lynn delivered the diamond necklace, "*containing forty two Diamonds on the string; being for the use of Captn Morgan*", to James Roche. That was the last heard either of the necklace or of the plate.

The 'Atterbury Plot' was foiled in the late Spring of 1722 by a combination of efficient spying by Walpole's agents and chance circumstances. It began to unravel with the death on 19th April 1722 of the Earl of Sunderland, an examination of whose papers by the authorities very soon after his death revealed him to be a Jacobite sympathiser in contact with 'James III'. At about the same time the Duc d'Orleans informed Lord Carteret (who reported to Robert Walpole) that an invasion of 3,000 men was planned for the following month, in support of a *coup d'état* led by the Duke of Ormonde on the Pretender's behalf. However, the French refused Ormonde permission to march his force to Calais or any other Channel port, and in any case Ormonde himself was held up in Spain. He was to have been taken to Bristol aboard a sloop, the *Ste Marie* (or *St. Mary*), commanded by Capt. John Monnrroy[464] (or Monery) and owned by none other than William Morgan. However, as bad luck (for the Jacobites) would have it, Morgan's vessel, having sailed from Roscoff in France to Corunna in Spain, had there been captured by English privateers in mid-April 1722. (Later that month Monnrroy made a declaration of the fact, to enable Morgan to claim compensation from the King of

---

[464] The spelling seems improbable, but is used consistently in the records.

Spain for the loss of the sloop.[465]) By 22nd July 1722, the planned *coup d'état* having failed to materialise, Morgan and his remaining two ships were back at Morlaix.[466]

It is inconceivable that, if he did not already have suspicions about William Morgan's activities, Francis Lynn could have remained unaware of rumours of them circulating after April 1722, and been very worried by them. He must then have decided that continuing to help Morgan, either directly by lending him money, or by assisting him in the collection of his debts, posed too much of a risk to his own reputation and too much likelihood of creating trouble for him with his employers – the Royal African Company – and with the Government. Quite what trouble is unclear, but Lynn wrote to a Mr Mackean, a lawyer who had been involved in the Holt case, on 1st December 1719 and on 26th January 1720[21] *"shewing the utmost Hazard he ran of utterly ruining himself & large Family, on Morgan's Acct, wch Lynn's unhappy Remains are now too sensibly convinced of"*. 'Mr Philpott', who seems likely to have been the same Nicholas Philpott who in 1713 had been appointed jointly with William Morgan as Receiver and Paymaster of the Reformed Officers, wrote to Francis Lynn on 5th March 1721[22], mentioning the Government's demands on Lynn and on his brother Samuel concerning Capt. Morgan. Samuel Lynn seems to have felt likewise, and wrote to Morgan's lawyer James Roche on 23rd October 1723 *"about Morgan's Accts, & ye Securities he enters into wth his Brother to ye Government, on Morgan's Acct"*. Samuel

465 TNA, SP 35/71/36.
466 TNA, SP 35/71/99.

wrote to his brother Frank five days later about Roche, Morgan, and the lawyer Walter Pryse, and about "*applying to ye Government for Protection, on Acct of their being Security for Morgan*". The list of exhibits in the *Galway v Lynn* case mentions another letter from Samuel to Frank, without giving its date, in which he refers to "*ye Hazard ye Lynns ran of being left in ye Lurch, on Acct of Morgan*".[467] For whatever reason, Francis Lynn had decided to wash his hands of William Morgan. (He may not have confided his concerns to his wife, hence her advancing three guineas to Morgan's son James in 1724.)

The list of debts owed to Morgan which Francis Lynn had compiled for him in March 1720 was amongst items shipped to Morgan in 1722 or 1723 – although probably not by Lynn – in a writing desk or 'scrutore' (i.e. escritoire), but did not arrive. An exhibit list compiled for the *Galway v Lynn* case of 1747-56 has a note[468] explaining that "*the said Scrutore was about that Time seized at Bilbao in Spain and was detained there*". It stayed detained for over twenty years, and was not delivered to Morgan – by that time living in Madrid – until about six weeks before his death in 1744.

James Roche wrote to Francis Lynn on 13th September 1723 on behalf of Morgan's wife Mary, who held Morgan's power of attorney:

"*Sir, Last night Mrs Morgan arrived here from France, where she intends to continue till all her affaries*[sic] *are*

---

[467] None of the originals of the letters mentioned in this paragraph has survived. Their contents are, however, summarised in the list of exhibits in the case, renamed *Lynn v Galway* – TNA ref C 111/207.

[468] TNA, C 111/207, Packet 1, item 28.

brought to a period. She came at a time when 'tis my misfortune to want even pockett money. This will be delivered you by Mr James Morgan to whom I pray, if you are in cash, lend Tenn pieces for the use of his Mother, which I shall take care to repay you, out of the first money We receive. I wrote to you long since about the affaire I once spoke to you of, but was not favoured with your Answer".[469]

There is no record of Lynn complying with this modest request. He may well have decided that as far as William Morgan was concerned, enough was enough.

James Roche wrote to Francis Lynn again on 27th September 1723 on behalf of Morgan's wife Mary, who held Morgan's power of attorney, but about a different matter, and in a distinctly more trenchant tone:

"*Mrs Morgan is very impatient to have her Affaires adjusted. The first Stepp to be taken is to prove Gen'l Echlins Will, which* [I] *this day have sent to D[octo]rs Commons. The next is immediately to file a Bill against her in your Name to redeem the Mortgage. The 3d that you'l be pleas'd at your leasure to make up Your Accts with her, & the fourth that the Mortgage to Mr Morgan from your Brother[470] be deposited in the hands of a third Person whom You shall Name in Trust for Mr Morgan & you till your Accts be ballanced. I doubt not our finishing these matters to our satisfaction by your intermediation.*"

Lt.-Gen. Robert Echlin, the former owner of

---

[469] Roche could be referring to any one of a number of deals involving both Lynn and Morgan.
[470] i.e. Samuel Lynn.

properties in Bacton and Cotton, Suffolk, in which Francis Lynn and William Morgan had direct or indirect interests, had evidently died very recently, still in exile, at 'Saint Paul'[471] in France. The exact date of his death is unknown, but it may well have prompted Mrs Morgan's return to England, which she reached on or before 13th September 1723. By his Will made in April 1715,[472] and in consideration of the "*great and signal services*" he had received from his "*worthy friend William Morgan*", particularly in helping to fund the purchase of the 'Boughton' and Cotton estates, for which Morgan "*had for his security only a Grant of the Equity of Redemption of the said premises*", Echlin made Morgan his sole residuary beneficiary, and appointed him as sole executor.[473]

The Will makes no mention at all of Echlin's wife, who when her husband died was still alive, and very much so when the Will was made in 1715 – if indeed it was not a later fabrication made by or for Morgan, as I suspect it may have been. An 'allegation', in anticipation of a likely probate lawsuit, was promptly lodged on Morgan's behalf.[474] One might have expected Echlin to have made a codicil after 1718, acknowledging even in some token way the substantial help he had received from Francis Lynn, to Lynn's considerable inconvenience, in connection with the Bacton-Cotton properties, but he did not, or if he did Morgan effectively suppressed it.

On 7th October 1724 the land agent Mr Samuel

---

[471] Saint Paul in Le Marais, Paris.
[472] TNA: PROB 11/607/424 and PROB 11/602/377.
[473] *Morgan v Hall* (1728) – TNA C11/73/39.
[474] TNA: PROB 18/37/168.

Waller wrote to Francis Lynn, expressing his concerns at the great risk Lynn was running of losing both the Suffolk estates and his money, although the precise contents of his letter are unknown.[475] Lynn must, however, have had similar concerns, and on 30th November 1724, possibly prompted by the death in London about ten days earlier of Mrs Mary Echlin (or 'Eklin'[476]), Lynn released to his friend and lawyer Walter Pryse his 'equity of redemption' in the Bacton and Cotton estates, or more accurately in the mortgage of them.[477] On the same date Lynn assigned to Pryse the £600 (and costs) judgment debt against Robert Echlin which William Morgan had assigned to him,[478] and William Morgan assigned to Walter Pryse all his interest in the Bacton and Cotton properties.[479] I have little doubt that at the same time Pryse, at Lynn's and Morgan's request, executed a deed intended to be kept off the title – a 'declaration of trust' – stating who was the true beneficial owner, although whether it was in favour of Lynn, or Morgan, or somebody else entirely, who can say?

William Morgan did not, in the event, obtain probate of Lt.-Gen. Robert Echlin's Will until 18th March 1726, and then not until the probate court had

---

[475] TNA C 111/207, *Lynn v. Galway*, Packet 1, list of exhibits, item 27.

[476] Mary Eklin, "*carr[ied] out*", was buried at (or near) the church of St Magnus the Martyr, north of London Bridge, on 21st November 1724.

[477] (TNA) Suffolk Record Office, Lowestoft branch, HA12/B4/8/10.

[478] (TNA) Suffolk Record Office, Lowestoft branch, HA12/B4/8/13.

[479] (TNA) Suffolk Record Office, Lowestoft branch, HA12/B4/8/12.

pronounced in his favour in a dispute[480] with Mary Echlin's daughter and heir, Catherine Faussett.

By that time Francis Lynn was busy fighting a legal battle of his own, back in Dulwich. *"The Commoner"*, Samuel Hunter – whom Lynn had long regarded as 'Uncle Hunter' – had died at Hall Place after a short illness on 21st April 1725, and the provisions of his Will were not at all what Francis Lynn had been led to expect they would be.

---

[480] TNA PROB 11/612/6.

CHAPTER 14

Uncle Hunter's Will

When Samuel Hunter died, Francis Lynn had not been living in Dulwich for over two years. As his 'diary' records, on 1ˢᵗ January 1722[23]: "*My Lord Duke of Chandos*[481] *gave me a House at Stanmore*[482] *near his Grace; & I thereupon removed from Dulwich*",[483] although of course he still had his 'tied' family apartment at the Royal African Company's headquarters in Leadenhall Street. Lynn must have heard of Hunter's illness, and reached Hall Place shortly before "*the Commoner*" died. As soon as Hunter had breathed his last, Lynn started searching among his papers for a Will. What he found

---

[481] The elder brother of Lynn's contemporary at Westminster School, Henry Brydges. The Duke's third wife, and widow, was the former Lydia Catherine Davall (died 1750), widow of Sir Thomas Davall and sister of Francis Lynn's former landlord in Dulwich, John Vanhattem. (TNA MS 2750, item 12.)

[482] about ten miles north-west of central London, in Middlesex.

[483] Dulwich road charges lists for 1724 and 1725 indicate that, following a period of non-letting, Lynn was succeeded as John Vanhattem's undertenant of 57/59 Dulwich Village by a Mr Peacock – possibly Edward Peacock, a London goldsmith with a young family.

caused him considerable shock.

There was, in Hunter's black writing-box, what appeared to be a Will, written on parchment in Hunter's own hand, with the usual preamble about being "*of sound and perfect memory*" although, Hunter had added, "*far advanced in years*" – he was no more than 73 – followed by the customary expressions of piety, but it was full of references to relations of whom Lynn had never heard. He also found a number of letters, including one dated only a week earlier, addressed from Lincoln, which began "*Ever honoured Sir*" and ended "*your most Dutifull & most Obedient Nephew John Hawkins*". Hawkins, and his cousin William Fenwick, were not only appointed executors of the Will, but were to be the residuary beneficiaries. Lynn, probably infuriated by this discovery but conscious of the correct protocol in such matters, penned and dispatched a letter to this John Hawkins, informing him of his uncle's death and of the main provisions of the Will. It cannot have been much later that, clearly still very angry, he wrote the following in his 'diary':

"*April 21st: 1725. Mr Hunter dyed like a Cheating false Villain, having many Relations wch he never ownd, to whom he left all he had, except the base Estate at Dulwich, & even the furniture of the House he left to be gatted*[484] *by them*".

Once he had calmed down, Lynn might have realised that he had a good deal for which to be grateful to Hunter. The chief asset was Hunter's lease from Dulwich College of the Hall Place estate, and

---

[484] 'gat' is an archaic form of 'got'.

this had been left to Lynn, for the better provision of his daughter Mary, the god-daughter of Hunter's late wife Mary. Perhaps Hunter felt that before he met his Maker it was time, after nearly fifty years, to make atonement for killing Mrs Mary Lynn's father.

As usual following a death, there was much to be done. Lynn "*caused Notice of the Testators Death to be advertized in the Publick news Papers*",[485] apparently at no cost (or none for which he subsequently sought reimbursement). "*Mrs Ellen*" (Eleanor Farmer) needed £1 15*s* 8½*d* immediately for house-keeping money, which Lynn paid on the day that Hunter died. (He paid her another four guineas three days later.) "*Oliver*" (Thomas Oliver) and "*Thomas*" (Thomas Allen) had to be kitted out for something suitable to wear for the funeral, and were given a guinea each by Lynn "*to buy in Hats, Shoes &c.*", and another £4 7*s* "*for Cloath*". The ladies ("*Mrs Ellen [Farmer] and Mrs Mary [Lynn]*") also needed funeral outfits, on which Lynn spent £4 5*s* 6*d* "*for Crape and linings*" and four shillings "*for fans*", as well as another eight shillings for "*Shoes 3s 6d and Gloves 4s 6d for Mrs Ellen*". Twelve mourning rings were bought from "*Mr Newton the Goldsmith*" at a cost of £10 4*s*, for those of Hunter's former colleagues, friends, and neighbours who were to attend his funeral, as well as for old Oliver and young Thomas.[486] Hunter had specified that his funeral was to take place at the College Chapel in Dulwich village, and that "*no more than two Coaches do attend my Herse for the carrying my Servants principally & such Relations as may attend the same*", followed by interment in the tomb where his "*dear*

485 *Stokoe v Lynn* (1727): TNA, C 11/693/20.
486 *Stokoe v Lynn* (1727): TNA, C 11/693/20.

departed wife" lay.[487]

The funeral duly took place on 1st May, and "*Gay the Brick-layer*"[488] was employed to open the vault to receive Hunter's coffin, and then close it up again. Robert Gay's services cost Lynn 8s 7d, and the funeral account itself was £40 3s 6d. With another £6 2s paid to Eleanor Farmer the following week for housekeeping, by 10th May Lynn had spent a total of £74 4s 3½d, but he was able to recoup most of this from a £50 note and £17 0s 2½d cash found in the house.[489] Hunter had been attended in his final illness by Dr John Beaufort (or Beauford), "*a Jacobite physician of considerable eminence*",[490] whose ten-guinea fee Lynn later paid.

If permitted, Hunter had asked for a plain plaque to be fixed over the pew in the College Chapel in which he and his wife habitually sat, with a suitable inscription composed[491] by his friend Francis Lynn for that and for the Hunters' tomb. Although it has not been used for burials since the 19th century, there are still over a hundred marked graves in the Old

---

[487] TNA, PROB 11/603/342. According to later evidence, none of Hunter's relatives (apart, possibly, from his two Executors) attended his funeral, simply because they lived too far away for the news of his death to have reached them in time.

[488] This was Robert Gay, lessee of *The Bricklayers Arms* (later renamed *The French Horn*) in Dulwich Village. He also occupied, as tenant of Mr John Righton, copyholder, one of two houses on the site of Allison Grove. (The other was occupied by Samuel Hunter's friend Thomas Normandy.)

[489] *Stokoe v Lynn* (1727): TNA, C 11/693/20.

[490] but no stranger to the bottle, according to various authors (all of whom seem to have copied from the same primary source).

[491] The inscription would have been in Latin, demonstrating Lynn's classical education.

Burial Ground in Dulwich Village, but now no trace of the Hunters' vault, and no trace of any plaque commemorating the Hunters in the Old Chapel.

It cannot have taken Francis Lynn long to notice that not only was Hunter's Will not dated – not in itself a fatal flaw – but it was not signed by Hunter himself or witnessed by anyone else. Normally three witnesses were required, or at least expected. And yet it had obviously been written by Hunter's own hand, was extremely detailed, and clearly expressed his considered wishes. Could it be ignored, or suppressed? From Lynn's point of view, and since neither he nor any member of his family could inherit on an intestacy as they were not related to Samuel Hunter by blood, this could only be if there were a previous Will, properly executed, which left Lynn a legacy worth at least that given by this last Will. We can safely assume that Lynn searched thoroughly for such an earlier Will, but could not find one because it did not exist. It was therefore in his interests to seek to have the putative Will admitted to probate, even though this would mean sharing Samuel Hunter's estate with people who to Lynn were perfect strangers.

Although the nephew John Hawkins was in business as a goldsmith in London, at the time of his uncle's death he was still in Lincolnshire. As soon as he received Lynn's letter he hurried south to the capital, where he met up with William Fenwick, who had also heard of Hunter's death (possibly from the announcement in one of the "*Publick news Papers*" which Lynn had arranged) and had travelled down to London from his home in Bedlington, County

Durham.[492]

So far as it is possible to establish the facts when the parties to litigation are, for their own ends, telling lies on which they do not think they can be caught out, or not telling the whole truth, or obfuscating whatever truth they are telling, it seems that after the two nephews met up in London, they set off together for Dulwich, where they found Francis Lynn and his family in occupation of Hall Place. Lynn eventually admitted to them that there was a Will, that he had it, and that Hawkins and Fenwick were appointed Executors, *"notwithstanding which the said Francis made several frivolous excuses to avoid producing the same"*. Hawkins and Fenwick were obliged to apply to a Proctor for Directions to Lynn to produce the Will. Despite getting such Directions, and informing Lynn's lawyer, Walter Pryse, of them, the Will was still not forthcoming, so that their next step was to obtain Further Directions from the Proctor, Mr Sandford Neville, and to issue a Citation against Lynn (requiring him either to produce a Will or to concede that it did not exist). This worked, and Lynn, or someone on his behalf, brought the putative Will to Mr Neville's office.

As soon as they read the Will, and consulted with their own lawyer about it, Hawkins and Fenwick would have realised that they too were in a quandary similar to Lynn's. If the unsigned, unwitnessed, and undated document was not submitted for probate, then in the absence of any earlier valid Will Samuel Hunter would be deemed to have died intestate, and his estate, or such of it as he was competent to

---

[492] *Lynn v Hawkins* (1726): TNA, C 11/277/32.

dispose of by Will, would be divisible between those entitled according to the rules of intestate succession. Admittedly Hawkins and Fenwick would, as the children of two of Hunter's deceased sisters, have been entitled to a share, but maybe not to as much – particularly in Hawkins' case – as they would if the Will were valid. That was because Hawkins and Fenwick, as well as being appointed executors, were also named as the only residuary beneficiaries, and Hawkins alone was also designated as beneficiary of some potentially valuable properties in Hampshire. It was therefore vitally important for them to find out as much as they could, as quickly as possible, about the assets and liabilities of Samuel Hunter's estate. They would have been reassured by Hunter's own statement in the Will that his debts "*thank God are very small*", but the gift of residue was subject to various bequests and legacies, the value of which had to be taken into account in calculating the likely residue.

If there were an intestacy, who would be entitled? Different rules applied to realty (essentially that meant freehold properties) and personalty (which meant everything else,[493] including leaseholds and personal chattels). In the absence – as in Samuel Hunter's case – of a surviving spouse, or issue, or parents, realty passed to the heir-at-law, who would normally be the eldest brother, but if there were no brother (and no descendants of any such brother) then any sisters were equally entitled as heirs. If any sister had predeceased, that sister's heir would also be decided in accordance with the rule of primogeniture, with preference given to males.

---

[493] except copyholds, which had their own special rules.

With personalty, the rules of intestate succession were subtly different, and derived from two statutes passed during the reign of Charles II, in 1670 and 1685, and known collectively as the 'Statutes of Distribution'. In circumstances such as those which applied in the Hunter case, these bore a striking resemblance to the intestacy rules which have applied to all types of property since 1925. In other words, the heirs were whoever was next-of-kin, which meant Hunter's four sisters, with the issue of those who had predeceased standing 'according to the stocks' (or, as lawyers used to say, '*per stirpes*') in their parent's shoes, share and share alike, regardless of gender. Since Samuel Hunter – as Hawkins and Fenwick soon discovered – owned both freehold and leasehold properties, as well as other forms of personalty, both sets of rules would be relevant.

Samuel Hunter is known from later litigation to have had four siblings, all female: Frances, Elizabeth, Deborah, and Catherine. There are baptismal records for three children of Thomas Hunter of Bishopwearmouth in Northumberland, namely Samuel (8th June 1651), Frances (10th October 1655), and Elizabeth (10th July 1656), but I have traced no birth or baptismal records for Deborah or Catherine Hunter, and no marriage records for any of them apart from Samuel. According to the court records, Frances Hunter had married Barnaby Fenwick, gentleman, of Bedlington, Durham, and had at least two children, William Fenwick and his unnamed sister. Elizabeth Hunter had married a Mr Hawkins, and had one child, John Hawkins. Deborah Hunter had married William Hall, of Ovingham, Northumberland, and had six children: Thomas,

Margaret (who was married to William Richardson), Elizabeth (who was married to George Johnson), Deborah (who had married John Fenwick, possibly a cousin), Dorcas (who had married Francis Wilson), and Catherine Hall. The fourth sister, Catherine Hunter, had married a yeoman, John Stokoe, of Greenside, Durham, and had three children: Thomas, John, and Stephen Stokoe. Of the four sisters, Elizabeth, Deborah and Frances had all predeceased Hunter (as had their respective husbands and John Stokoe senior). Samuel Hunter's other sister, widow Catherine Stokoe, was still alive.

Of the nieces and nephews, John Hawkins, Thomas Hall, Margaret Richardson, Elizabeth Johnson, Deborah Fenwick, Dorcas Wilson, Thomas, John and Stephen Stokoe, and William Fenwick, were all living at Hunter's death. William Fenwick's unnamed sister may or may not have predeceased Hunter. Catherine Hall had married one George Slater,[494] but had died, survived by her husband George and five children: Ann (who was married to Robert Cutter, of Berwick Hill, Northumberland), John, Deborah, Catherine and Elizabeth Slater, who were all "*infants*" (i.e. minors, under 21).[495]

Thus, if Samuel Hunter had died intestate, those entitled to share his 'real' estate would be:

---

[494] It would be remarkable if this were the same George Slater who in 1715 was landlord of the Dolphin Inn in Dover – see Chapter 8 – but the name is not that uncommon.

[495] Hunter's family tree can be constructed from the pleadings in the litigation which ensued over his Will, particularly *Hall v Fenwick* (1727): TNA, C 11/1742/1.

- as to one-quarter: John Hawkins (as heir-at-law of Elizabeth Hawkins, one of Hunter's deceased's sisters);

- as to one-quarter: Thomas Hall (as heir-at-law of Deborah Hall, another of Hunter's deceased sisters);

- as to one-quarter: Catherine Stokoe (as Hunter's surviving sister); and

- as to the remaining one-quarter: William Fenwick (as heir-at-law of the late Frances Fenwick, the last of Hunter's deceased sisters).

Those entitled to share Hunter's 'personal' estate in the event of a deemed intestacy would be:

- as to one-quarter: John Hawkins (as sole child of Elizabeth Hawkins);

- as to 5/24ths: equally between Thomas Hall, Margaret Richardson, Elizabeth Johnson, Deborah Fenwick, and Dorcas Wilson (as surviving children of Deborah Hall);

- as to 1/24th: equally between Ann Cutter, John Slater, Deborah Slater, Catherine Slater, and Elizabeth Slater (as children of Deborah Hall's other child, Catherine Slater deceased), who were thus entitled to 1/120th each;

- as to one-quarter: Catherine Stokoe (as Hunter's surviving sister); and

- as to the remaining one-quarter: equally between William Fenwick, his unnamed sister (or, if she had predeceased, her children in equal shares), and any other children (such as John Fenwick) of the late Frances Fenwick, the last of Hunter's deceased sisters.

If the Will was not admitted to probate, then all the bequests and legacies in Hunter's Will would fail. There was the provision for Hunter's housekeeper (now "*Elenor Farmer* alias *Woodroff*") in the 1715 Deed of Covenant already mentioned, as varied by the Will. Hunter's Will left his "*sister* [Catherine] *Stokoe*" an annuity of £15 a year, and on her death £200 was to be divided between her children (one of whom, John Stokoe, was forgiven the £50 debt he owed Hunter). The children of his "*Sister* [Deborah] *Hall alias Wallis*" were to share another £200, and the daughter of his "*sister* [Frances] *Fenwick deceased*" (or her children if that daughter predeceased) was to get (or were to share) £60. £100 was left to Trinity House, Hunter's former place of work, for the interest to provide each year for "*five poor Superannuated Pilots or their Widows*" not already receiving a pension. His wife's relatives Abigale Vickers and Robert (son of Levit) Thompson were to receive £10 each. There was £6 for six "*of the oldest and most necessitous poor of Dulwich*" £2 between the Poor Brothers and Sisters of the College (the men to get twice as much as the women) and a shilling each for the twelve Poor Scholars. Elenor "*my maid Servant*" (i.e. Eleanor Farmer) was to get £10, and Hunter's other servants (including Thomas Oliver and Thomas Allen, "*yeomen*", who later attested to knowledge of his handwriting) £5 ("*to buy them mourning*") and three months' wages each.

Francis Lynn, "*my friend and relation … to the intent he may make the better provision for my Wifes God-daughter Mary*" was left "*the Lease that I hold of Dulwich Colledge of which my dwelling house is a part together with all the other Edifices Land and appurtenances thereunto belonging and my pretended*[496] *right of Renewing the said Lease at the present Rent*". He was to be let into possession on the Quarter Day six months from the Quarter Day following Hunter's death (June 24th, St John's Day), which meant at Christmas 1725. There was a catch, however. The gift was subject to a condition that before he took possession Lynn was to purchase an annuity or rentcharge of £8 a year, secured on some suitable property, for Hunter's servant Eleanor Farmer *alias* Woodroff.

Hunter had also left a number of poignant personal bequests. Francis Lynn was to have the diamond-and-turquoise ring "*which I commonly wear*", Lynn's wife Mary "*my two Guilt Cupps and Covers*", their daughter Elizabeth "*a pair of Diamond Shot-bucklers of my Wifes*", their "*before mentioned*" daughter[497] Mary "*the wrought Bed in the best Chamber with its appurtenances and the Chairs thereunto belonging*", and their daughter Sophia "*the Stitcht Quilt wrought by my Wife*". There were no gifts to Lynn's son Philip or daughters Ann and Arabella, but perhaps that was only because at the time of Hunter's Will and death they were respectively only 16, 14, and 9, and could not have given the executors a valid receipt for any bequests personal to them.

There was yet another gift intended for Eleanor Farmer, in consideration of her "*long and faithfull Service*". Hunter directed that "*for her better maintenance in her old age*" she was to enjoy a life interest in "*my*

---

[496] i.e. 'claimed'.
[497] This is the only internal evidence that by his earlier reference to "*my Wifes God-daughter Mary*" Hunter meant Francis Lynn's "*before mentioned*" daughter Mary, not Lynn's wife Mary.

Copyhold Estate … in Dulwich … now in the occupation of Thomas Ireland together with the Rents and Profits ariseing from those other Grounds intermixed with the said Copyhold and rented by me of the said Colledge and Joyntly occupied by the said Ireland and I do direct that my Executors do pay the Fine required for her admittance to the said Copyhold", and after her death the same was to be applied in establishing "*a Schoolmaster or Mistress for the teaching gratis four Male and four Female Children of the Inhabitants of Dulwich such as are poorest and under the degree of Farmers the first to read perfectly the new Testament and the latter the Bible perfectly as also to serve and do other plain needlework after which it is expected that the School Master of the Colledge according to his duty*[498] *will for the allowance directed by the Founder sufficiently teach the male Children aforesaid the English Tongue Writing and vulgar Arithmetick*". As we shall see, none of that happened.

Hunter left to his nephew John Hawkins his interest in lands "*at Charleton near Andover in Hantshire*". These, if you recall, had been inherited by Elizabeth Thurman from her father James Vickers, given to her daughter Mary on her marriage to Samuel Hunter, forfeited to Robert Thompson after Hunter killed Thompson's son Robert, inherited (again) by Elizabeth Thompson (formerly Thurman) on her husband's death, inherited by Mary Hunter (nee Thurman) on her mother's death, and inherited on Mary's own death by her husband Samuel Hunter. Lands which Hunter had inherited or purchased at nearby Sutton Scotney (including an inn called *The King's Head*), adjoining a copyhold which Hunter also owned (again, probably among the

---

[498] This was a dig at the Rev. James Hume, Schoolmaster-Fellow of Dulwich College, with whom Hunter had fallen out.

Hampshire properties inherited from his wife) and of which he claimed he had already made John Hawkins life tenant, were also left to Hawkins, whose estate in it was to be enlarged to the copyhold equivalent of a fee simple.

Finally, the nephews John Hawkins and William Fenwick were to share the residue *"whether in South Sea or other Stock Annuities bonds household Stuff or other Effects"*.

Allowing the intestacy rules to apply would have the advantage for Hawkins and Fenwick of denying any benefit to Francis Lynn, as the Hall Place lease would form part of residue and pass according to the Statutes of Distribution. On the other hand, although Samuel Hunter may not have got around to signing the Will, it was in his own hand and clearly reflected his considered wishes. Would it be morally right for them to disregard it? Could it be admitted to probate anyway, regardless of the patent defects in its execution? The answer to that question was, 'Yes, it could.'[499]

All these factors had to be considered, and no doubt after further discussion with their lawyer Hawkins and Fenwick decided to apply for probate of the Will in 'Common Form'. In this, although from very different motives, they would have had the support of Francis Lynn. It would still be possible for anyone with an interest on intestacy,[500] who felt that a

---

[499] This remained the case until the Wills Act of 1837 tightened up the requirements for signing and witnessing Wills.

[500] These included Eleanor Farmer. The 1715 Deed of Covenant was still valid, even if the Will might not be. Eleanor must have come to the conclusion that her potential benefits under the Will

challenge to the validity of the Will would be worth their while, to issue proceedings which would result either (if they were successful) in having the initial grant of probate revoked or (if they were not successful) in having the Will admitted to probate in 'Solemn Form', rendering it impervious to any further challenges.[501] Despite the two executors still not having full information about the assets and liabilities of the estate, the Will was duly submitted to the Masters of the Prerogative Court of Canterbury, and once the court was satisfied that the document was indeed in Samuel Hunter's own handwriting (for which his two man-servants supplied the evidence) it was admitted to probate, on 5th June 1725.[502]

At the beginning of September William Fenwick returned to Northumberland, either because he was obliged to or because he preferred to, and did not return to London until 7th August 1726, eleven months later. John Hawkins was left with the task of dealing with as much of the administration as he could, which included investigating what assets existed. He asked Francis Lynn to provide an Account of what he knew, which he later claimed Lynn several times promised, but failed, to do.

Francis Lynn and his family stayed at Hall Place for about six weeks after Samuel Hunter's death, then on or about 9th June Lynn handed over all the keys

---

were more valuable than those under the intestacy, or she may not have considered the point at all.

[501] The terms 'Common Form' and 'Solemn Form' are still relevant to probate practice today, but almost all Wills are admitted to probate in Common Form only.

[502] TNA, PROB 11/603/342.

(except for one, to a room which Lynn intended to retain for his own use) to John Hawkins, together with almost all of Hunter's goods and papers that were still on the premises – he kept the turquoise-and-diamond ring which Hunter had left him. (He later admitted that during those six weeks he and his family and friends had consumed about half a dozen bottles of Hunter's wine, which does not seem much.) Hawkins immediately returned to Lynn such of the papers as related to Hall Place itself, telling Lynn, so Lynn later claimed, "*that they were rightly his*", and allowed him the temporary use of Hunter's black writing-box – now emptied of its former contents. Soon after Hunter died another trunk, box, or portmanteau belonging to him, containing who knows what, had gone missing. Mary Lynn, Francis' wife, later swore that she knew nothing about it, save that Hunter's trusty elderly servant, Thomas Oliver had been seen to remove such an item shortly after Hunter's death, and when she was told about it – by which time Oliver was "*at some considerable distance from the House*" – she assumed that he was using the trunk to carry away goods of his own, or to which he was entitled. (Francis Lynn kept quiet on the subject of the missing trunk, and by the time it was raised, in 1729, old Oliver was dead.) The only paperwork that Lynn said he had retrieved from Hall Place (apart from the Will and the letter from John Hawkins) were two receipts for ten shillings each from the Sun Fire Office of London, the most recent dated a week before Hunter's death.[503] It was of course in Lynn's own interests that the property should be adequately insured.

---

[503] *Fenwick v Lynn* (1729), TNA C 11/1479/26.

However, there were still enough *"Deeds, Evidences and Writeings"* to enable Hawkins to piece together the main elements of Samuel Hunter's estate. The principal asset was the Hall Place lease, and even if he could not immediately gain legal possession Lynn did at least employ a gardener, Preslee,[504] to tend the grounds, and paid him £6 3s *"for Work, Seeds Plants &c which Mr Hawkins reaped the benefitt of"*.

Hall Place c.1860 (by which time it had been renamed 'The Manor House'), painted by local artist Tom Morris.

The house would not have looked very different from the one built in c.1701 by Samuel Hunter on the site of the original medieval building.

---

[504] This was probably William Presley, whose daughter was baptised in Dulwich College Chapel in 1723.

Apart from the personal chattels and Hunter's investments (about which we are told only that it amounted to a *"considerable personall Estate more than sufficient for the payment of his Debts and Funeral expenses"* and comprised *"Mony, Mony out at Interest on Mortgage & of Bills Bonds Notes & other Securityes for Money besides Debts on Simple contract & other Ways"*), were Hunter's freehold, leasehold, and copyhold properties. Hawkins made a list of them. There was the freehold estate at Sutton Scotney near Southampton, let to a local, Thomas Smith, at £15 a year. Then the *King's Head* Inn at Sutton Scotney, also let to Smith (at £26 p.a.), but Hunter had held only a 99-year lease, of which about 40 years were unexpired. Thirdly, there were lands in or near Charlton and Wildherne in Hampshire, which appeared to comprise merely an annuity or rentcharge on the reversionary interest in lands in the possession of one Giles Carter as lessee of a 99-year lease, and payable by Carter. Fourthly, there was a copyhold estate in Sutton Scotney, in the possession of one Mary Doiley or her undertenant, in which Hawkins believed Samuel Hunter had only ever had a life interest, and which never came into Hawkins' possession (despite Hunter claiming in the 1715 Deed of Covenant that he had already made Hawkins life tenant of it). Next, was the 6-acre copyhold in Dulwich, *"now or late in the possession of Thomas Ireland"*, for which Hunter had paid a quit rent of 1s 3d a year, and in which his Will directed that Eleanor Farmer was to have a life interest. (There was no mention, however, of the adjoining 5 acres for which Hunter paid Dulwich College £3 5s a year, but that was because the land was held *"at will"*, and not under a formal lease.) Last, but certainly not least, was *"One Lease hold Estate being a Mansion house with some out houses Tenements & Lands adjoyning held by Lease for Twenty One Years from Dulwich Colledg aforesaid*" at £22 a year.

As already mentioned (in Chapter 5), the Hall Place estate comprised not only the mansion house known as Hall Place, but lands and at least two other houses within the curtilage of the main house that were occupied by Hunter's sub-tenants. Mr James Causey had a house, Mr George Thompson had another, and Henry Budder (who had recently succeeded his father, Robert Budder, as tenant in his own right of a house on the north side of Dulwich Common, and 43 acres called Cokers on the south side) farmed the 29 or so acres south of the mansion house and garden. Causey paid £13 a year for his house, Thompson £7 a year for his house, and Budder £20 (less £5 for "*the Kings Tax*", leaving a net £15) for his land.

On or about 18ᵗʰ December 1725 Francis Lynn settled Eleanor Farmer's £8 p.a. annuity, which he purchased for £80 from his lawyer Walter Pryse,[505] secured on two brick-built freehold tenements owned by Pryse in St Paul's parish, Covent Garden.[506] Having therefore complied with the condition attached to his inheritance of the Hall Place estate, Lynn expected the executors to make immediate arrangements for the lease to be assigned to him. However, they took no such steps, and as Lynn recorded in his 'diary':

"*Decr: 29ᵗʰ. 1725 Mʳ Hawkins & Fenwick Execʳˢ of Mʳ*

---

[505] In his 'diary' Francis Lynn gives the date as 23ʳᵈ December 1725.
[506] *Lynn v Hawkins* (1726), TNA C 11/277/32.

Hunter refused to give me possession of [the] *Dulwich Estate left me by his Will, so I was forced to go into Chancery with them.*"

Samuel Hunter – one assumes unwittingly – had created the conditions for a perfect storm of litigation, which is what now ensued.

CHAPTER 15

Litigation, litigation, litigation

As his 'diary' indicates, between the very end of
1725 and the middle of 1729 Francis Lynn and his
wife Mary and daughter Mary were involved in a
series of court cases with Samuel Hunter's executors
and Northumbrian relatives.

The first of these was *Lynn v Hawkins*[507] (1726),
when Francis Lynn and his daughter Mary sued the
two executors, John Hawkins and William Fenwick,
complaining that the executors had not, despite Lynn
having complied with the condition in the Will
requiring him to purchase an £8 p.a. annuity for Mrs
Woodruff, transferred the lease to him, and had
damaged the property by having, Lynn alleged, "*carried
& taken away several Materials & Ornamentals which were
part & parcel of and comprised in or past by the said Will …
as appendant or appurtenant to the said Capital & other
Messuages*", in other words fixtures and fittings, and
had sold or otherwise disposed of several trees,
loppings of trees, and hay (which the executors

---

denied), and "*depastured the Meadow Grounds ... and received considerable sums of Mony for the same for which they ought to accompt ...*". Young Mary had also not received the bequest of the wrought bed and matching chairs in the "*best Chamber*". (As no mention was made of the bequests to Lynn's wife Mary and to their daughters Elizabeth and Sophia, I assume that those gifts had been retained by them when the Lynn family temporarily quit the premises in June 1725.) John Hawkins admitted that the wrought bed and chairs were in his possession, but said that he would be happy to deliver them to Miss Mary Lynn "*when ever she shall send or come to fetch them upon any reasonable Notice*". John and Eleanor Woodruff, joined (clearly unwillingly) as parties, confirmed that Eleanor was receiving her secured annuity and that they hoped that Francis Lynn would soon have possession of Hall Place. They asked to be discharged from any further involvement in the case (and could they, please, be indemnified for their costs?).

In a Further Answer John Hawkins later claimed that Francis Lynn and his family had remained at Hall Place for "*upwards of Twelve Months after the Death of the Testator before they quitted the same*", and that rather than let the property he (Hawkins) "*hath been at considerable Expence in keeping a Person upon the Premises to look after the same & prevent any damage*", and had laid out "*small sumes of Money for necessaries and Repairs in & about the sd Mansion House*", as well as paying Dulwich College £19 3s 9d for rent due from Christmas 1725 to Michaelmas 1726 (including three years' quit rent for the copyhold, at 1s 3d p.a.).[508]

---

[508] *Lynn v Hawkins* (1726), TNA C 11/277/32.

Next, in May 1727, came *Stokoe v Lynn*.[509] This time the plaintiffs were Samuel Hunter's only surviving sister, Mrs Catherine Stokoe, her nephew Thomas Hall and, perhaps surprisingly, the executor William Fenwick, suing Fenwick's co-executor John Hawkins, Francis Lynn, and Eleanor Farmer (now Woodruff). Hawkins, so the plaintiffs alleged, "*Combineing and Confederateing together*" with Eleanor Farmer, spinster (as she had been), and with Francis Lynn, had conspired with persons unknown to deprive Hunter's relatives of their just entitlements, and had failed to provide them with any Accounts or with any details of the estate's assets. The plaintiffs asserted that any disposals of those assets which had taken place since Hunter's death were "*Utterly Voyd*", because the so-called Will under which Hawkins and his confederates purported to act was invalid. Although Hawkins' and Lynn's respective Answers, denying the allegations, are in the archives, that of Eleanor Woodruff (formerly Farmer) is not, although I expect she claimed that none of this was anything to do with her, and could she have her costs, please?

The two executors, Hawkins and Fenwick, appear to have patched up their differences, if indeed they had really had any, and in the same year sued Francis Lynn's lawyer, Walter Pryse, in the case of *Fenwick v Pryse*.[510] Joined as defendants were Francis Lynn, his wife Mary, and their daughter Mary. However, the Northumbrian relatives were far from done, and in February 1727[28] the entire family (with the minor great-nephews and great-nieces represented by their

---

[509] TNA, C 11/693/20.
[510] TNA, C 11/1733/6.

uncle, Thomas Hall) issued proceedings[511] against both executors (John Hawkins and William Fenwick), Francis Lynn, John and Eleanor Woodruff, and Samuel Hunter's near neighbour and friend Thomas Normandy. We have the Bill of Complaint and the Answers of the two executors, but none of the other Answers. I think we can guess the gist of the Woodruffs' Answer in what was now the third case into which one or both had, for no good reason, been dragged.

The family's case was essentially that Hunter's supposed Will *"is void by the Statute of Frauds & Perjuryes in regard the said Will is not either Executed datyed signed nor Attested"* as that Statute required, and that accordingly, as regards the leasehold properties, *"the same ought to be distributed according to the Statute for distribution of Intestates Estates"*, and as regards the freeholds and copyholds *"not surrendered to the Uses of his Will which … none of it is"*, they ought to be divided as to 25% *"for each sister or her descendants"*. Consequently, Lynn should not be allowed to claim lost rents for Hall Place for eighteen months from Christmas 1725, as he had done. The bill for £233 17s 1d which Lynn had presented to the executors included (apart from Dr Beauford's ten guinea fee, Preslee's £6 3s gardening bill, and the £7 4s 1d still owed to Lynn after paying the funeral expenses) not only the rents for eighteen months totalling £60 (at respectively £13, £7 and £20 p.a.) due from Mr Causley and Mr Thompson for their respective houses within the grounds of Hall Place, and from Henry Budder for the Hall Place land that he farmed, but a notional £150 (at £100 p.a.) which

---

[511] *Hall v Fenwick* (1727), TNA C 11/1742/1.

Lynn claimed he could have received if the executors had not allowed Hall Place itself to remain empty for the eighteen months to midsummer 1727. Although I am sure that the property could have been sub-let for a great deal more than the £22 rent charged for it by Dulwich College, I suspect that Lynn was being optimistic, and that he knew it.

Francis Lynn's Answer sheds further interesting light on his relationship with the late Samuel Hunter. While conceding that the Northumbrians might very well share the ties of blood with Samuel Hunter that they claimed, Lynn averred that Hunter had often declared to him "*that he had no relation save Mary this Defendants Wife whom he always called his Kinswoman*" and that Lynn having in 1697 "*intermarried with his Said Wife Mary with the privity and Consent of the sd Samuel Hunter*[512] *he thereupon and frequently after … made great Protestation and Professions of Friendship to this Defendant and his said Wife declaring that this Defendants said Wife was the only relation he had and that he lay under many Obligations particularly one very Extraordinary on Account of her fathers death to provide for her and her family and often declared that when he dyed all he had in the world should be hers or to that Effect and having engaged this Defendant to live near him this Defendant at the Instance and request of the sd Samuel Hunter and purely to gratify him in his Desire took a house at Dulwich in the County of Surry as near the said Samuel Hunter as he conveniently could and resided there as often as*

---

[512] Although Mary Thompson would not have required Samuel Hunter's consent to marry Francis Lynn, this does at least indicate that Lynn and Hunter were acquainted by April 1697.

his business would permitt".[513]

The litigation dragged on, and on. In 1729 the executors, Hawkins and Fenwick, issued proceedings[514] against Francis Lynn, his wife Mary, their daughter Mary, Lynn's lawyer Walter Pryse, John and Eleanor Woodruff – what did they have to do to keep out of a dispute which no longer concerned them? – James Roche, and Thomas Powell. Roche was, of course, William Morgan's lawyer, although he may have been brought into the case on his own account, and Thomas Powell's involvement is not explained. Lynn took the opportunity of explaining the circumstances in which he had found the Will (and the two insurance receipts), and telling what he knew (which he claimed was nothing) of how Hunter's trunk or portmanteau had gone missing.

In the midst of all this unpleasantness, Francis and Mary Lynn became grandparents. Their eldest daughter Elizabeth had married a young Irish widower, Robert Cotes, who in 1716-17, when he was supposedly only 21, had been Mayor of Galway, Ireland. Charged with failing to enforce anti-Catholic laws there, he was obliged to flee to London to contest the accusation (which he did, successfully). Here he became an apothecary, with premises in increasingly fashionable Bond Street. In 1721 Cotes married for the first time, but his wife Anna (*née*

---

[513] Lynn later, in 1729, provided a further Answer, which has been filed in the National Archives as *Hall v Lynn*, TNA C 11/264/20.

[514] *Fenwick v Lynn* (1729), TNA C 11/1479/26 and C 11/1731/41.

Fowler) died in 1722,[515] and on 24th August 1724 Robert Cotes married Elizabeth Lynn.

William Morgan belatedly (in February 1726) offered congratulations to the father of the bride: "*I am heartily glad to hear my frind Mrs Betty is Marryed. I hope my Washerwoman will have soone a hapey and good husband*". The 'Washerwoman" was a reference to the Lynns' next-eldest daughter, Mary, usually known as 'Polly', but what service she had done for Morgan to earn this *soubriquet* can only be guessed at. In February 1719[20], in his last extant letter to Morgan, Lynn (who occasionally demonstrated a dry sense of humour) had written "*if you can find good Husbands for Your Washerwoman & her Elder Sister who will take them without Fortunes, you will not only very much oblige them but me too*". In the event, Mary Lynn never married.

The Cotes/Lynn marriage was soon to be blessed with issue. As Francis Lynn recorded in his 'diary':

"*May 20th: 1726. My daughter Cotes was brought to bed of a Son at ¼ past 3 in ye Morning who was Christened Francis, Myself and Mr Tho: Cowper[516] being Godfathers and Mrs Bowles[517] Godmother.*"

---

[515] From '*Dictionary of pastellists before 1800*', an essay by Neil Jeffares, augmented by information from the 1818 obituary of Samuel Cotes in *The Gentleman's Magazine*, vol. 88, part I.

[516] Perhaps a colleague of Lynn's at the Royal African Company, but otherwise the connection between the two men is unknown.

[517] I know of three mid-1720s references to a 'Mr Bowles' (first name unknown) in the Dulwich records, but then nothing until the late 1750s, when Leonard Bowles and his wife Martha appear as Dulwich tenants, successively. Mrs Martha Bowles survived until 1791. If this was the same 'Mrs Bowles', she must have been very young in 1726.

More of that grandson, Francis Cotes, later. The birth of a second grandson was recorded barely a year later:

"June 11ᵗʰ: 1727. My daughter Cotes was brought to bed of her second child a Son, about 4 a clock in the Morning, Christened Robert."

The parish register of St Mary-le-Strand (the church in which Elizabeth Lynn and Francis Cotes had been married and had both their sons baptised) records the burial on 24ᵗʰ November 1730 of Robert Cotes, *"a child"*. By that date Francis Lynn had ceased making entries in his 'diary', either because he had lost interest or because illness prevented it. There was to be a third son, Samuel, born to the Cotes in 1734, by which time Francis Lynn was dead. That son was to enjoy a very long life.

What Francis Lynn's 'diary' also failed to record was the death of his mother-in-law, Mrs Elizabeth Moreland (formerly Thompson, *née* Ashby) in August 1727. She was buried on the 16ᵗʰ of that month at St Giles Church, Camberwell (and not, perhaps significantly, with her late husband in his family vault in Strood, Kent).

Lynn was still Secretary to the Royal African Company, which after its encouraging re-start in 1720 was now struggling. Lynn tells us that at the beginning of May 1726 *"... Mʳ Joseph Cleeve Cashier to the Compᵃⁿʸ being forced for some ill practices to quitt & to leave the Kingdom, the Court of Assistants appointed me to Act as Cashier, without giving any Security, but at no Settled Salary and at Xtmas had 30 Guineas as a Gratuity"*.

However, the Company's fortunes did not improve, and on 24th June the following year, 1727, Lynn recorded that "*Upon a further Reduction in the Office My son Philips Salary (tho but £15 per annum) was taken away, And £60 a Year only allow'd Me as House keeper, out of wch I was to pay for Coales, Candles, Serv^{ts} Wages &c – And my Salary continued at £200 per annum*". His only consolation was that at Christmas 1727 the Court of Assistants ordered that he be paid a bonus of thirty guineas "*for acting as Cashier ye Year past*".

It must have been galling for Francis Lynn, whose school and university days had been filled with such promise, whose career had begun so well, to find himself in his late fifties as little more than a glorified janitor. He had been cheated (as he saw it) by Samuel Hunter, and completely misjudged "*the best Friend I ever had in the World*", William Morgan. Further evidence that he had is provided by William Morgan himself, in letters to his wife Mary, including one dated 17th November 1728, from France. Mary Morgan had informed her husband that Francis Lynn's lawyer Walter Pryse had furnished a second Stated Account which she (as her husband's attorney) and Lynn had signed on 19th December 1727.[518] (There had been an earlier one, finalised on 6th April 1726.[519]) Lynn was claiming expenses of £100 for entertainment, and not allowing interest on £800 that Lynn had received from Samuel Waller in respect of the Bacton-Cotton estates and which it seems to have

[518] TNA C 11/2201/5 refers.
[519] *Ibid.*

been conceded belonged to Morgan.[520] Morgan's response was, to say the least, disingenuous:

"I *am surprized that my old friend Frank Lynn should Charge me with his Tavern Expences when every Night of his life it was his useall Coustom to goe to a Tavern. And since he Never did me the lest Service, to the Contrary he Neglected Every thing that concern'd me, In Short he soe Neglected his freindship to me, that he lett Brigadr Corbetts Mrs Administer, & received 380£, onely for want of shewing the Power he had. And as for the Mony he received for me, surely if he Charges Mee Intrest for what Money he paid me he will think it Just to Deduct prenciple & Intrest for what Mony he received for me, at lest I am Sure Mr Prise will think it reasonable to stop it for me, and your Justice to your family will require you to Insist upon it.*"

Almost incredibly, these issues were still unresolved a decade later, long after Francis Lynn's death, when on 13th December 1739 Morgan, who by now had fallen out with his lawyer, possible cousin, and former friend, James Roche, again wrote to his wife:

"*Yoᵘ tell me that yoᵘ were goeing to a La[w]yor that Was Named Arbitrator twixt yoᵘ. and the Widdow of Frank Lynn, pray if they should Insist upon the 100£, that was Demanded for Frank Lynns Tavern Expence, let them shew Any one Act of his where he Ever served me. He had a power to receive a Debt Due from Brig Corbet of About 380£ which he had Onely to ask or put in His Claime, and which Mony Corbet's Whore received because Noe boddy else put in for it, -*

---

he Never Either Caled Waller to Acc^{tt}. Nor removed him from receiveing the rents. but left him to goe on untill he ran a thousand or Elleven hundred Pounds in Debt. Afterwards when he Desired to have Mr Roch Joyned wth him in Another Letter of Attorney, he let Roch doe all he pleased, and received the Money that he Ought to receive himselfe & which Might have long agoe bring[sic] him in yor Debt, instead of yor being in His Debt. Mr Pryse knows all this very well. It is much that the Executors of Waller cannot be brought to Justice. Pray in your next [letter] let me know where Waller lived & the Name of the next great Towne to him, & who were his Executors &c^{ra}."

William Morgan's lack of gratitude for what Francis Lynn had tried to do for him, admittedly with mixed success, is breathtaking. His economy with the truth was to have the unfortunate effect of misleading his heirs after his death in 1744, to the extent of them issuing a claim against Francis Lynn's estate for what they thought was a balance of funds still due to Morgan's estate.

However, I am running too far ahead, and should return to the litigation of the late 1720s. By 1728, as he recorded in his 'diary', Francis Lynn had at least achieved one ambition:

May 31. 1728. I took possess^n. of [the] Dulwich Estate by Order of [the] Court of Chancery.

The book in which the 'diary' is written contains many more leaves, but these are entirely blank, and the above is the very last surviving entry. The bottom half of the page on which it has been written, and which at one time clearly contained seven lines of writing of which only the first letters are partially visible, has been carefully cut away, although why, and whether by Lynn himself or by one of his descendants or of the document's later owners, is of course impossible to say. Lynn still had nearly three more years to live, during which one of his grandsons and his mother-in-law died, yet apparently he was unable to record these significant events in his 'diary'. He may perhaps no longer have felt that the details of his life were of any interest to anyone, including himself.

Samuel Hunter, you may recall, had left Francis Lynn not only his existing lease of Hall Place, but "*my pretended*[521] *right of Renewing the said Lease at the present Rent*". Hunter was not the first, and would not be the last, to be under the false impression that although Dulwich College could not, by its Statutes, grant leases for longer than 21 years it would, if the tenant observed his covenants and appreciably improved the premises, be bound to renew the lease at its expiration at the same rent. The practice had evolved of the College issuing '*recommendams*' to this effect, but there was no legal obligation on it to do so. One particularly active College Fellow, James Hume, who arrived in post in 1706, tried (with eventual success) to get the practice banned, as it meant a considerable loss of potential income for the College. Hunter ought to, indeed must, have known better, for when his lease of Hall Place had been renewed in 1703 the '*recommendam*' passed by the College Audit Meeting in 1701 was ignored, despite the substantial improvements he had made, and the rent was raised from £20 to £22 p.a. Evidently that had still rankled

---

[521] i.e. 'claimed'.

with him. As it happened, Lynn's lease of Hall Place did not come up for surrender and renewal until 1739, several years after his death, and for the remainder of his life he continued to pay Dulwich College £22 a year for the property.

Although the gift in Hunter's Will of the net rents from the five leasehold acres in Napps (sub-let to Thomas Ireland, from whom a piece of manor waste called 'Ireland Green', through which Half Moon Lane now runs, took its name) was as effective as any of the others, that of the adjoining 6 acres would not have been unless Samuel Hunter had previously surrendered the copyhold to the uses declared in his Will, which contained no such specific provision. The direction that after Eleanor Farmer's death the net rents and profits of both parcels were to be applied in funding a schoolmaster for local children not at Dulwich College hints at an *animus* against the College Schoolmaster. James Hume and Hunter had had a prolonged and heated argument regarding the latter's idea of allowing Dulwich's copyholders, of whom of course Hunter was one, to acquire parts of the Common, preferably those parts fronting their existing premises. (This was in fact essentially what happened anyway, following the Act of Inclosure of Dulwich Common eighty years later.) As Dr Jan Piggott relates, in his definitive '*Dulwich College: A History 1616-2008*':

"*In crossing an important tenant such as Mr Hunter …, Hume brought down upon himself and the College an act of revenge. According to Young,*[522] *Hunter's aim in instigating a*

---

[522] William Young, '*The History of Dulwich College, Down to … 1857*', I, p.230.

*Visitation of the College by Archbishop William Wake[523] was
simply to gain a revision of the statute restricting leases such as
his to a term of 21 years. It would appear, however, that he
also sought the elimination of the Dividend payments,[524] the
intrusion of the 'Junior Fellows' who had been legally dispensed
with in 1628, and, above all, the dismissal of the Schoolmaster.
Hume was accused on five grounds… . Hunter must have
considered Hume a very serious obstacle to his ends to have
concerted such a powerful attack against him; and for this we do
not have to rely on Hume's evidence alone. An anonymous
letter,[525] possibly by Hunter, among Archbishop Wake's
papers is directed against the Schoolmaster's failure to carry out
the preaching role assigned to his post, and promises to go
beyond the Archbishop to Parliament, the Lord Chancellor
and, if necessary, the Crown to attain this end."*

Hunter may be forgiven for failing fully to
understand the rules relating to inheritance as applied
to Dulwich copyholds, which were far from
straightforward, although he should have learned
something from his previous dealings with his
Dulwich holding following the death of Elizabeth
Thompson in 1700 when, as the copyholder, he
surrendered his Dulwich copyhold to his wife Mary
and himself for life, thereafter to the uses declared by

---

[523] According to Alleyn's Statutes, the Archbishop of Canterbury
for the time being was *ex officio* to be the College 'Visitor', with
power to oversee the running of the College and to settle
disputes between its Members.
[524] The Master, Warden, and Fellows of the College were entitled
to share the profits of its estates, according to a formula laid
down by Alleyn's Statutes.
[525] *Wake MSS, Christ Church, Oxford: Epistles 27, pp. 218-20,*
tracked down by Allan Ronald.

the Will of the survivor. As Hunter's relatives were not slow to point out, his Will was silent regarding the Dulwich copyhold, and it was doubtful whether the clause disposing of residue covered it. The custom of the manor did not allow for the possibility of life tenants, let alone the setting up of charitable trusts, so if Hunter's intentions that Eleanor Farmer should enjoy a life interest in his six copyhold acres (near the north end of Croxted Lane, now Croxted Road), followed by an educational trust, were to be realised, it would be necessary for those who were entitled to be admitted as tenants, according to the customary rules, to agree that the net rents and profits of the land should be so applied. Who were those persons, anyway? The Homage – those villagers who decided such matters – were faced with a situation without exact precedent. Samuel Hunter had died without issue. If he had left sons and daughters, the youngest son, according to the custom of the manor, would have been entitled to inherit. If he had left only daughters, they would have inherited equally. For a copyholder who had died without a spouse, issue, or surviving parents, and who had not previously surrendered his copyhold to the uses declared in his last Will – which Samuel Hunter could not have done, or events would have taken a different turn – one looked for an heir to the deceased's siblings. In this case those siblings were all female.

The Steward of the manor – a lawyer employed by Dulwich College – would have been asked by the College to look through the available manor rolls for a copyhold admission as similar to the Hunter case as he could find. He is likely, in his researches, to have encountered the case of Richard Wright, a copyholder whose death was reported at the manor court held on 10th May 1574. Wright had left five daughters, aged from 16 down to 9 months, and they were all admitted as his heirs.[526] On that analogy, if Samuel Hunter's four sisters had all survived him they would all have been admitted as equal tenants-in-common, but only one of them, Mrs Catherine Stokoe, was still alive. The Homage therefore had a choice between adopting the rules of inheritance relating to leasehold properties, or those relating to freehold properties. When the members of the Homage looked at Hunter's family tree, and realised that adopting the former solution would result in having a minimum of fourteen persons, some of them minors, admitted as tenants of Hunter's copyhold, they must have baulked at the idea. Perhaps justifying its decision on the basis that Dulwich copyholds, being heritable, were more akin to freeholds than leaseholds, the Homage took the pragmatic approach: to treat the heir-at-law of each deceased sister, and the surviving sister, as the joint and several heirs. Thus the copyhold heirs were agreed to be Mrs Catherine Stokoe (as the surviving sister), John Hawkins (as heir of Elizabeth Hawkins), William Fenwick (as heir of Frances Fenwick) and Thomas Hall (as heir of Deborah Hall), and they were duly admitted. I doubt very much whether they, or any of them, agreed to execute a declaration of trust in favour of Mrs Eleanor Woodruff, to enable her, as Samuel Hunter had intended, to receive the rental income paid by Thomas Ireland for the property, let alone so that the net rents or profits should be applied after Mrs Woodruff's death to fund a

---

[526] DCA, Court Roll CR I1(v), ll.34-38 and I2(v), ll.84-86.

Schoolmaster for local children. They derived their title from rules of customary inheritance, not from Hunter's Will, so there was no reason why they should have agreed otherwise.

First, however, there was the question of a 'Heriot'. This was the deceased copyholder's 'best beast', or a payment of its equivalent value in lieu. Hunter's coach horse, or one of them, was delivered to the College and sold for £15 19*s*, as appears in the Warden's Accounts for 27th August 1725.[527] That was followed three days later by the payment of the requisite Entry Fine by the four incoming copyhold tenants.[528] One assumes that at the next manor court they, or their representative, made fealty in accordance with ancient custom. By 1744, as it happens, all four tenants-in-common had died, and over the following year their respective heirs were admitted at the manor court to their respective one-quarter shares.

The birth of his first grandchildren and the complications following the death of Samuel Hunter must have prompted Francis Lynn to think seriously about his own mortality, and on 20th October 1727 he made his last Will, giving his address as African House, Leadenhall Street. Without, as was still customary among testators, commending his soul to Almighty God or expressing any hope of resurrection to eternal life – his faith as a "*zealouse*" Church of England man in 1714 appears to have dwindled away to nothing – Lynn left his entire estate – apart from £10 given to his daughter Elizabeth Cotes "*to buy her*

---

[527] DCA, Bickley's Catalogue 30.
[528] *Ibid.*

mourning" – to his *"deare and well beloved Wife Mary Lynn"* upon certain trusts to which I will return in the next Chapter, and appointed her to be sole executor. I would guess that he made his Will without the benefit of qualified legal advice, as although short and apparently simple, the Will[529] is not without its problems, and sparked later litigation between Lynn's widow and one of their daughters.

Lynn and his family still used Hall Place when they were not living at African House, and having already been the victims of a break-in there in 1719 they – or specifically Mrs Lynn – suffered another theft early in 1731. Mary Lynn, *"wife of Francis Lynn of Dulwich, gent."*, laid information before the authorities that a quilted silk petticoat, a linen gown, an old handkerchief, and *"several other things"* had gone missing from her house, and she suspected Elizabeth Taylor – a maidservant, one assumes – of being the culprit.[530]

Mary Lynn was having a bad year, as her husband Frank was dying, if not already dead. *The Gentleman's Magazine and Historical Review*[531] reported that *"Francis Lynn Esq., Secretary to the Royal African Company, died this day"*, 5th April 1731. Like his father,[532] he died in his 60th year.

---

[529] TNA, PROB 11/644/349.

[530] Surrey History Centre, TNA ref: QS2/6/1731/Eas/12.

[531] vol. I, p.173, col. 1.

[532] Actually Francis Lynn may have been mistaken about his father's age – see Chapter 1. The only possibly relevant entry I can trace is for John Lyn, son of Peter Lyn, baptised at St Margaret's Westminster in April 1630, which would make John Lynn 61, and in his 62nd year, when he died on 18th December 1691.

CHAPTER 16

'Philly', 'Samick', and Capt. Morgan

Francis Lynn's wife and children were all in England at the time of his death on 5th April 1731, with one exception – his only surviving son, of whom fifteen years before, when Philip was only seven, Lynn had expressed the belief that he "*will never make a soldier*". Philip Lynn, whether by temperament or physical constitution, was evidently not cut out for a military career (despite having been commissioned as an Ensign in the Army before he was four years old!).

Aged eight, 'Philly' was "*putt to School to Mr Hume at Dulwich College*"[533] on 24th July 1716. He was not actually enrolled at the College, as that privilege, if at the time it could be so considered, was reserved for 'Poor Scholars', preferably orphans or with parents 'on the parish', born in one of the four London parishes for which the College's Founder, Edward Alleyn, had provided in his Statutes. Their number was limited to twelve at any one time, but the College Statutes also provided that, in addition to teaching the

---

533 Francis Lynn's 'diary'.

twelve Poor Scholars "*good and sound learning, wryting, reading, grammar, musique and good manners*", the Schoolmaster and the Usher (two of the College's four Fellows, under the Master and the Warden) "… *shall freely, without recompence or reward, teach and instruct the children of the inhabitants within Dulwich … in writing and grammar*"[534], provided that in doing so they did not neglect their duty to the Poor Scholars.

The Schoolmaster, or Second Fellow, had since 1706 been the Revd. James Hume, son of a Scottish Episcopalian minister. After graduating from the University of Edinburgh and being ordained in London (by the Bishop of London), Hume was formally appointed by, most unusually, an Order of the Archbishop of Canterbury (who was, *ex officio*, the College 'Visitor'); the customary method established by Alleyn, but not used on this occasion, was of winning a ballot by drawing the slip bearing the device *'God's Gift'*.

One of the most intelligent and energetic men to hold office in the Old College – not that the competition in those respects was that strong – Hume set about improving the College's lax organisation and increasing its revenues from its estates. The College's practice of issuing *'recommendams'* to enable existing tenants to have their leases renewed after 21 years at the same rent, was a particular bugbear of his. As we have seen, he made an enemy of Samuel Hunter in this respect and in others, and met with opposition, or at least apathy, even from some of his colleagues.

---

[534] *Statutes and Ordinances* (dated 29th September 1626), Item 65. Printed in full in W. H. Blanch's *'Ye Parish of Camerwell'* (1875), Appendix pp. xiii-xxxiv.

Hunter (or a supporter of his) alleged that Hume refused to give free teaching to the children of Dulwich inhabitants, as required by the Statutes. In admitting the charge in his response to Archbishop Wake's Vicar-General, Hume asserted that to do so would demean his status and that of the College. He thought that the task would be better carried out at a dame-school.[535]

Hume may have objected to giving free tuition, but evidently saw nothing wrong with charging for his services, albeit modestly. Francis Lynn paid him ten shillings a quarter for his son's education. Hume would have tutored other private pupils, probably including William Andrews, grandson of Lady ('Dame Rosamund') Booth and two or three years older than Philip Lynn. Perhaps it was on a visit to the College to settle up with Hume that Lady Booth ran into Francis Lynn on a similar mission, and arranged for him and James Hume to witness her signing of her Will,[536] in June 1718.

By then Philip Lynn had left James Hume's pedagogic care, and according to his father's 'diary' was sent in early May 1718 to board at a school in Chiswick (near to his uncle Samuel's house in Little Sutton) run by a Mr George Hay, at the considerably increased charge of £20 a year. His military prospects had vanished. When his regiment was disbanded at Christmas 1712 he had been put on half-pay, and on 27th June 1717, being a minor (he was still only nine)

---

[535] For a more detailed account of James Hume's background and career at Dulwich, see Dr Jan Piggott's '*Dulwich College – A History 1616-2008*' (2008).
[536] TNA, PROB 11/565/218.

was "*struck out of that likewise*".[537]

We hear nothing more of Philip Lynn[538] until 25th March 1724, when no doubt thanks to his father's influence he was admitted as a clerk in his father's office at the Royal African Company, of which Francis Lynn had been the Chief Secretary since 1720. Initially Philip was on a salary of £30 a year, but the Company was struggling to make profits, and a year later his salary was halved. The Company's affairs did not improve, and in June 1727 Philip's salary, "(*tho but £15 p.a.) was taken away*". There was nothing for it but to use his father's connections and his own wits, and try to earn a living by commissions rather than on a salary.

So Philip Lynn sailed away to join the Royal African Company's establishment on the Gold Coast as a 'factor', or merchant, on what was then considered to be Guinea and is now partly in Ghana, where there were numerous forts and trading posts, some French or Portuguese but mostly either English or Dutch. Prior to mid-March 1731 he was stationed at the large English fort of Cape Coast Castle, but on 17th March he arrived at the Company's smaller outpost at Dixcove[539] (formerly Dick's or Dickie's Cove), some sixty miles to the west, where he immediately assumed joint responsibility with the new station 'Chief' for "*all the Goods Merchandize & Provisions Slaves for Shipping &[cete]ra belonging &*

---

[537] Francis Lynn's '*diary*'.

[538] In a letter to Francis Lynn of 6th November 1720, William Morgan asked to be remembered to his wife, daughters, mother-in-law, and "*the little Yonker*" (i.e. 'young person'), by which he must have meant Philip, now 12.

[539] Now preserved as Fort Metal Cross, Ghana.

appertaining to the Royal African Company of England &
w[hi]ch Remained in the warehouses of their Fort of Dixcove".
These included *"midling"* perpets,[540] trading guns and a
birding gun, 990lbs of gunpowder, 657lbs of lead
shot, quantities of brass pans and kettles, bars of iron
and copper, sheets, 36 gallons of rum, seersuckers,[541]
beef, elephant tusks (described as *"Large Teeth"*) and
teeth (*"Small Teeth"*), corn, a five-handed canoe and a
seven-handed canoe, one female slave, and an ounce-
and-a-half of gold. Some of these goods, and more
which had arrived from Cape Coast Castle with Philip
Lynn, were over the next few days bartered with
native chiefs for more gold, three elephant tusks, five
male slaves, six more chests of corn, and 62½ gallons
of palm oil. Whichever Company vessel or hired
canoe had brought Philip Lynn to Dixcove returned
two days later to Cape Coast Castle with William
Shuckworth the retiring Chief (who was replaced as
such by Vincent Rice, probably the son of Francis
Lynn's old adversary, Col. John Rice)[542] – and the
female slave.

When fully garrisoned, the fort at Dixcove could
hold a complement of several dozen men, but
relations with the local tribal chiefs – principally of
the Ashanti – must have been relatively stable, as

---

[540] Perpets were lengths of perpetuana, a durable woollen twill
fabric. Among its uses were bed-covers, coat-linings, and
draperies.
[541] Seersucker was (and is) a thin cotton fabric, suitable for light
clothing.
[542] Vincent Rice would certainly have remembered Philip's father
Francis Lynn from Westminster School. Lynn had been Senior
Scholar there in 1689, as Rice was in 1695, and both went on to
Cambridge on scholarships, Lynn in 1691 and Rice in 1699.

apart from Rice, Lynn, and a Corporal/gunner, there were but five soldiers stationed there at this time.

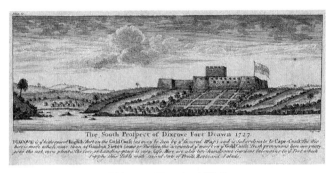

Dixcove Fort in 1727.

Every few days merchant ships would arrive from England, some from Liverpool or Bristol but mostly from London, bringing goods and provisions and taking on board slaves bound for the West Indies. During Philip Lynn's brief time at Dixcove the *'Garraway'* and the *'William & Joseph'* arrived in late March, and the *'Suffolk'* on 1st April, all from London. The *'Mermaid'* moored up the following day. On 13th April the *'Success'*, under Captain Robert Cummings, arrived. Its port of origin is not given, but was probably London, in which case Capt. Cummings would almost certainly have brought a letter for Philip Lynn from his mother, telling him of his father's death.

But Philip himself was mortally ill, and the Dixcove Journal records that on 29th April 1731 *"Mr Philip Lynn, Factor, dyed"*. He was not yet 23, and had outlived his father by barely three weeks. We are not told what caused his death, but yellow fever and malaria, both of them mosquito-borne and with similar unpleasant symptoms and usually fatal consequences, were (and to a lesser extent still are) endemic on the Gold Coast.[543] At Lynn's funeral his colleagues, despite their brief acquaintance with him, marked the occasion with twenty pounds of gunpowder and five gallons – supposedly between only six drinkers! – of rum. (Three months later the 'Chief', Vincent Rice, also died,[544] and although his death was likewise marked with a gunpowder salute, nothing was spent on rum, possibly because none was left.) [545]

Thus passed the last surviving son of Francis and Mary Lynn, and grandson of Lt. Robert Thompson and his wife Elizabeth. A wretched and premature end to a life rather less distinguished than his late father must have hoped.

Back in England, Francis Lynn's widow and daughters had by now learned the contents of Lynn's last Will, made in October 1727, if they did not already know them. They might reasonably have expected Lynn to have regarded his son Philip as his principal heir, subject perhaps to legacies for each of his daughters, with suitable provision, perhaps in the form of a life interest in residue, for his wife. This, they discovered, was by no means the case. Apart from the £10 legacy to the eldest daughter Elizabeth

---

[543] Nine days earlier one of the Dixcove soldiers, Patrick Read, had died, probably from the same cause.

[544] Again, probably from malaria or yellow fever.

[545] The information relating to Philip Lynn's time in West Africa is from the Dixcove Journal (TNA ref: T 70/1466), to which my attention was drawn by a reference to his death in late April 1731 *"at Dixcove on the Gold Coast of Africa"* in the Bill of Complaint in the case of *Kelsey v Lynn* (1746), TNA ref C 11/2299/40.

Cotes, Mrs Mary Lynn was left an unfettered life interest in the entire estate, on the understanding that she would use it to provide *"for the Maintenaunce and Education of such of my Children as at the time of my decease are unmarryed, shall nott have beene marryed, or be unprovided for"*, as well as for herself, and that on her own death whatever was left would go *"betweene such of my said Children as shall have beene unprovided for as aforesaid, in such proportion as my said wife shall ... appoint and direct"*. If his wife failed to exercise that power of appointment, the residue was to go *"betweene such of my Children unprovided for, share and share alike"*. His *"deare and well beloved Wife Mary"* was appointed sole executor and trustee. William Hagar, Gentleman, of St Bride's parish, London, and James Forbes, of the parish of St Katharine Cree, London (where Lynn had attended services and where his daughter Elizabeth was married), as acquaintances of Lynn's of more than ten years' standing, both testified to the Will (which was not formally witnessed) being in Lynn's hand-writing, and it was duly admitted to probate on 31st May 1731.

Francis Lynn may have supposed that his son Philip's constitution was too weak to make it likely that he would survive for long – in which case he was right – and his daughter Elizabeth, on whose marriage to a well-respected and prosperous apothecary, Robert Cotes, her father had settled a marriage 'portion' of at least £500,[546] could hardly expect to receive from his estate anything more than her £10 legacy. However, all of Lynn's other surviving children were unmarried. Perhaps Lynn felt that his children did not show their

---

[546] *Kelsey v Lynn* (1746), TNA C 11/2299/40.

mother sufficient respect,[547] and the Will was intended by him as a device to enable her to exercise control over them. Thus if they hoped eventually to inherit anything from their father's estate, they had to be nice to their mother.

Samuel Lynn, Mary's brother-in-law, owned his leasehold house in Spring Garden until at least 1728, and on 18th June 1723 had mortgaged it for £600, ostensibly to a London mercer, James Colebrook.[548] However, on the same date Colebrook made a declaration of trust[549] in favour of a London haberdasher called Joseph Cam. Most declarations of trust, being as it were 'behind the title', do not survive, but this one has, so we know that the money was in fact advanced by Cam, for whom Colebrook was acting as intermediary, probably without Lynn's knowledge. On 27th March 1728 Lynn remortgaged the property for £3,000 to William Chetwynd of Dover Street, Hanover Square. Of the £3,000, £1,907 15*s* 4*d* was paid to Lynn and the remaining £1,092 4*s* 8*d* to Joseph Cam, and as security the various lease terms were assigned by James Colebrooke to Chetwynd.[550] From the fact that William Chetwynd was not listed among Samuel Lynn's creditors after his death, one assumes that by then the property had been sold and the mortgage paid off.

---

[547] From a man who to his friends referred to his wife as 'Puddy', signifying 'short and stout', this might be considered somewhat hypocritical.

[548] LMA, ACC/0530/ED/14/003.

[549] LMA, ACC/0530/ED/14/004.

[550] LMA, ACC/0530/ED/14/006.

Samuel's wife Elizabeth – 'Goody' – had died on 15th January 1723[24] *"of a long & lingring Sickness"* (according to her brother-in-law Francis Lynn.)[551] A happier event occurred exactly six months later, when their daughter Henrietta was married to Richard Holford, of Avebury in Wiltshire.[552] Holford's grandfather, Sir Richard Holford (who was 'Goody' Lynn's mother's brother, so Henrietta and Richard were in fact second cousins), had been a Chancery Master, and young Richard was himself a lawyer, admitted to Lincoln's Inn in June 1719.[553] As usual on such occasions, there was a marriage settlement, as part of which Samuel Lynn was supposed to settle £1,500 *"as the portion or fortune"* on his son-in-law. However, he not only failed to do so, but during the course of the next ten years had to borrow £1,500 from Holford. To put it bluntly, Samuel Lynn was broke, and Richard Holford was obliged to sue his-father-in-law for the full £3,000, for which he obtained judgment in the court of King's Bench in Michaelmas Term 1734.[554] Lynn must have accepted the justice of this, as he subsequently appointed Holford to be one of his executors.

Whether his Tidmarsh estate failed to produce the income it should have done, or whether he lived beyond his means, or both, Samuel Lynn spent most of the last fifteen years of his life in debt, with only the Tidmarsh estate as acceptable security for anyone

[551] Francis Lynn's *'Diary'*.
[552] Marriage Allegation, TNA ref: DL/A/D/004/MS10091/074.
[553] *The Records of the Honorable Society of Lincoln's Inn, 1420-1799*, vol. I (1896).
[554] *Lynn v Cotman* (1739), TNA, C 11/784/44. Answer of Richard Holford.

from whom he wished to borrow money. According to his son-in-law Richard Holford, Lynn "*did in his life time take up divers sumes of Money of severall persons at Interest And that for securing the payment thereof he did make and Execute One or More Mortgage or Mortgages of the said Manor Lands and Premises And that he did by Judgments and otherwise subject the same to the payment of divers other summes of Money …*".[555]

Early in 1730 one Mary Granger of Bedford, Widow, was looking for "*some good Security*" on which to lend £1,600, and Samuel Lynn (probably introduced to Mrs Granger by Samuel Child, a London banker) proposed his manor of Tidmarsh as suitable. Thereupon, by indentures of lease and release dated 25th and 26th February 1729[30] Lynn mortgaged his Tidmarsh estate to Mrs Granger in return for her loan of £1,600, subject to his right to redeem on payment by a specified date (which did not happen) of £1,672. With interest, the amount increased to £1,679 10s, at which point Lynn applied to Samuel Child to lend him the £1,679 10s and another £520 10s (to make £2,200 in all) upon the existing security, to which Child agreed. Accordingly, by another lease and release dated 1st and 2nd April 1731, Samuel Lynn mortgaged the Tidmarsh estate to Mr Child, and Mrs Granger received her £1,679 10s.[556] Later, on 21st May 1735, Lynn borrowed another £800 from Child, to make the loan £3,000 in all, and since no capital or interest had been returned

---

[555] *Lynn v Cotman* (1739), TNA, C 11/784/44. Answer of Richard Holford.

[556] On her instruction this was paid to her brother, Mr Francis Disney, Apothecary, of Great Suffolk Street near Charing Cross. Apothecaries seem to figure a good deal in this story!

by Lynn's death the amount claimed as then outstanding was £3,470.[557]

In June 1730 Samuel Lynn had borrowed £500, at 4% interest, from his former Deputy Muster-Muster, Richard Carter, then of Pangbourne Lane, St Mary's parish, near Reading, Berkshire. As security for the loan, Lynn granted Carter a mortgage of part of the Tidmarsh estate, comprising a house and farm, and about 100 acres of land, occupied by William Plumb. Whether or not he disclosed to Carter the existence of the mortgage of the whole estate to Mrs Granger, which took priority, is open to doubt. Whether Carter, who was supposed to be holding the 1715 mortgage of the property as a trustee, disclosed this latest twist in the saga to the beneficiaries of that trust, is also a subject for speculation. The transaction was sealed by the usual device of a lease and release dated on consecutive days, 23rd and 24th June. Lynn, as usual, failed to repay the loan and fell behind with the interest payments, and when Carter sought to call in the total due of £580 four years later Lynn applied to Wilson for help. Wilson lent him £600 on the same terms, and the matter was completed using the same device of a lease and release (dated 25th and 26th June 1734). However, by the time that Samuel Lynn died nothing had been paid on this either.[558]

Besides Richard Holford's judgment debt of £1,500, other debts had been incurred by the time Samuel Lynn died, not all of them charged against the

---

[557] *Lynn v Cotman* (1739), TNA, C 11/784/44. Answer of Samuel Child.

[558] *Lynn v Cotman* (1739), TNA, C 11/784/44. Answer of Alexander Wilson.

Tidmarsh property. Some were secured by Bonds: £200 to Henry Simeon, £100 to the Revd. Walter Chapman, £100 to Sarah Lyford, £100 to Elizabeth Goddard, and £60 to Mrs Joan Moss.[559] Henry Simeon also claimed "*about £300*" for "*Business done and money laid out*" for Samuel Lynn.

A cache of letters between William Morgan (in France or Spain) and his wife Mary (in England), dated between 1728 and 1740, was brought into evidence in the *Galway v Lynn* case of 1747-56.[560] There were originally at least fifteen of them, several of which are no longer extant but were listed as exhibits.[561] Much of the content of those which have survived is concerned with mundane family matters. There are many allusions to people whose identities are as often as not obscured to the point of anonymity, and insufficient clues are given as to why either Captain or Mrs Morgan should be concerned with them.

The sequence starts with a letter[562] from Mary Morgan (care of Mrs Painter's, Red Lion Street, near Red Lion Square) to her husband William on 11th January 1727[28], telling him that 'Harry' (their future son-in-law, Henry Leslie)[563] had got home to England,

---

[559] *Chapman v Lynn* (1744), TNA C 11/869/13.

[560] TNA C 11/1622/22, and C 111/207 (exhibits).

[561] TNA C 111/207.

[562] TNA C 111/207, packet 1, item M(15) refers. Original not extant.

[563] The parish register for St George's church, Bloomsbury, records that on 4th July 1738 Henry Leslie and Julia Morgan, both of that parish, were married by licence.

possibly to stay, but not with her, that her unnamed brother had little hope of success in his affairs, whatever they were, and that Mr Howard, whoever he was, had got married.

William Morgan replied[564] on 16th February 1727[28]. After announcing his resolve to dispense with the services of his lawyer James Roche – *"He wants to have a Yearly Allowance which Ile noe more give him, then I will to Frank that in his life did me noe maner of service"* – Morgan continued:

"This Court has don noe business of a great while by the Indisposition of the King,[565] soe that I am just as I was, for I cannot get a peney of my Money as yet, and if you had not releived me I should be in want, I thank you for it my Dear. God knowes every penny I spend goes against my Nature, because it is not spent with you.

My health is very good, and I leive with all the satisfaction that I can doe from you. I have these 12 Months past leived with Co.ll Lauless, your Brother knowes him – one of the best Men Leiveing, wee are as like Man & wife as 2 Men can be, extream regular, he keepes a Coach & leives comfortable without making great figure, he always sends you his service by the name of his rivale, for he passes for my Wife.[566]

---

[564] TNA C 111/207, packet 1, item M(15).

[565] Morgan is referring not to the Old Pretender, by now living in Rome under the Pope's protection, but to Louis XV of France.

[566] One hopes that Mrs Morgan had a sense of humour. Either Col. Lawless or his son later married the Morgans' daughter Anna, and the couple was living in Barcelona in 1744. In 1734 an Irish Captain Lawless was Major of the garrison at Avignon, and was described when encountered by two cousins undertaking the Grand Tour that Summer as a *"very good natur'd affable man"*. A

All our other frinds are well, I have only to begg of you my Childe to endevour to be easey and not to frett your selfe, confident that wee have a chance … to end the rest of our old dayes with comfort with one another."

Mary Morgan wrote to her husband (care of Mr Waters, his banker, in Paris) on 9th October 1728,[567] in reply to his[568] of 15th September. She had, in place of the out-of-favour James Roche, instructed a Dublin lawyer, Mr Lacy, to act for her and her absent husband, but *"not having on[e] peney of rents from the Tenants, and them friends I once depended on is now so shie of me, will denie seeinge me"* was having trouble paying his fees. *"The Tenants"* were of properties in Newark, Nottinghamshire, which Mrs Morgan had apparently acquired on her own account, and with whom she was in dispute over repairs and rent arrears. Mary Morgan's letter continued with news of mutual acquaintances:

'I must Tell you Mr Pryes's Last Wifes Grand'son is dead in His Craules abroad, and Left Mr Pryes[569] Eight Hundared pd a year, he's still in the Country. … your Cousin Rochs Nephew is dead the Eldest Brothers son, & his daughter in Town Told me 700£ a year Came to Her father by His Death, the Truth of it I Cannot afirme, having Little beleivf of

---

drawing by J.M.W. Turner features, on a rock on the road along the western shore of Loch Lomond. a memorial tablet to a Colonel Lawless, presumably a casualty of the Jacobite Rebellion of 1745.

[567] TNA C 111/207, packet 1, item (16).
[568] TNA C 111/207, packet 1, item (16) refers. Original not extant.
[569] Walter Pryse, lawyer.

what they say. …"

In Morgan's reply of 17th November, he reported hearing that the only son – *"a young boy"* – of the Dublin lawyer Mr Lacy *"was Dround a few Dayes agoe"*. As for James Roche …

"I fear Noething will succeed wth him, but I am glad he getts any fortune to suporte him tho I despise his vanity, folly, and Injustice. I am heartily glad of any good fortune that my friend Mr Prise may have, & I wish him Joy of it, the more he getts, the more usefull he can be to his friends …".

Mary Morgan noted on the outside that she answered the letter on 4th December, but that letter has not survived. Nor have any between the couple during the next ten years, apart from one dated 7th March 1734[35] from Morgan to his wife, in reply to hers of 27th January:

"I hope my Dear that yow nor Mr Prise will not parte with Mr [Samuel] Lynn's Mortgage Deede out of yor hands untill the Money is paid yow, Not that I question his Integrity, but wee are all Young & Old layable to be surprized by Death, and in that case wee must rely upon his Children &c. If Mr Lynn could rais Money to pay yow, it would help to clear … what is due to yow from Wallers Executors."

After more obscure gossip, Morgan turned to domestic news:

"Yor family here are well, your Grand Son[570] *t[h]rives, he is very quiet sleepes a great Deal and cryes but litle which*

---

[570] This must be the son of Ann Lawless and her husband. Whether the child survived I do not know.

makes his Mother say often that he will not leive long – but he is very well and lively, and like the father."

Morgan mentioned those of their acquaintance who wished to be remembered to Mrs Morgan *"especially Mr Butler"*.[571]

"I am teased by Sir John Hely[572] to give yow his Service and to beg of yow to send him a glass such as yow once gave him at Sevile, he sayes that the glass that fitts yor sight will fitt his."

There is then another gap of several years until a letter from Morgan to his wife dated 13th December 1739. The cold weather *"has begon here already after such violent raines & Storms which never was seen here before."* He referred to her visit to a lawyer appointed to act as arbitrator between her (on his behalf) and *"the Widdow of Frank Lynn"*. The letter ends with the usual rash promise that they would soon be together again.

Mrs Mary Morgan was, not for the first time, in poor health. On 9th March 1739[40], in response to hers of 22nd January, Morgan wrote to her:

"I am glad you are recovered of your Violent fitt of the Gravill,[573] … but Nothing will cure a perplex't and Melancoly Minde. All this I brought upon you, and now it is just I should pay for it."

Morgan did not pay for anything, if he could help

---

[571] 'Mr [Richard] Butler' was a *nom de guerre* of the Duke of Ormonde.
[572] Hely or Healy; created a Jacobite baronet in 1728.
[573] indicative of kidney stones.

it. He continued:

"Jemey has sent you some Olives … I am almost perswaded he will this Spring goe to the Indies, soe pray endevour to get a little Mony for him."

Morgan's last known letter to his wife is dated 29th August 1740. She had reported that her health was *"pretty good"*, despite the *"Crosses & Disappointments"* she had borne on his behalf. She pleaded poverty, but Morgan rather insensitively told her that her *"want of money is comone every where, especially since this Warr*[574] *has soe drain'd us, that … wee must be reduced to live in garetts and eate browne bread"*. If his affairs did not turn out as he hoped, *"I promise you that I will find a way to meete you and to end Our Dayes togeather … Adieu my Dearest"*.

There is a note on the cover by Mary Morgan to the effect that she answered this letter on 14th September 1740. That is the last heard of or from her, although on 8th March 1742[43] Mary Morgan *"of St James Westminster"* was buried at St James's Church, Paddington, and that may well have been William Morgan's long-suffering wife.

---

[574] The so-called 'War of Jenkins' Ear' (1739-48) between Britain and Spain, which from 1740 ran concurrently with the War of the Austrian Succession.

CHAPTER 17

Yet more litigation

Mrs Mary Lynn had continued as lessee of her Dulwich property, Hall Place, still at the 1703 rent of a mere £22 a year. However, Dulwich College (largely thanks to the influence of James Hume) was becoming more 'savvy' about the rents it could obtain from its properties, and Mrs Lynn could not have spent sufficient sums on improvements to justify renewal at the old rent, so when she applied for a new lease on the surrender of her existing one in September 1738 the College Audit Meeting ordered that the new lease – for 21 years from Lady Day 1739 – should be at a rental of £50 a year, although there must have been further negotiation, as that Order was revoked – the entry was struck through – and replaced at the following March Audit Meeting with a new one, at £40 a year. The deleted Order had stipulated that £100 should be spent on the premises before March 1739, and this was replaced by a requirement that £80 be spent before the present lease was surrendered and the new one granted. Bizarrely, both Orders refer not to Mrs Lynn, but to

293

'Mr Lynn', as if the College was unaware that Francis Lynn had died, and equally oddly the College rent records between 1731 and 1738 refer neither to Francis or Mary Lynn, but to the previous lessee Samuel Hunter, who had died in 1725.

The actual lease granted to Mrs Lynn in 1739 is in the Dulwich College Archives,[575] and was of the messuage or mansion house called Hall Place, with its barn, stables, outhouses, yards, gardens, orchard, and backsides, with a moat round about the said messuage, two bridges with gates at the east and west entrances to the property, and also two messuages near adjoining thereto "*nearly south and by east the said mansion house*" and another messuage near adjoining thereto "*nearly north and by east the said mansion house*" with that dwelling's yard, gardens, stable & outhouses. The Hall Place 'compound', including those three other dwellings, was measured in all at 2*a*.2*r*.3*p*., and there were also the six parcels of pasture lying south of the premises, 29*a*.3*r*.31*p*. marked **A:I:** on the College Survey Map of 1725,[576] a total of 32*a*.1*r*.34*p*., with common of pasture for horses, neat cattle and sheep only, etc., for 21 years, at the agreed rent of £40 a year.

Samuel Lynn had made his last, and possibly only Will on 24th March 1736[37]. Apart from £2,500 "*in lieu of the several individual Parcells contained in the Articles of my Marriage dated the 18 December 1699*", to be

---

[575] DCA, Env XLIIIA.

[576] This detailed Survey Map, sadly, no longer exists, and probably ceased to do so by the end of the 18th century.

invested and held by the current trustees of his marriage settlement, the Will (and a Codicil to it of the same date)[577] left various bequests, including "*my Silver Decanter given to me by the Widows of the Army And my Silver Tobacco Box with subscription on it*" to his son Thomas (appointed as another of his executors), items "*which were my Daughter Harriots*" to his widowed son-in-law Richard Holford, "*the Silver Bohee Teapott Lamp Tea Spoons Strainer and Tongs and Tea Box*" to his son Samuel, "*my Tobacco Box with the Buste's upon it my Writing Candlesticks Snuffers and Stand markt H.St.J.*"[578] to his other surviving son Richard, £5 for a mourning ring for each of his nieces, and "*to my Niece Mary Lynn Daughter of my Brother Francis All that Debt both Principall and Interest due to me by Bond from the late Mr Moreland*[579] *which my said Brother promisd me should be paid in case his and Mrs Morelands Effects should ever come to his hands as they afterwards did*". He left "*all my Books and Papers in Manuscript*" a bible, a Book of Common Prayer, and an equal share of his residuary estate, to each of his three surviving sons.

Presciently, in William Morgan's letter to his wife of March 1735, he had expressed the hope that neither she nor the lawyer Walter Pryse would part with possession of Samuel Lynn's £1,500 mortgage to Morgan of his Tidmarsh property until it was paid off, as everyone could be "*surprized by Death …*".

---

[577] TNA PROB 11/686/385.

[578] i.e. Henry St. John, 1st Lord Bolingbroke – Samuel's former employer (and house-guest).

[579] No other record of this loan to Christopher Moreland, Francis Lynn's wife's stepfather, exists. There is of course an implied criticism here of Frank Lynn for having held on to his brother's money.

Whether or not he was surprised by it, Samuel Lynn's death occurred on 8th October 1737.

There was a problem with the Will. One would have thought that, aware of the difficulties that Samuel Hunter's unexecuted Will had caused his brother Frank, Samuel Lynn would have been careful to ensure that his own Will was properly signed and witnessed. It was neither. Consequently, even if admitted to probate, it could not change the provisions of the 1699 marriage settlement, as Samuel had apparently intended it should, nor (so it was thought) could it dispose of his real estate – namely the manor of Tidmarsh and the freehold land held with it. The Tidmarsh estate was essentially Samuel's only asset – he died possessed of "*only a very small personall Estate not near sufficient to pay his debts*".[580]

However, all was not lost. As the only potential sharers of residue, the three brothers – Samuel junior, Thomas and Richard – could "*in consideration of the naturall love and affection*" between them effectively bring the Will into full effect, or indeed vary it, by agreeing to do so – the equivalent of the modern 'deed of family arrangement' or 'deed of variation'. They duly did so, by the then usual method of executing deeds of lease and release on consecutive days – 8th and 9th November 1737. Richard Holford and Henry Simeon were also party to the deeds, in which, as the heir-at-law, Samuel junior released his rights in the Manor of Tidmarsh and all that went with it to Holford and Simeon, as trustees, upon trust to sell it, pay off all and any mortgages and judgement

---

[580] *Lynn v Cotman* (1739) – TNA C 11/784/44: evidence of Richard Lynn.

debts "*charged or chargeable*" on it, and set aside and invest £2,500 from what was left to satisfy the terms of the 1699 marriage settlement (into which Samuel Lynn the elder was supposed to have invested property, but had failed to do so). The balance – if any – of the proceeds of sale of the Tidmarsh property was to be shared equally between the three brothers, as *quasi* residuary beneficiaries of their father's Will. The £2,500 trust fund would be held for Samuel junior and "*the heirs of his body*", or in default for Thomas and his heirs likewise, or if none then for Richard and his heirs likewise.[581]

Despite its problems, the Will was proved in Common Form by Thomas Lynn (with power reserved to the other executors) on 16th December 1737. However, in view of their uncertainty (which, it transpired, was fully justified) as to whether Samuel Lynn's estate would be sufficient to fund even the £2,500 trust fund, Richard Holford and Henry Simeon declined to take any steps to sell the Tidmarsh estate without the comfort of a court order requiring them to do so.[582] As was so often the case with anyone connected with Francis Lynn, litigation ensued.

On 8th March 1737[38] Samuel's youngest son Richard Lynn (the eldest, Samuel junior, having just died) issued proceedings against his surviving brother Thomas (who was himself at death's door), his father's non-proving co-executors Richard Holford and Henry Simeon, his aunt Mary Lynn (Francis Lynn's widow), Captain William Morgan (by his appointed attorney,

---

[581] *Ibid.*
[582] *Ibid.*

Andrew Galway), and Captain Alexander Wilson,[583] requiring each of them to show how much his father's estate owed them, and asking for an order that the estate should then immediately be sold to satisfy such claims and to enable the net proceeds to be distributed in accordance with the Will.

Soon afterwards Thomas Lynn also died, leaving Richard as Samuel Lynn senior's only surviving son, and on 10th July 1738 Richard obtained a grant to his father's unadministered estate (the other executors, wishing to avoid a fight, having renounced probate). In view of the deaths of both his elder brothers, Richard Lynn was obliged for the sake of form to re-issue proceedings, which he did on 22nd March 1738[39],[584] as the only surviving heir of his father Samuel Lynn, as administrator and heir of his recently-deceased brother Samuel 'the younger', and as executor of his other recently-deceased brother Thomas, against the same parties, with the addition of Samuel Child (a son of the founder of the banking house Child & Co.,[585] and possibly the inventor of the pre-printed cheque), John Hawkins (Samuel Hunter's surviving executor), Sarah Cotman and Jane Carter (as daughters of the late Richard Carter, Samuel Lynn's former deputy Muster-

---

[583] Probably the 'Wilson' who had attended a meeting with the Lynn brothers and others at Brown's Coffee House on 2nd February 1719[20].

[584] TNA ref C 11/784/44. The TNA listing cites the case as *Lynn v Cotman*, although Mr and Mrs Cotman were only minor participants in it. There *is* a case, from 1742, listed as *Lynn v Holford* – C 11/625/25 – but this concerns unrelated proceedings issued by Richard Lynn against Ann and Staynor Holford.

[585] which still exists, as part of the Royal Bank of Scotland group, with its head office in Fleet Street.

Master, who when he had died on 15th July 1735 was the surviving trustee of the Tidmarsh estate)[586] and Sarah's husband Joseph Cotman.

Two Bills of Complaint were issued on Richard Lynn's behalf (an amended Bill was filed on 28th June 1739), and eight Answers by the various Defendants, the first (from Capt. Wilson) dated 8th June 1739, followed the next day by that of Richard Holford. Those of Mrs Mary Lynn, William Morgan and Samuel Child followed on 3rd July, and that of Henry Simeon on 7th November. Finally, those of the Cotmans (and Miss Carter) and John Hawkins, all of whom pleaded ignorance of everything connected with the case, followed on 10th November 1739. All of the defendants who had claims to make against the estate of Samuel Lynn the elder took the opportunity to update those claims with additional interest due, and to his previous claims Henry Simeon added legacies of £42 and £21 which he should have received, but had not, under the Wills of Samuel Lynn the elder and Thomas Lynn respectively, and £57 2s 6d due on two promissory notes from Thomas Lynn, although any claims he had against Richard Lynn as Thomas Lynn's executor were nothing to do with the present action. Even more cheekily, he also claimed the cost (£10) of "*mourning*" for the elder Lynn.

Amongst 'Master Brougham's Exhibits'[587] is a Bill of Costs, entitled "*Lynn ag[ain]st Holford & Others*", covering the period 1739 to April 1743, which gives an almost blow-by-blow account of this case, nowadays listed as *Lynn v Cotman*, from the point of

---

[586] The other trustee, James Fury, had died "*many years since*".

[587] TNA ref C 111/207.

view of two of the defendants, Mrs Mary Lynn and Captain William Morgan. They, and probably Samuel Child as well, used the same Solicitor, John Meackham, and the same Counsel, Charles Waller.

Meackham took Mrs Lynn's instructions and her Answer was drawn, submitted in a fair copy to Counsel, discussed with Counsel, engrossed, sworn on 3rd July 1739, and submitted to the court. Mrs Lynn, not having any of the relevant documents in her possession, could not swear to how much was owed by her late brother-in-law to her late husband's estate, but thought that a Bond the former had entered into with the latter on 28th January 1729 in the sum of £1,320 was evidence that £660, and interest thereon, was still owed by Samuel to Francis, and that the £660 was part of the original £1,500 lent by her husband to his brother. She believed, although she could not prove it, that William Morgan had assigned his right to his half-share of the £3,000 mortgage to her husband, as part of the financial dealings between them.[588] She drew attention to the 'Account Stated' signed by Francis Lynn and William Morgan's wife Mary dated 19th December 1727, showing a balance then due from Morgan to Francis Lynn of £1,023 2s 0d, which she expected to receive, together with interest on that and on the £1,500.

Capt. Morgan did not personally swear to his

---

[588] Since this showed a potentially serious dispute between Mrs Lynn and Capt. Morgan, Mr Meakham should at this point have declared a conflict of interest, and ceased to act for either. However, lawyers at that time were evidently considerably more relaxed about such matters than The Law Society would allow today's Solicitors to be!

Answer, and an additional cost was incurred for Counsel to obtain the court's permission to accept Morgan's Answer "*without Oath*". (Morgan's son-in-law, Capt. Henry Leslie or Lesley, was by this time acting as his attorney, either alongside or instead of Capt. Andrew Galway.) Morgan asserted that "*the Sume of Two Thousand pounds and upwards*", despite various payments of interest (several of which are endorsed on one of the original 1715 mortgage deeds), remained owing to him.

All this was done in Trinity (i.e. Summer) Term 1739. The wheels of justice ground, as usual, exceeding slow, and nothing happened in Michaelmas Term, but in "*Hillary 1739*" (i.e. Lent Term 1740), on 1ˢᵗ February, a Hearing took place before the Master of the Rolls, who "*(amongst other things) decreed that an Account should be taken before William Kinaston Esquire one of the Masters of this Honourable Court of what was due to the said Morgan, Lynn, Wilson and others for Principall and Interest on their respective Mortgages*" and ordered the sale of the Tidmarsh Estate, by private auction (i.e. by inviting best bids by a specified date).[589]

On 31ˢᵗ January 1740[41], Mrs Mary Lynn entered into an Arbitration Bond (in the sum of £3,000) with William Morgan, whereby she agreed to appoint Charles Waller of Lincoln's Inn (her barrister, but apparently no longer Morgan's) and Francis Garvan of the Middle Temple as "*indifferent arbitrators*". Waller and Garvan were "*to State Settle and Adjust all … Accounts Claims and Demands*" between Mrs Lynn and Morgan, and if they failed to do so by 25ᵗʰ March 1741 then

[589] Recited in *Galway v Lynn* (1747), TNA, ref: C 11/1622/22, Andrew Galway's Bill of Complaint.

Waller and Garvan were to appoint an independent "*Umpire*", who was to complete the job by 12th April 1741. Mrs Lynn promised to accept the validity of such an award, in which case the Bond (to ensure her compliance with this promise) would be void.[590]

By Hilary Term 1740[41] an Account of the principal and interest due to the mortgagees "*&* *Incumbrancers*" and "*Bond Creditors*" of Samuel Lynn's estate and of the Tidmarsh estate in particular had been drawn up and the creditors prioritised. On 5th February, the court convened to hear the Plaintiff Richard Lynn report that the best bid so far was one of £10,500, from himself. The Defendants must have regarded this as insufficient, if not suspicious, as it was not approved. A month later the Lord Chancellor issued a judgment (or "*decree*") in the matter.[591]

In Easter Term 1741 there was an examination of the Stated Account between Samuel Lynn and Francis Lynn, which had to be copied. (Since it was "*very long*", Mr Meackham charged 7*s* for this service.) Another 6*s* 8*d* was charged for "*Attending Captn Wilson several times at his house in Westminster to take an Account of Money paid by him for the Pl[ain]t]iff']s Father in discharge of the Def[endan]ts demand*".

The Solicitors for the Defendants Mary Lynn, William Morgan (by his attorney) and Richard Holford agreed with the Plaintiff Richard Lynn to "*concert measures for procuring a better Purchaser for the Estate on the bidding being opened*", and on 30[th] April £10,700 was bid for the Estate by Capt. Wilson

---

[590] TNA: C 111/207, packet 1, item G-25.
[591] TNA: C 111/207, packet 1, no. 27 refers.

himself. This was also regarded as insufficient, and the property was re-advertised. This resulted in fresh but inconclusive bidding on 26th June, and it was not until 26th November that an acceptable bid of £10,800 was made by a Mr Surtees. However, either he withdrew or there was some objection to him, and Capt. Wilson was reinstated as the successful bidder, at £10,700.

Little seems to have happened in Hilary (Lent) or Easter Terms 1742. Trinity (Summer) Term 1742 was more eventful. On 1st July Mr Meackham attended on Mr Coppinger (another lawyer), Richard Lynn, and Henry Simeon for four hours "*at the Blew Post Tavern in Portugall Street to settle the Queries in Defts Charge & Plts Discharge*". Several queries were unresolved, and Mr Simeon was commissioned "*to make Inquiry in the Country in relation thereto*", presumably in the Tidmarsh area. While he was there he sent "*many Letters … relateing to the Queries*" on which the Solicitor had to pay the postage totalling 2*s* 6*d*.[592] On 8th November, in Michaelmas Term 1742, Counsel Mr Waller attended on the Master "*to settle the priority of the Creditors Demands*". The bill of costs mentions all the creditors (apart, oddly, from Samuel Child and Henry Simeon), but their order of priority has not survived.

Although the case was not finished, during Hilary Term 1742[43] Mrs Lynn for some reason withdrew instructions from John Meackham. His bill of costs or acting for her and Capt. Morgan since 1739, including ten shillings charged at the end of almost every Term for "*C[ounse]l & Soll[icito]rs Fee*" (presumably as a

---

[592] Prior to the introduction of the penny post in 1840, postage was paid by the recipient, not the sender.

retainer), totalled £58 7*s* 4*d*. Credit was given for two guineas paid on account, but it was not until November 1746 (by which time Mr Meackham was dead and his executor John Bowman was dealing with the matter) that Mrs Mary Lynn (or rather Robert Cotes on her behalf) paid another £40 "*on Account*". Whether she, Capt. William Morgan's executor, or anyone else ever paid the balance of £16 5*s* 4*d* is not recorded.

Master Kynaston issued his Report on 28th November 1743. The original Report is missing, but some of its contents can be reconstructed from other documents, particularly Andrew Galway's Bill of Complaint in the case of *Galway v Lynn* (1747).[593] Kynaston found "*that the said Samuel Lynn in his Life time had paid to said Francis Lynn his part of all the Money due to the said Francis Lynn on Account of Principall or Interest on the Mortgage aforesaid; that the said Samuel Lynn had also paid unto the sd William Morgan all Money due on Account of Interest for his part of the sd Sum of three thousand pounds*" but only up to 25th December 1715; and that since then "*the said Samuel Lynn had also paid to the said Mary Morgan (as attorney to her husband the said William Morgan) and to other persons by his Order at several times*" sums totalling £1,196 4s 5d, which after deducting it from the £1,500 and interest, on 25th March 1742[43] left principal and interest of £2,208 3*s* 7*d* (and costs of £23 0*s* 8*d*), in all £2,231 4s 3d, due to Mrs Mary Lynn from William Morgan. (It must therefore have been accepted that Morgan had assigned his half-share of the £3,000 mortgage to Francis Lynn.) The Master also certified that Francis Lynn had lent

---

[593] TNA, ref: C 11/1622/22.

Samuel Lynn a further £600, secured by Samuel Lynn's Bond dated 20th January 1729[30]. Master Kynaston's Report and Decree were made "*absolute*" by the court of Chancery on 3rd December 1743.[594] Based on their previous evidence and other sources, the list below should reflect the amounts adjudged due to the creditors of Samuel Lynn's estate:

- Mrs Mary Lynn, as prior mortgagee ... £2,231 4s 3d;

- Mrs Mary Lynn, on a Bond ... £600 plus interest;

- Capt. William Morgan ... £0;

- Capt. Alexander Wilson ... £600 plus interest and costs;

- Richard Holford ... £3,000 plus interest and judgment costs;

- Samuel Child ... £3,470, plus costs;

- Henry Simeon ... £200 plus costs; plus £42 plus interest;

- Mrs Elizabeth Goddard ... £100 plus interest and costs;

- Miss Sarah Lyford ... £100 plus interest and costs;

- Mrs Joan Moss ... £60 plus interest and costs;

- Revd. Walter Chapman ... £100 plus interest and costs.

Memorial to Samuel Lynn in St Laurence's parish
Church, Tidmarsh, Berkshire.

Ignoring interest and costs, the total is a minimum of £10,503, so the net proceeds of the Tidmarsh estate would have to be at least that amount for the creditors to have any hope of being paid in full. Once interest and costs were added nothing, let alone £2,500, would be left for the 1699 marriage settlement trust fund, and there was certainly no prospect of any residue for Richard Lynn and the estates of his two recently-deceased brothers to share. Nevertheless, Richard Lynn arranged – presumably at his own cost – for an elaborate tablet to be placed in Tidmarsh parish church as a memorial to his father. It is still there.

On 25th April 1744[595] William Morgan Esq., Colonel[596] aggregated to "*the Regiment of Ireland*", resident of Madrid, native of Bantrey in Ireland, lawful son in marriage of Dennis Morgan Esq. and of Mrs Christina Morgan *née* Gallwey (both deceased), in the Roman Catholic faith, "*being sick (but without keeping his Bed) of the Bodily disease with which God our Lord has been pleased to visit him, but in his natural Senses and understanding*", handed to Don Julian de Hermosilla, the 21-year-old local Lieutenant-Corregidor (a judicial and administrative official), a "*paper stitched up and sealed … which he said was his last Will and Testament*", to be opened and published after his death. He did so in the presence of de Hermosilla and others who were acquainted with Morgan (including a scrivener, Pedro Martinez Colmenar, a journeyman shoemaker Blas Ruano, aged 18, a journeyman coachmaker Bartholomew de Gravdenboz, aged 60, and Morgan's servant Manuel de Sesto y Scipo, aged 25).

---

[595] according to the Gregorian ('New Style') calendar, eleven days ahead of the date in England, which still used the Julian Calendar.
[596] Presumably promoted from his British rank of Captain by the Old Pretender.

William Morgan may have been prompted to revise his Will by the fortuitous arrival some two weeks before of the 'scrutore' – the *escritoire* or desk – which contained many of his papers from England, and which had been confiscated at Bilbao over twenty years before, shortly after Morgan's Jacobite escapades had come to an end. We know that he had made at least one previous Will, as in December 1716 he had asked Francis Lynn to give it, enclosed, to Andrew Galway, who was coming out to France to see Morgan, "*without telling him what it is*". I would be very surprised indeed if Galway did not know exactly what it was by the end of that journey, if not when he started out. Galway was present with Morgan when the desk and its contents eventually turned up.

On 24th May 1744, at about 11 a.m., Morgan died in his house in Calle de Pez, "*of natural causes*", as was attested to by Sr. Colmenar, his clerk Domingo Antonio de la Ruam, young Blas, old Bartholomew, Morgan's servant Manuel, Don Ignacio de Haro, Don Miguel Hostatrique, and Sebastian de Avila. All of them were present at the time, and almost immediately provided Colmenar with depositions to that effect, but not before de Hermosilla had, at Andrew Galway's request, taken a pair of scissors, snipped the threads binding the Will, and opened it. He ordered that the Will be "*read and published*" by Colmenar to those assembled, but Colmenar declined. The Will was in English, in which language Colmenar claimed that he was insufficiently fluent. It was therefore immediately dispatched to the Translator-General of Madrid, Don Miguel Joseph de Aoyr, who translated it into Spanish and promptly returned the original to Colmenar, who received it the same day, to be put into Colmenar's *"Register of Publick Deeds"*. Don Miguel sent with it a copy of the translation, which was certified immediately by five local English-speaking merchants as being accurate.

Having declared *"that I have lived and dye in the Roman Catholick Apostolick Religion"*, Morgan's Will appointed *"the Reverend Father Edmond Doran as likewise my dear and beloved Cousen Mr Andrew Gallwey and Captain Daniel O'Leary for Executors"*. He left his servants Petronilla dela Fuente and Manuel, aside from any arrears, a year's wages as *"gratification"*, $60 to *"my Friend and physician Dr Gregory Jones … for his Assistance during my Sickness"*, and several minor legacies for religious purposes. Abbot O'Sullivan was to be paid *"what appears due on my Note"*, Messrs Patrick Jones & Co. were to have $100 *"of 15 Rials vizt due to Mr Butler[597] of Sevile for the import of Mr Andrew Gallwey's Bill upon Mr O'Leary of whom I received funds to pay said Bill"*, and *"my Friend and Relation Mr Daniel O'Leary"* was to be paid *"the remainder of his Accompt"*. Morgan's financial affairs had clearly lost none of their complexity.

Morgan's estate in England was to go to his only son James, who was currently in Havana, Cuba, for life. This was *"Jemey"*, who had previously been an enthusiastic and active supporter of his father's Jacobite endeavours. However, Morgan envisaged some difficulties in getting in the English estate, over which his son-in-law Henry Leslie had been given (and apparently misused) a power of attorney. That power was to be regarded as revoked, and Jemey and the executors were to recover what they could from

---

[597] 'Mr Butler' was a pseudonym of the Duke of Ormonde.

Capt. Leslie. On James's death Andrew Galway was to receive one-third (limited to £100) of the income from the English estate, and James's heirs the remainder, but if James had no issue then, subject to Juliana (or Julia) Morgan Lesley receiving, at the trustees' discretion, a pension of £50 p.a. "*in case her Husbands Estate should be confiscated or that she should be in want of the same*", the English estate was to be equally divided between Julie and Nancy, or their issue if they predeceased. If they left no issue, then the estate in England was to be sold and the net proceeds "*equally divided amongst my three Sisters Children Margaret Julian and Honor*[598] *at the discretion of my Executors and their heirs*".

Morgan's property in Spain was to be divided equally between his three children James ('Jemey'), Juliana ('Julie') Lesley, currently in England, and Ann ('Nancy') Lawlis, currently in Barcelona. As an afterthought, Morgan left his son "*my Gold headed Cane and Gold Watch and Silver hilted Sword and what other Furniture of the House he shall require*".

After an unaccountable delay of two years, a certified copy of the Spanish translation of Morgan's Will found its way to London and was on 31ˢᵗ May 1746 translated back into English by a Notary Public "*and Tabellion*" (an official scribe) fluent in Spanish,

---

[598] I *think* this means "my sister's three children …", not "the children of my three sisters …", the ambiguity being a consequence of lawyers' disinclination, then as now, to use punctuation. Perhaps in the course of being translated from English into Spanish and then back into English, the original meaning was obscured.

John D'Costa.[599] This latest copy, certified as true, was admitted to probate by the Prerogative Court of Canterbury on 3rd June 1746. The only proving executor was Andrew Galway, with 'power reserved' to his two co-executors Father Edmond Doran and Captain Daniel O'Leary.[600]

Andrew Galway must have spent part of those two years since William Morgan's death mulling over the contents of the 'scrutore' and Morgan's other papers. By March the following year Galway had persuaded his co-executors to join him in suing Frank Lynn's widow for whatever was still due.

The litigation was very far from over!

---

[599] Of course, if D'Costa had a copy of the original Will in English, he might have saved himself some time and trouble, without loss of fee, by simply copying that out.

[600] TNA, PROB 11/747/306. In subsequent proceedings *O'Leary* is often rendered as *O'Leaty*, which I have assumed to be an error.

CHAPTER 18

'We are all Mortall'

Mary Lynn did not die until 1756, but she made a one-paragraph Will[601] in 1734 (when she still occupied a grace-and-favour apartment at African House) and never afterwards changed it. In it she left her entire estate (without saying anything about her late husband's estate, which should have been kept separate) *"unto my three Daughters Mary, Sophia and Arabella, to be equally divided between them share and share alike"*, with Mary and Sophia appointed as Executors. But both in 1734 and when she died Mrs Lynn had five, not three, daughters: Elizabeth (who had married well, and did not need to be provided for), Mary, Sophia, Arabella – and Ann. On 4th October 1732 Ann Lynn married (as his second wife – he had a young daughter, Elizabeth, from his first marriage) Simon Kelsey, a colleague of Francis Lynn's in the Royal African Company, and eventually to be its Deputy Accountant, before he switched careers and

---

[601] TNA, ref: PROB 11/820/253.

became a wine dealer.[602]

For some reason Mrs Lynn took a dislike to her new son-in-law, who also had an apartment in Africa House, or to her own daughter Ann, or to both of them. The ill-feeling seems to have been mutual, for in 1746 the Kelseys – without, perhaps, giving sufficient thought to the probable consequences – sued Mrs Lynn in the court of Chancery. Ann Kelsey protested that her mother "*hath taken some unreasonable Dislike to your Oratrix having refused to give your Oratrix any thing on her said Marriage … though your Oratrix never did any thing to offend her said Mother*[603] *and always behaved towards her in the most Dutiful and Proper Manner*". Nor had Mrs Lynn furnished the Kelseys, as they had sought to insist, with any account of her late husband's "*considerable*" personal estate of more than £4,000, and had indeed refused to do so. Technically, as a trustee of it, she should have kept such an account, even if there was no-one with a legal right to see it, but since Francis Lynn had appointed no co-trustee to act with her, there was no-one to force her to do so, unless the court did. Nor, in theory, because of the wide discretionary power given to her by her husband's Will, was there anything or anyone to prevent Mrs Lynn spending the entire trust fund on herself, which is exactly what she threatened to do, adding that if any of her children attempted to deny her this right she would "*cut them off with a Shilling*". In Ann's case, her mother did not leave her even that much, and she would eventually receive nothing from either parent's estate. Apart from Elizabeth Cotes, Ann's sisters never

---

[602] according to his 1755 Will – TNA PROB 11/822/155.
[603] apart from suing her, of course.

married, and evidently, from whatever motive, remained on their mother's good side.

That year, 1746, Mary Lynn had more litigation to deal with, which was to dog her for the rest of her life. On 16th August, ten weeks or so after probate of William Morgan's Will was obtained, Mrs Lynn entered into another £3,000 Arbitration Bond, similar to that between herself and Morgan in 1741, save that this time the other party was Morgan's executor Andrew Galway (allegedly of St Paul's Covent Garden), and the appointed arbitrators were Benjamin Periam (a member, since 1731, of the Court of Assistants of the Royal African Company, and therefore well known to Mrs Lynn) and Dennis McCarthy, a London merchant (and presumably an acquaintance of Galway). The deadline for completion of the arbitration was 10th October 1746, but there was no provision for an independent 'Umpire' to be appointed if the figures could not be agreed.[604] Evidently, they could not.

In Easter Term 1747 proceedings were issued in the name of Capt. William Morgan's three executors: Galway (still supposedly of Covent Garden), and (Father) Edmund Doran and (Capt.) Daniel O'Leary (both late of London, now of Amsterdam, Holland), against Mrs Mary Lynn, her son-in-law Robert Cotes, and (Capt.) Alexander Wilson, in the case initially known as *Galway v Lynn*.[605] The Plaintiffs "*did therein pray the said Mary Lynn might Admitt Assetts of the said Francis Lynn her deceased Husband or might set forth an*

---

[604] TNA: C 111/207, packet 1, item H-26.
[605] TNA, ref: C 11/1622/22. Subsequently (on appeal?) *Lynn v Galway*, TNA, ref: C 11/2201/5.

Account of his Personal Estate and that the said Defendant Wilson might pay the Plaintiffs a certain sum therein mentioned and that the said Mary Lynn might Come to a General Account with the Plaintiffs for the Money received by Francis Lynn on Account of the said William Morgan".[606]

Soon after the final court order in *Lynn v Cotman*, Capt. Wilson had been let into possession of Samuel Lynn's former Tidmarsh estate. The required conveyances, to some of which William Morgan was to have been a party, were drawn up, but Morgan died before seeing them. According to Andrew Galway, Wilson and his Solicitor were *"very impatient"* to have matters finalised. Although it appears that the rest of the purchase price had been paid into court and then distributed to the other creditors, Wilson had withheld the £2,231 4s 3d which the judge in *Lynn v Cotman* had decided was due to Mrs Lynn. He had his reasons, at least in respect of £970 of it, as was to become apparent.

Andrew Galway's closely-written Bill of Complaint, including three Schedules, is over three feet wide by nearly nine feet long, and has to be unrolled and spread sideways over two long tables in the Map Room at the National Archives in Kew to have any hope of being transcribed. The first Schedule is a copy of the list[607] compiled by Francis Lynn's of debts totalling £10,291 11s 7d due to William Morgan (in Notes and Bonds) as at 16th March 1719[20]. The second Schedule is a copy of the Stated Account from 6th April 1726,[608] showing Debit

---

[606] TNA, ref: C 11/2201/5.
[607] The original is TNA ref: C 111/207, packet 1, item G-28.
[608] The original is TNA ref: C 111/207, packet 1, item E-8.

capital (i.e. what Francis Lynn advanced to William Morgan or to his order) of £3,601 19*s* 11*d* and interest of £1,611 19*s* 5¾*d*, total £5,213 19*s* 4¾*d*, and Credit capital of £1,808 6*s* 4*d* and interest of £905 11*s* 1*d*, total £3,713 18*s* 5*d*, leaving a balance of £1,500 0*s* 11¾*d* due to Lynn. The third Schedule is a copy of the Stated Account dated 19th December 1727,[609] and carries down the £1,500 0*s* 11¾*d*, contains two minor adjustments (one of £80 and interest "*due to Mr Walter Pryse on Mr Lynns Bond*") totalling £90 14*s* 8*d*, leaving £1,404 6*s* 3¾*d*, and calculates interest on that (at 5% p.a. for 618 days) as £118 15*s* 8¼*d*, making £1,523 2*s* 0*d*, less £500 "*Rec'd of William Morgan Esquire by the hand of Mary Morgan his Wife and Attorney*" on the same day, leaving a balance then due from Morgan to Lynn of £1,023 2*s* 0*d*.

The Defendants responded, led by Mrs Mary Lynn on 9th November 1747. Her Answer is almost as long as Galway's Bill, and even harder for a researcher to transcribe – a crease in the rolled parchment along the right-hand edge is now, after 270 years, permanent, and one paragraph near the end has been inserted, evidently as an afterthought, in the most miniscule hand-writing. However, one can gather the gist of it, which is that Mrs Lynn did not believe that there was anything more due from her or her late husband's estate to William Morgan or his estate, in fact quite the reverse.

Next up, on 28th November, was Mrs Lynn's son-in-law, Robert Cotes, who had very little original to say. What is remarkable about his rather shorter Answer is the very shaky signature appended to it,

---

[609] The original is TNA ref: C 111/207, packet 1, item F-9.

strongly suggesting that, although he was to live for another twenty-seven years, Robert Cotes was suffering severely from what we would now call Parkinson's Disease. On the backs of many of the exhibits in the case are comments (for the guidance of the court, one supposes) in a similar shaky hand, which may well have been his.

Finally, several months later on 14th May 1748, came the Answer of Capt. Alexander Wilson. He was indeed, he said, very anxious that the conveyance to him of the Tidmarsh estate should be completed as soon as possible. He questioned Andrew Galway's right to speak for all three executors, as he had not seen any evidence that the two executors now living in Amsterdam had appointed Galway as their attorney. Despite claiming to knowing nothing of the financial arrangements between William Morgan and Mary Lynn, Wilson's Answer is of comparable length to the latter's. Appended to it is a Schedule of payments claimed to have been "*lent and advanced*" by Wilson to Mary Lynn between 17th January 1739[40] and 29th July 1746. An initial loan £170, followed by various small sums not exceeding £50 each, came to £785 0s 0d up to 8th April 1746. With interest (£154 12s) and a final payment of £30 18s, the total was exactly £970.

The Plaintiffs responded, and "*several Witnesses having been Examined the said Cause came on to a hearing*"[610] on 5th March 1749[50], when the Lord Chancellor (Lord Hardwick) ordered the case to be referred to a Master of the court, Henry Montague, who was tasked not only with examining the two

---

[610] TNA, ref: C 11/2201/5.

Stated Accounts of 6th April 1726 and 19th December 1727 and to work out what on the latter date was due from either party to the other and to calculate interest at 5% per annum on it, but also to consider any evidence tending to 'falsify' the Accounts (i.e. prove them false), by taking *"an Open Account of All Dealings and Transactions between said William Morgan and said Francis Lynn in their Life Time and Between William Morgan and … Mary Lynn after his Decease"*.[611]

The first task should have been simple, as Master Montague's predecessor Master William Kynaston had already done it. At 19th December 1727, according to the agreed Stated Account of that date, Morgan owed Francis Lynn £1,023 2s 0d. Earlier Stated Accounts between Lynn and Morgan dated 25th December 1715,[612] 5th September 1717,[613] and 6th November 1725[614] were still available, and although others are missing the opening balance of the Stated Account of 6th April 1726 should have reflected all that had gone before.

The other part of Montague's brief would involve considerably more work. There were all the letters written by Lynn to Morgan, by Morgan to Lynn, by Morgan to his wife, and by Lynn to others and others to him. There were accounts and receipts relating to William Young, Joseph Knight, John Rice and others, and to the Bacton-Cotton estates. The sheer quantity

---

[611] *Ibid.*

[612] TNA: C 111/207, packet 2, item No. 7, showing an agreed balance then due from Morgan to Lynn of £385 0s 8d.

[613] TNA: C 111/207, packet 1, items D-2 and D-3, showing an agreed balance then due from Morgan to Lynn of £1,298 19s 4d.

[614] TNA: C 111/207, packet 2, item 9, showing an agreed balance then due from Morgan to Lynn of £443 14s 5d.

of material to be examined and cross-referenced was huge, and the cost to each side of preparing the evidence for consideration by its opponents, by Master Montague and by the court, must have been commensurately enormous.

The item which may have given Master Montague most food for thought was the list compiled by Francis Lynn for William Morgan as at 16th March 1719[20], showing a grand total of debts (many marked "*bad*") due to Morgan of £10,291 11*s* 7*d,* and ending with the line "*Recd. then the Bonds & notes as before mentioned for wch I promise to be accountable. Fra: Lynn*".[615] Common sense suggests that Lynn could only have meant to be "*accountable*" for those debts, if any, which he managed to collect in, but Master Montague may have applied a stricter interpretation. That would have meant that Mrs Lynn owed Morgan's estate a net £9,268 9*s* 7*d*, plus interest on £10,291 11*s* 7*d* from March 1720 to 19th December 1727 and on £9,268 9*s* 7*d* for the twenty-odd years since then. Although Master Montague's Report – which in February 1756 was still awaited – is now missing, assuming it was ever filed, I do not think that he could reasonably have come to such a conclusion, in which case there must be some explanation other than appealing the decision for the names in the case to be reversed, so that *Galway v Lynn* became, by 1756, *Lynn v Galway*.

Matters were further complicated by the bankruptcy late in 1750 of Alexander Wilson, whose appointed trustees, Edmund Bradshaw and George Ross, were substituted for him in the *Galway v Lynn*

---

[615] TNA: C 111/207, packet 1, item G-28.

case. By 1746-47 Wilson was acting as Regimental Agent for an astonishing number of units – 24 out of a possible total at the time of 88. "*Unfortunately for the agents, such large empires were of brief duration, for with the coming of peace young corps were broken and old corps reduced, …*".[616] Thanks to the reforms instigated by Georges I and II, former opportunities for fraud and 'creative accounting' – claiming for dead or fictitious rank-and-file soldiers was a common ploy – were no longer available, which presumably helped cause Wilson's bankruptcy. The following year, 1751, he was the subject of a claim made in the Scottish Court of Sessions by one of his creditors, Adam Fairholm, concerning a Bond which Wilson had given the Earl of Rothes in September 1750, but the court decided that since Wilson, although "*originally from Scotland*", had been resident in England for many years, he was no longer subject to Scots law.[617]

Capt. Wilson had not been Mrs Mary Lynn's only source of loans. Walter Pryse, Francis Lynn's Solicitor and friend, had in January 1738[39] lent Mrs Lynn fifteen guineas (£15.75 in modern money). At the same time, apparently at her request, he submitted a bill for legal work done for her late husband, on the

---

[616] '*Oeconomy and Discipline: Officership and Administration in the British Army 1714-63*' by Alan J. Guy (M.U.P., 1985), p.60.
[617] '*The Decisions of the [Scottish] Court of Sessions …*' (1802), p. 2778. One of Wilson's trustees in bankruptcy, George Ross, was involved as such in the inheritance case of *Clarke v Ross* (1779), where property had been left by one J. D. Mason to a succession of beneficiaries 'in tail', and in the event (which occurred) that they left no qualifying heirs, then to Capt. Alexander Wilson (probably Mason's son-in-law) and his heirs. Sadly for Wilson, his bankruptcy prevented him from personally enjoying this inheritance.

understanding that she would settle it out of the mortgage money she was due to receive from the estate of her brother-in-law Samuel Lynn. Walter Pryse died in July 1745, still owed the fifteen guineas and the £108, but his son and executor, Lewis Pryse (of Woodstock, Oxfordshire), was still willing to wait, at least he was until word reached him that the Tidmarsh estate had indeed been sold but still there was no sign of his father's money, which he thought including substantial other loans to Mrs Lynn. Despite not being able to put a figure on the precise amount (due to his father's papers and accounts being "*left in Confusion and Disorder*" at his death), he issued proceedings for its recovery in July 1751, seeking to join as defendants Andrew Galway and Alexander Wilson – somewhat pointlessly, because the former was constantly abroad and out of the court's jurisdiction, and the latter was now an undischarged bankrupt. Lewis Pryse was hoping that Wilson would be able to pay to Mary Lynn at least £1,231 4s 3d (the amount certified by Master Kynaston as being due to Mrs Lynn in respect of her late husband's mortgage on the premises, less £1,000) "*of the purchase money*" remaining in Wilson's hands following the sale to him of the Tidmarsh estate, so that she could then pay him what was owed to his father's estate. In Mary Lynn's 'Answer', dated 17th March following, she acknowledged that the fifteen guineas and probably also the £108 were due, but she denied (possibly on the assumption that no-one could prove otherwise) having borrowed any other sums from Walter Pryse. Besides which, she was unable to say what was due from or to anybody until Master Montague had made his final report to the court, which she (and no doubt all the other interested parties) were still waiting for him to do.[618]

At some time between 25th March and 29th September 1753 Mrs Mary Lynn assigned her lease of Hall Place and all that went with it to one Jeremiah Joye or Joy. Joye had been living in Dulwich, and probably at Hall Place itself as Mrs Lynn's tenant, since at least 1743, and on 12th October that year he married Marie Margaret Le Clerc de Virly (of Huguenot extraction) in the College Chapel.[619] By 1758 his main business address was in Great Winchester Street, earning his living as a "*stock broker, brokering financial services*".[620] Joye's name appears in the College rent tables[621] from Michaelmas 1753, and at the Audit Meeting on the following 4th March it was ordered that in view of his "*making great Improvements at this time there*", he should, on surrender of the existing lease, have a new 21-year lease of the premises, at £40 a year – the same rent as Mrs Lynn had been paying.

It seems likely that Joye would not have demolished the house built by Samuel Hunter in about 1701, but may have extended it. We still have no physical description of the main house, and do not know what "*great improvements*" Joye made to it, but we do have a set of auction particulars prepared when in May 1773 Joye's successor William Kay – Joye had left Dulwich for Wolton, near Dorking, in 1763, and

[618] *Pryce v Lynn* (1751), TNA: C 11/1654/3.
[619] Dulwich College Chapel Register.
[620] *The Universal Pocket Companion*, 3rd edn., 1760, and *A Compleat Guide to All Persons Who Have Any Trade or Concerns Within the City of London, and Parts Adjacent*, 10th edn. [2nd impr.], 1767.
[621] DCA, BC:30.

died in late August 1766 – put the property in the hands of Mr Christie, of Pall Mall, after Kay had had the first of his many disputes with Dulwich College. These particulars refer to Hall Place as "*including A commodious Mansion, with proper Offices, Coach House, Stables, Gardens, thirty Acres of rich Pasture Land, together with A genteel Dwelling House contiguous, Pleasantly situate at Dulwich, on the verge of the Common*".

On the ground floor of the main house in 1773 was a Hall, "*centrically*" placed, an "*Eating Parlour with a neat China Closet adjoining*", "*a handsome Drawing Room and Tea Room*" each with a marble chimney-piece, a kitchen, cellars, laundry-room, well-equipped brew-house, larder, dairy, and butler's pantry. At the end of the "*range of rooms*" was "*a well-contrived Green House*" and two small rooms on a mezzanine floor. A large staircase led to the first floor, containing "*Three pleasant Bedchambers, with Dressing Closets, hung with fashionable Papers, finished with Marble Chimney-pieces*". Back stairs led to three Garrets on the top floor, no doubt used as servants' quarters.

Nearby, but "*at a proper Distance*", was a "*new-erected Brick building*" (probably on the site of one of Samuel Hunter's out-buildings) "*forming a double Coach House*", with stabling for three horses each, lodging rooms (for the groom) and hay loft, a Cow-house (which could be used as a three-horse stable) and "*A Room paved with Tyles*". There was a "*Court*" in front, and two large yards adjoining, with cart houses, poultry houses, and the like.

The "*adjacent house*" (north-east of the main house) "*of a compact size*", was also on three floors, with "*a Parlour, Kitchen Wash-house, Pantry and Cellars, etc.*" on the ground floor, *"Five neat apartments"* on the first floor, and two Garrets on the top floor, with a *"Coach and Stable for three Horses, and other inferior Offices"* adjoining nearby.

Samuel Hunter and his successors, and their respective tenants, must have lived in considerable comfort, if not luxury.

Early in January 1756, still mired in litigation, Mary Lynn, the widow and relict of Francis Lynn, died, and on the 12th of that month she was buried at Westminster. Seventeen days later probate of her 1734 Will was granted to her spinster daughter Mary, with power reserved to Mary's sister Sophia to prove it if Mary died before the administration was completed. The following month Mary and Sophia Lynn jointly applied to be allowed by the court to substitute for their late mother in *Lynn v Galway*.[622] How the case was ever resolved is unknown, but I think it highly likely that, even if the Lynns won (as I think they deserved to do), they would never have recovered a penny in costs from Andrew Galway or his co-executors, who would have been careful to keep out of England, beyond the reach of their creditors and of the court.

Francis Lynn's son Philip and daughters Mary, Sophia, and Arabella all died unmarried and without issue. Only Elizabeth and Ann married, the former to Robert Cotes and the latter to Simon Kelsey. Ann Kelsey had no children who survived to adulthood,

---

[622] TNA, C 11/2201/5.

but Elizabeth Cotes had three sons: Francis (1726-1770), Robert (1727-1730) and Samuel (1734-1818).

By the time Ann's husband Simon Kelsey, former Deputy Accountant with the Royal African Society, made his last Will in September 1755 (when he was "*in an ill state of bodily health*"), he had become a "*Dealer in Wines*". In the Will he left his estate between his daughter (by his first marriage) Elizabeth, his wife 'Anne' (*née* Lynn), and "*such Child or Children as my said Wife may be ensient*[623] *with at the time of my decease*", in equal shares. As Anne (or, more usually, Ann) was nearly 45 years old at the time, this was somewhat optimistic, and in the event the childless Ann and her step-daughter Elizabeth shared the estate. The Will was proved[624] in April 1756, and since the appointed executor (James Maud) had renounced probate Ann Kelsey was, as a residuary beneficiary, granted letters of administration 'with the Will annexed'. Ann moved to Saffron Hill, survived her husband by only six months, and was buried at St Andrew's Church, Holborn, on 24th September 1756. She appears to have died intestate, in which case, having no issue of her own, her heirs would have been her surviving sisters Elizabeth Cotes, Mary Lynn, Sophia Lynn, and Arabella Lynn. Heaven knows, at least three of them badly needed the money.

Of Elizabeth and Robert Cotes' three children, only their sons Francis and Samuel survived into adulthood, and Samuel until 1818. His obituary referred to his elder brother Francis, a celebrated artist, who had in his day been considered to be '*the*

---

[623] '*Enceinte*' is a somewhat archaic synonym for 'pregnant'.
[624] TNA, PROB 11/822/155.

Rosalba of England. Certainly Francis Cotes' expertise in crayon or pastel matched that of the Venetian artist Rosalba Zuanna Carriera (1673-1757), but '*The Gentleman's Magazine*' is alone[625] in thus describing Cotes. Horace Walpole, whose portrait had been painted by Rosalba Carriera, apparently coined the epithet '*the English Rosalba*' for Cotes' near contemporary Catherine (or Katherine) Read (or Reid). Catherine Read (1723-1778) shared (like Cotes) Rosalba's preferred medium, style, and abilities, and (unlike Cotes) her gender, although Read was Scottish, not English.[626]

Francis Cotes' artistic talents were evident from a young age, and he trained with the portraitist George Knapton in the early 1740s. Initially he used a room in his father's apothecary shop in Cork Street as a studio. His success as one of the most fashionable portrait painters of the day enabled him in 1763 to buy a large house in Cavendish Square, later occupied by George Romney.

There are no extant works by Francis Cotes dated earlier than 1747, and it must be a matter of regret that Francis Lynn did not survive long enough for either of his surviving grandsons to capture his likeness in some form. (Samuel Cotes was also a noted artist, specialising in miniatures.) It is of course possible that such a picture by another artist exists – so many 17th- and 18th-century paintings are

---

[625] apart from all those secondary sources which have copied and adapted the quotation, referring to Cotes as '*the Rosalba Carriera of England*'.

[626] Most of what is generally considered Read's best work was, however, done in her studio in Welbeck Street, London.

captioned, if they are captioned at all, only as 'Portrait of a Gentleman', '… of a Lady', '… of an Officer', etc. – but as it is we have no identifiable portraits of Francis Lynn, or for that matter of Mary Lynn, Samuel Lynn, Samuel Hunter, Captain William Morgan, or any of the other main characters who feature in these pages, or indeed any physical description of any of them (apart, arguably, from Mrs Lynn). There is but one portrait by Cotes of an identified member of his family – that of his father, Robert Cotes, which hangs today in the dining room at Burlington House – but it seems highly likely that, if only to practise his art, he would not have missed the opportunity to paint from life other Lynn relatives – his aunts, perhaps, if not his grandmother.

Mrs Mary Lynn lived until January 1756, when her grandson had switched from crayons or pastels (his initial medium of preference) to oils, and there is one painting thought to be his work, catalogued as 'Portrait of a Lady' (reproduced above) which conforms closely to her nickname of 'Puddy', signifying short and stout, and could be of her. At least, I like to think so.

In 1761 Francis Cotes was one of the founders of the Society of Artists of Great Britain, a precursor of the Royal Academy of Art, of which he was also a founder in 1768. He died on 16th July 1770, in Richmond, Surrey, aged only 44. Among the bequests left by his Will, admitted to probate[627] on 30th July 1770, he left a pastel self-portrait to his "*honoured Father*" and his gold-headed cane to his "*Dear Brother*" Samuel. To his wife Sarah he left the rest of his personal chattels (including her choice of his other paintings) and £1,000. There were minor legacies, including £5 "*to each of my Aunts Mary Sophia and Arabella Lynn Spinsters*". Everything else, including the lease of the house in Cavendish Square where he and Sarah both lived, was to be sold at auction by the executors and the proceeds invested upon trust to pay out £34 a year to his parents or to the survivor of them. The income from the rest of residue was left to his wife for life, then to his parents (who both survived him) for life, then to his brother Samuel for life, with remainder to Samuel's children (if any) at 21. If Samuel left no children, half of residue was then to go to some friends and relatives of his wife's, and the other half to his three aunts Mary, Sophia and

---

[627] TNA, PROB 11/959/99.

Arabella for the lifetime of the survivor, with remainder for his wife's two nieces. Clearly, he and Sarah had no children.

When Robert Cotes made his last Will a month later, in August 1770, he left almost his entire estate (apart from a mourning ring for Sarah, Francis Cotes' widow) to his wife Elizabeth for life, with remainder to his surviving son Samuel, charging him to show "*the most dutiful and affectionate regard to the best of Mothers*". The Coteses had moved from Cavendish Square to nearby Charles Street by the time Robert Cotes died in November 1774, and the Lynn sisters were all living in rented property in Bond Street which he had paid for. Indeed, the final clause of his Will says:

"*Lastly tho' my Wifes three Sisters are very largely in my Debt by money at different times lent their Mother and advancing several sums on Account of a very troublesome and expensive Law Suit in Chancery*[628] *a large Book Debt besides and paying Rent for them in Bond Street All amounting to Many hundred Pounds Yet I desire my Wife to give each of them two Guineas*".[629]

Elizabeth (then living in Lumley Court, Covent Garden) was the first to go, in January 1776, followed by Sophia in April 1777, Mary in August 1778, and finally Arabella, aged 83, at the beginning of 1799. (Her body was brought from St Pancras parish and

---

[628] Art historian Neil Jeffares identifies the case as *Kelsey v Lynn* (1746), but as mentioned above I think it more likely to have been the long-running and far more expensive case of *Galway v Lynn* (1747-56).
[629] TNA, PROB 11/1002/323.

buried on 7th January at Whitefields Memorial Non-Conformist Church.)[630] However, all four sisters seem to have died intestate. On that assumption, Elizabeth Cotes' estate, such as it was, went to her surviving son Samuel, Sophia's estate passed equally to her surviving sisters Mary and Arabella, and on Mary's death Arabella, as sole survivor, would have had over twenty years to enjoy whatever was left, living, one imagines, in a state of genteel poverty. On her death, intestate, her nephew Samuel Cotes would have been her sole heir.

Samuel Cotes, the youngest grandson and last surviving descendant of Francis Lynn, lived on until 1818, dying without issue *"in his 85th year"* according to the obituary for him which appeared in *The Gentleman's Magazine* that September. Since he survived all three of his aunts, while they were alive they would have derived no benefit (other than a £5 legacy each) from his brother's estate, of which he was life tenant. His own Will, made in 1816 when he was living in Paradise Row, Chelsea, and proved on 8th September 1818, left all his property to William Yatman, Esq., of Arundel Street, Strand. Yatman was a lawyer, of the Inner Temple, and may also have been an artist, albeit an amateur, as his son, also William (and also a lawyer), became a noted artist in his own right.

Yatman junior became the owner of Highgrove House, near Tetbury, Gloucestershire, the present (2017) residence of the Prince of Wales. It may have been Yatman senior who was responsible, by way of sale or gift, for Francis Lynn's 'diary', inherited by

---

[630] Ancestry.co.uk.

Yatman from Samuel Cotes or from Cotes' aunt Arabella's estate, coming into the possession of the Duke of Sutherland before 1834, when it first re-surfaced and extracts from its early entries were published. If Yatman senior retained any of Samuel Cotes' other personal chattels, including family portraits, they would have perished in a fire which destroyed the interior of Highgrove in 1893.

Such are the accidents of history. Francis Lynn almost certainly did not intend his 'diary' for publication, but he must have hoped that it would be read by succeeding generations of his family. Fate decided otherwise, and although six of his ten children survived to adulthood, only one of them had children, and none of those children left issue. There are today no living descendants of that remarkable man, Francis Lynn, to whose memory I dedicate this book.

ABOUT THE AUTHOR

Until he retired in 2015, Patrick Darby was a Solicitor (specialising in probate and trust work), initially in private practice, and for the last twenty years working successively for two national charities as their Legacies Administration Manager.

Considered (not least by himself) as a leading authority on the history of Dulwich before 1800, he has spent most of his life in the area, and he and his partner David now divide their time between Dulwich and Braintree (Essex).

Printed in Great Britain
by Amazon